CONTENTS

Foreword vii

01 Principles of public relations theory and practice 1

The role of theory 1
The evolution of public relations 3
Practice paradigm 6
Defining public relations 6
Modes of PR practice 9
Grunig's primacy 11
Questions to discuss 12

02 Evaluation and communication psychology 13

Number one practitioner topic 16
Defining evaluation 17
Objectives of evaluation 19
Complexity of evaluation 20
Methodology problems 21
Effects-based planning 22
Principles of evaluation 22
Questions to discuss 24

03 The history and culture of PR measurement and evaluation 25

Early influences 26
Mid-century 27
Increasing discussion 27
The 1980s and 1990s – debate widens 28
New century 29
Questions to discuss 34

04 Gathering and interpreting information 35

The scope of research 38
Primary and secondary research 40
Research methods 41
Action research 42
Case studies 42

Experiments   44
Surveys   44
Interviews   46
Focus groups   47
Questionnaires   49
Sampling methods   50
Questionnaire design   51
Content analysis   52
Questions to discuss   54

05   Evaluation structures and processes   55

Preparation, Implementation, Impact (PII)   56
Macnamara's Pyramid Model   57
Public Relations Effectiveness Yardstick   58
Research and planning   61
The Unified model   64
Practitioner-derived models   67
Short term and continuing programmes   68
Universality of application   70
Dashboards and scorecards   72
Questions to discuss   74

06   Developing a media evaluation system   75

Setting up a simple media monitoring system   75
A dimensional model of media evaluation   91
Case study: in-house media evaluation system   96
International media analysis   100
Questions to discuss   101

07   Evaluation in practice – case studies   103

Philips: strategic use of measurement   103
The Pepsi Refresh Project: evaluating the outcomes   107
Crime fighting PR: success on a low budget   109
St John Ambulance: promoting first aid training   111
Medicare Open Enrolment: changing behaviour through PR   113
Westminster City Council: using evaluation to improve services   114
Conclusions   116
Questions to discuss   117

08   Objectives and objective setting   119

Objectives in context   120
Aims, goals and objectives   122

Management by objectives   125
Hierarchy of objectives   126
Specifying objectives   127
The nature of objectives   129
Process objectives   132
Questions to discuss   134

09   Relationship management and crisis communication measurement   135

Measuring relationships   137
Evaluating communication in a crisis   139
Questions to discuss   143

10   Evaluating social media   145

What should we be measuring?   147
Exposure/reach/impressions   148
Engagement/sentiment/tone   150
Influence/respect/relevance   153
Action/impact/value   154
Social media planning   154
KPI/metrics   156
The move towards standards   160
Questions to discuss   161

11   Linking PR activity to business   163

Return on Investment   163
Practitioner interest in financial metrics   167
New financial metrics – BCR and CEA   168
Valid metrics framework   169
Communication controlling   170
The Six Influence Flows   182
Questions to discuss   184

References   185
Index   193

PR in Practice Series

**Published in association with the Chartered Institute of Public Relations
Series Editor: Anne Gregory**

Kogan Page has joined forces with the Chartered Institute of Public Relations (CIPR) to publish this unique series, which is designed specifically to meet the needs of the increasing numbers of people seeking to enter the public relations profession and the large band of existing PR professionals. Taking a practical, action-oriented approach, the books in the series concentrate on the day-to-day issues of public relations practice and management rather than academic history. They provide ideal primers for all those on CIPR, CAM and CIM courses or those taking NVQs in PR. For PR practitioners, they provide useful refreshers and ensure that their knowledge and skills are kept up to date.

Professor Anne Gregory PhD is Director of the Centre for Public Relations Studies at Leeds Metropolitan University, UK. She has authored over 70 publications; as well as being editor of the Kogan Page/CIPR series of books which she initiated, she is Editor-in-Chief of the *Journal of Communication Management*. Anne also leads specialist commercial research and consultancy projects from the Centre working with prestigious public and private sector clients. She is a non-executive director of Airedale NHS Foundation Trust. Originally a broadcast journalist, Anne spent 12 years as a senior practitioner before moving on to academia. She was President of the CIPR in 2004, leading it to Chartered status and was awarded the CIPR's Sir Stephen Tallents Medal for her outstanding contribution to public relations in 2010. In June 2012 she became Chair of the Global Alliance of Public Relations and Communications Management, the umbrella organization of over 60 public relations institutes from around the world.

Other titles in the series:

Creativity in Public Relations by Andy Green
Crisis, Issues and Reputation Management by Andrew Griffin
Effective Internal Communication by Lyn Smith and Pamela Mounter
Effective Media Relations by Michael Bland, Alison Theaker and David Wragg
Ethics in Public Relations by Patricia J Parsons
Internal Communications by Liam FitzPatrick and Klavs Valskov
Online Public Relations by David Phillips and Philip Young
Planning and Managing Public Relations Campaigns by Anne Gregory
PR and Communication in Local Government and Public Services by John Brown,
    Pat Gaudin and Wendy Moran
The PR Professional's Handbook by Caroline Black
Public Relations in Practice edited by Anne Gregory
Risk Issues and Crisis Management in Public Relations by Michael Regester and
    Judy Larkin
Running a Public Relations Department by Mike Beard
Writing Skills for Public Relations by John Foster

The above titles are available from all good bookshops. To obtain further information, please go to the CIPR website (**www.cipr.co.uk/books**) or contact the publishers at the address below:

Kogan Page Ltd
2nd Floor, 45 Gee Street
London EC1V 3RS
United Kingdom
Tel: 020 7278 0433
www.koganpage.com

FOREWORD

Evaluation remains one of the hottest topics in public relations. Yet it seems that for every two steps forwards there is one step back. While certain evaluation basics such as those captured in the Barcelona Declaration of Measurement Principles (2010) have been talked about and broadly accepted for the last 15 years or so, and the multi-faceted nature of evaluation established beyond reasonable dispute, the quest for the mythical 'magic bullet' or single-measure evaluation still persists.

Evaluation in public relations is necessarily and inherently difficult since it concerns measuring how humans change in reaction to communication. All kinds of factors complicate this assessment. What about context? Susceptibility? Disaggregating your communication effect from that of others? Accepting that human motivations for attitude, feeling and behaviour change are complex and unpredictable and so are the outcomes arising from them, it is rather odd that there is still the compulsion to try to define one simple measure for public relations effectiveness and usually this measure is Return on Investment (ROI). This search in many ways devalues the effort of public relations professionals and is against the trend in business reporting. The newly launched (December 2013) International Integrated Reporting Framework shows very clearly that intangible assets, as opposed to financial and physical assets, account for about 80 per cent of the value of organizations. So why the pursuit for a single measure based on financial return when intangible assets such as intellectual property, reputation and relationships are patently more valuable, but also obviously more complex to evaluate?

The complexities of evaluation and ways to respond to them are well laid out in this book by Tom Watson and Paul Noble. In this thoroughly revised edition there is a great deal of new material and the approach is more comprehensive and sophisticated. Starting with a discussion of the definitions (and hence purpose) of public relations – important if you are to evaluate it, this book then moves on to a detailed exploration of communication psychology and an expanded and comprehensive overview of the history of evaluation. This then sets the scene for a detailed examination of the importance and techniques of research – the underpinning for evaluation.

Over the years a number of structures and models of evaluation have been developed, which are well described in the book, and it is remarkable how the same factors come to the fore in most of them: the need for a variety of measures, the fact that there are different levels of activity and the requirement for continuous monitoring within programmes, not only end-of-programme evaluation. Media evaluation has long been a focus for commercial and in-house evaluation efforts and this is reflected in the space devoted to the topic and the practical methods that are explained.

The latter part of the book is devoted to some key topics in evaluation, including objective setting, measuring crisis communication, linking public relations to business objectives and, new in this edition, a substantial section on social media evaluation.

Throughout the book there are some excellent mini and more extended case studies that bring the principles under discussion to life. These show the richness of public relations evaluation measures that are now being deployed and which in turn reflect the diversity and complexity of public relations activity.

Tom Watson and Paul Noble have done an excellent job in updating and extending *Evaluating Public Relations*. It is now an essential on the reading list of any practitioner and academic who not only wants an excellent review of the topic, but wants to know the detail of best practice.

Professor Anne Gregory
Consultant Editor

01
Principles of public relations theory and practice

I n this chapter, public relations is introduced and set in the historical perspective of its evolving practice. The nature and extent of public relations theory are explored and definitions of public relations are discussed.

Ask any group of PR practitioners around the world to list the major issues facing their discipline, and it is almost certain that evaluation of PR activity will be ranked very highly, if not the number one topic. The measurement of activity and outcomes has many facets which will be described throughout this book. To set the context of evaluation, the theory and debate over the discipline of public relations need to be explored. For some practitioners, theory is 'stuff' that gets in the way of 'doing PR'. Yet theory is developed from observed practice and helps predict outcomes. This, in turn, gives greater strength to practitioners in developing robust campaigns. Evaluation helps them define campaigns, monitor their progress and provide evidence of outcomes. So theory and sound evaluation practices can and should go hand-in-hand.

The role of theory

Public relations is a relatively new professional activity that is still developing its body of knowledge and theoretical approaches. At present, the role that theory plays in public relations practice is limited. As practice expands worldwide, the demand for greater agreement on concepts, embodied in models and theory, is expected to grow, if only for reasons of clarity of communication from one nation to another.

The adoption of the scientific research process for the study of public relations issues and problems offers many advantages to practitioners in the creation of effective campaigns and other public relations activities. Robustly researched theories offer prediction, understanding and replication. Prediction gives greater assurance to planning and execution of activities and a practitioner could, therefore, buttress his or her professional experience with the application of relevant theory to explain that, if a certain course of action is followed, it is likely that certain consequences may follow. That a practitioner can apply proven theory will help in the making of 'intelligent practical decisions'. When there is a lack of theory, it is exceedingly difficult to create a consistent decision-making methodology for use in planning and evaluation, let alone make predictions on outcomes of public relations activities.

Public relations practice is in the humanistic, social science framework and therefore unlike the more precisely measured natural sciences. Because public relations activity uses a multiplicity of communications techniques, it does not operate in isolation (as would a natural science experiment in a laboratory) from other communications influences and so concepts and theories are likely to be based on observed practice. However, predictive understanding has already been identified as an important value of theory for use by the practitioner. Whether objective knowledge can be obtained, in the style of natural science, is a challenge for future research programmes. At present, it is most probable that understanding based on observation is likely to create the path forward for public relations theory as it has done for much of social science (see, in particular, the discussion of action research in Chapter 4).

Practitioners are often closely involved in the mechanics of their activities and need to develop a structured understanding of the issues they are influencing in order to understand the attitudes of others. They also need the rigour of predictive understanding to verify the phenomena (such as publics, communities and media) with which they plan to communicate.

Replication is another attribute of theory that has value for planning of public relations programmes. If theory provides clear guidance to 'explain and predict phenomena of interest to us', the theory should be applicable in many similar situations. It can thus be replicated in practice and in future research activities.

For public relations, the methodology of the scientific research process in its social sciences form offers the opportunity to create model theory that can be applied to current practice. Practitioners of public relations are active in an industry that has evolved rapidly by borrowing concepts from a wide range of other disciplines. There is an increasing opportunity to develop theory that is relevant to practice.

The evolution of public relations

Where and when did 'public relations' start? There are two answers frequently offered to this question. The first is that PR-like activities (often called proto-PR) go back to the ancient Babylonians and Sumerians (in modern Iraq) who are often held up as instigators because of messages on mud-brick walls around 3,000 years ago. The second answer is that the term 'public relations' was probably first used in late 19th-century United States. There have been several claims of first use and it is contested as to which person or organization actually invoked the term first, but for the sake of simplicity, public relations was applied as a term around the turn of the 20th century.

In the United States, historians have pointed to public relations having two quite separate beginnings – the publicity and press agentry of the circuses that provided popular entertainment, and the railroads, oil companies and public utilities. The circuses provided the route towards today's celebrity PR and product publicity while the less exciting but economically richer organizations have led to modern corporate PR and corporate communications. The US historian Scott Cutlip identified a Boston publicity agency, The Publicity Bureau, which set up in 1900 as the first PR agency business in that country. It started with business clients and gained the account for the telecommunications monopoly American Telephone & Telegraph in 1903. The third to start was Parker & Lee, in which the famed pioneer, Ivy L Lee, was a partner. The firm issued its Declaration of Principles in 1906 which accentuated a public right to know. Cutlip says it 'was, over time, to have profound influence on the evolution of press agentry into publicity and publicity into public relations'. Lee left in 1908 and went to Pennsylvania Railroad. He later worked for the oil magnates, John D Rockefeller Sr and Jr, as a strategic adviser.

There are, however, parallel histories of PR's establishment in Europe. In Germany, the industrial giant Krupp had set up a news bureau in 1893 and there are other examples of organized business and governmental communication activities and operational units in the first 30 years of the 20th century. In the United Kingdom, the Marconi Company had sent out its first news release in 1910. The first PR agency, Editorial Services, was set up in London in 1924 and the first holder of a 'public relations officer' post was appointed in 1925. However, public relations and corporate communications in both countries did not take off until after the Second World War.

In the United States, public relations became established between the world wars. Although the focus is often on the 'great men', pioneers like Ivy Lee, Edward Bernays, and Pendleton Dudley, the business application of public relations developed most in major organizations like the railways and transport organizations, oil companies and parts of government. Leadership came from major figures such as Arthur W Page in AT&T who took a holistic view of public relations as being a whole-of-organization set of behaviours that were not restricted to communications practices.

From the mid-20th century onwards, there was greater emphasis on the development of public relations in Europe, especially through the formation of national associations (Finland was the first on the continent in 1947/48, shortly before the United Kingdom) and the International Public Relations Association (IPRA) which had very wide European influences in its formation in the early 1950s and on through its development in the 1950s and 1960s.

It is notable that the concept of 'international public relations' was fostered primarily by Europeans, many of them reflecting the pain of war and seeking a platform for international understanding and promotion of democracy through public relations strategies and practices. When IPRA started in 1955, it had representation from France, Netherland, Norway, the United Kingdom, and the United States. Belgium and Finland joined shortly afterwards. Although IPRA's membership seldom rose above 1,000, it was an important influence in the spread of public relations across Europe in the 1950s and 1960s. It was responsible for the first codes of professional practice and ethics (the Codes of Venice and Athens) which were adopted widely from 1965 onwards.

Although some European PR pioneers looked to the United States for ideas and guidance after World War 2, it was the expansion of the major US consultancies, such as Hill+Knowlton, Burson-Marsteller and Barnet & Reef, outside North America in the 1960s that began the internationalization of public relations in Europe. These consultancies followed their US-owned multinational clients as they expanded into the consumer and governmental markets of Europe and the emerging Middle East. Most started by creating networks of local consultancies and then acquiring them.

Other important influences on PR's growth were the formation of European transnational companies, which led to the setting-up of corporate communication departments and the rise of marketing-led PR or consumer PR with its tactical publicity style. Although the United States had a wide range of university courses in public relations from the 1940s onwards, Europe was slow to follow. Indeed, most public relations training was provided by the national public relations bodies that sprang up in the 1950s and 1960s. At this time, public relations was not a graduate entry industry. Typically, journalists moved across into the information and communication roles. Women, even with university degrees, came in through secretarial and assistant positions.

Through the 1960s and 1970s, public relations was mainly focused on media relations. This was a reflection of the journalistic background of many of the recent entrants and of their employers in companies and governments. This remains a major part of PR practice today.

In the 1980s, university education commenced in Europe. In the United Kingdom, the initial group of universities started teaching cohorts of aspirants in the latter years of the decade. Other countries were in parallel or followed soon after.

After the fall of the Berlin Wall in 1989 and the collapse of the former Eastern Bloc, public relations began to flourish in these countries. For some this development is seen as 'new PR' which arose from the introduction of democratic governments while others see it as a continuation of practices from the formerly socialist countries. They argue that many of the former governmental communications and propaganda people left their old jobs and became PR entrepreneurs using many of the same techniques and contacts.

In the 1990s, Europe led the PR world in two areas. The first was the formation of the International Communications Consultants Organization (ICCO) which brought the world's PR trade bodies together and the second was the interpretation of the Quality Assurance (QA) movement into the public relations field. One of the factors that had supported growth of PR employment and budgets had been the formation of national public relations trade and professional bodies. In addition to ICCO, the PR professional bodies formed the Global Alliance for Public Relations and Communication Management later in the same decade. IPRA was behind the formation of the International Quality in Public Relations organization which promoted QA approaches to public relations. This was picked up in the United Kingdom and from it the Consultancy Management Standard was created and adopted by several countries.

In the 1990s, there was rapid expansion of public relations in consultancies, government and corporations. One driver was the privatization of governmental entities which fuelled further internationalization of consultancies and corporate communication operations as companies moved rapidly into new markets through acquisition. Another driver was the rapid growth of technology PR from the mid-1990s onwards. This brought new types of expertise and communication methods, as technology PR practitioners used e-mail and the nascent internet as communication and promotional tools. This was the period of Web 1.0 and the beginning of the biggest transformation of public relations practices and strategies since the end of World War 2. Until then, technology change was relatively slow with fax machines only recently replacing telex and post. With Web 1.0, the pace of change accelerated.

Although the bursting of the dotcom bubble around 2001 slowed the growth of public relations, it was only temporary as public relations employment continued to expand. For example, in 2004, it was estimated that 45,000 people worked in PR in the United Kingdom. By 2013, it had risen to about 62,000. Similar growth has been experienced across Europe. For example, the annual European Communication Monitor survey is sent to over 30,000 mid- to senior-level corporate communicators in 43 countries.

So, by the second decade of the 21st century, public relations has become a major communication practice in Europe and around the world. The very small beginnings in the United States with the first PR agency business in 1900 have led to widespread employment, extensive use of its practices and a burgeoning research and academic field. It is a long way from a few circuses, steam railways and telephone companies publicizing their activities through a very limited range of print media.

Practice paradigm

The renowned US theorist James Grunig has defined four descriptors of public relations activity: press agentry/publicity, public information, two-way asymmetrical and two-way symmetrical. Press agentry/publicity has already been described. Public information is the distribution of positive information undertaken by 'journalists in residence'. These are both one-way models in which the practitioner does not seek information from the public through informal feedback or research.

His two-way asymmetrical model uses research to identify messages most likely to produce the support of publics without the organization's behaviour changing. Grunig says 'the effects are asymmetrical because the hoped-for behavioural change benefits the organization and not publics'.

One of Grunig's main contributions to public relations theory is the symmetrical model of public relations. He described it as 'benefiting both organization and publics'. It is public relations with a social conscience and is closely linked with some of the more altruistic aspects of public relations. There is further discussion later in the chapter.

Defining public relations

What is public relations? For many, the simplistic answer is getting their name (company, client, self) into newsprint, on air or on social media as a report, article or third party reference; for others it is publicity that attracts response through name recognition or rising sales. Governments see it as dispersal of information, for example in a health promotion campaign. These may be descriptions of some everyday public relations activities, but they do not define the public relations process nor explain the meaning of the term 'public relations'.

Public relations has been defined in many different ways and Rex Harlow in a 1976 article reckoned that there were around 400 definitions. Time has not reduced the output of definitions but many have common characteristics. Some commentators see the surfeit of definitions as a weakness of public relations; others appreciate the debate that surrounds them as an indication of vigour in the field. It is relevant that recent efforts to create definitions have actively sought the input of practitioners in order that the results are more acceptable.

The management function of public relations is most frequently expressed in definitions. One of the most widely taught, especially in the United States, is that of Cutlip and Center (Broom and Sha, 2013: 26): 'Public relations is the management function that establishes and maintains mutually beneficial relationships between an organization and the publics on whom its success or failure depends.'

There are several phrases to note in this well-known definition. They first describe public relations as a 'management function', which implies it is a deliberate, planned action that has an outcome in mind. This is reinforced by 'establishes and maintains', which demonstrates research and a continuum of activity. 'Mutually beneficial relationships' relates to a two-way communication process through which the organization will act in the interests of both itself and the groups or publics with which it interacts. This definition goes one stage further than others do by defining publics as those 'on whom its success or failure depends'. This verges on tautology as publics by their very nature are of central importance to an organization by giving it a reputation and a commercial, governmental or other organizational raison d'être. However, this is a comment that queries an aspect of this definition, not its central thrust of being a managed process of two-way communications.

Coombs and Holladay (2006: 26) have a wider approach to relationships in their definition: '(public relations is) the management of mutually influential relationships within a web of stakeholder and organizational relationships'.

By using the term 'stakeholder', they emphasize interdependence and the complexity of relationships in which organizations are engaged. Although definitions have a reductive purpose to simplify and explain, this definition emphasizes that communication management can be messy and not simply bilateral.

In 2011/12, the Public Relations Society of America (PRSA) initiated an international crowdsourcing campaign and subsequent public vote that produced this definition: 'Public relations is a strategic communication process that builds mutually beneficial relationships between organizations and their publics'. PRSA says that it is 'simple and straightforward (and) focuses on the basic concept of public relations – as a communication process, one that is strategic in nature and emphasizing "mutually beneficial relationships"'.

PR commentator Paul Holmes, however, criticized the definition for its emphasis on communication and its lack of ambition:

> My biggest problem with the definition, not surprisingly, is the emphasis on 'communication'. It's an emphasis that diminishes what PR people do; that reduces it to the tactical rather than the strategic. It implies, to the long-term detriment of the discipline, that public relations is merely the art of explaining policy rather than an essential consideration in setting policy.

In the United Kingdom, the Chartered Institute of Public Relations (CIPR) supported the PRSA initiative but has retained its definition which has a reputational emphasis:

> Public relations is about reputation – the result of what you do, what you say and what others say about you.
>   Public relations is the discipline which looks after reputation, with the aim of earning understanding and support and influencing opinion and behaviour. It is

the planned and sustained effort to establish and maintain goodwill and mutual understanding between an organization and its publics.

This definition is also debated because many parts of organizations will 'look after reputation', not just public relations or corporate communication functions. Arguably, well-managed companies and organizations seek to 'establish and maintain mutual understanding' in all that they do. Public relations is thus reduced to communication and not policy-making or enactment.

It does, however, share the continuum element of 'planned and sustained effort' with objectives of establishing and maintaining goodwill and understanding, also an aspiration for two-way communications. As in the Cutlip & Center definition, there is a strong aspirational element that presupposes there is a nirvana of perfect communications which could be reached, if only 'goodwill and mutual understanding' were established.

By contrast, in an earlier era Edward Bernays emphasized the persuasive element in his definition that 'public relations attempts to engineer public support' (Bernays, 1955: 4–5). This is a one-way definition and is probably closest to practitioner attitudes. Bernays developed his theories of public relations from his interpretation of social sciences and psychology, in particular. He considered that knowledge of psychology was important because practitioners had to understand the diversity of human behaviour. By understanding behaviour, public relations programmes could be designed to meet the needs of both client and the target publics. There is no aspirational element offered because Bernays' definition is action-oriented. Not surprisingly, his contribution to public relations theory has been strongly criticized as encouraging the manipulative and being anti-democratic.

US academics Carl Botan and Vincent Hazleton (1989) observed that: '[Public relations] serves as the definitional label for the process of attempting to exert symbolic control over the evaluative dispositions (attitudes, images) and subsequent behaviours of relevant publics or clienteles'. This is one of the few definitions that offer a conceptual approach to the process as opposed to the majority which describe the objectives of public relations practice. It also firmly places public relations in the persuasive, asymmetrical model because of its emphasis on controlling communications to meet an organization's objectives.

Two conclusions can be drawn from these many definitions of public relations. One is that there is a clear gap between the two-way communication models advocated by academics and the reality of one-way models adopted by practitioners. This is a divergence that runs parallel throughout comparisons of academic research and actual practitioner behaviour. The second, referred to above, is the debate between the managerial view of public relations practice, which is not confined to one-way or two-way definitions, and the altruistic/ethical approach that is exemplified by many two-way definitions.

Modes of PR practice

When considering definitions, their relevance to practice needs to be taken into account. Broadly, and without considering specialisms, public relations can be conceived and practised in five modes:

1 as a marketing discipline (part of the marketing mix): the most common model in which PR is expressed as brand publicity;

2 as the management of reputation: used operationally by major consultancies since the mid-1990s and included in CIPR's current definition;

3 as the management of communication and relationships between an organization and its publics: as defined by leading US academics and the (US) Institute for Public Relations;

4 as a practice which contributes to the performance and success of organizations: a widely-held view in Europe also proposed by UK commentator Philip Sheldrake (2011);

5 as a strategic activity in which communication and relationship-building are related to core organizational objectives: the communication management expressed most strongly in Germany (see discussion of 'communication controlling' on page 170).

Modes 3 to 5 have many overlaps and will often be undertaken simultaneously. They also relate to Excellence Theory (see box). It can be seen that most definitions cover some of the modes but not all.

Excellence Theory

The core purpose of Excellence Theory, the main normative theory of public relations, can be summarized as: By undertaking the communication management role, practitioners can contribute to the overall effectiveness of the organization. Thus, PR is part of organizational planning and decision-making (a management function) and helps the organization achieve its strategic plans.

As a normative theory, it prescribes how a PR department should be structured and operate. If a PR operation chooses not to be 'excellent', the outcomes are likely to be that it does not take part in the 'dominant coalition' of management and is restricted to publicity and crisis communication. There will be greater emphasis on technician roles and providing a service.

Three elements make up the core purpose of the theory:

- Public relations contributes to organizational effectiveness when it helps to reconcile the organization's goals with the expectations of its strategic constituencies. This contribution has monetary value to the organization.

- Public relations contributes to effectiveness by building quality, long-term relationships with strategic constituencies.

- Public relations is most likely to contribute to effectiveness when the senior public relations manager is a member of the dominant coalition where he or she is able to shape the organization's goals and to help determine which external publics are most strategic (Grunig, 1992: 6).

Research that helped establish the theory studied over 300 organizations in order to identify the factors that made public relations contribute most to organizational effectiveness. The principles of Excellence Theory were recognized and can be expressed in eight themes. 'Organizations which embrace these principles will be more effective' (Heath and Coombs, 2006: 200):

- *Value of communications:* CEOs and top management must understand the value of PR and communications.

- *Contribute to strategic functions:* PR is part of the organization's strategic planning; it is part of the decision-making group in the organization; it acts to represent the views of stakeholders to other members of management.

- *Perform a management role:* There are two roles in PR: technician and management; technicians create materials, organize events, and do writing tasks; managers are involved in planning and decision-making (they are knowledgeable in use of research). Organizations are more effective when their top PR people act as managers.

- *Use two-way symmetrical model of PR:* There are four models of PR: press agentry, public information, two-way asymmetrical and two-way symmetrical. Two-way uses research to understand stakeholders; it aims at creating dialogue between the organization and stakeholders; both sides influence each other and understand each other's perspectives.

- *Potential to practice the ideal model:* The excellent PR department has practitioners with research and strategic management skills and knowledge.

- *Activism as positive energy:* Activism is when stakeholders communicate the need for change to the organization. Excellent PR departments have a high level of activism, drawn from the dialogue between the organization and stakeholders. This helps them better represent needs and issues to management as part of the strategic monitoring and planning process.

- *Organizational culture and structure:* Rigid, hierarchical structures discourage communications; so excellent PR thrives in more flexible organic organizations. The organizational culture must be participative and empower employees to make decisions.

- *Diversity as a strength:* PR departments are stronger when they are diverse in terms of gender and race. Those who reflect the diversity of stakeholders can better understand and represent their interests.

Excellence Theory has continued its development for more than 20 years. It has critics who consider it to be very corporatist, dated in the social media world and ignoring the reality of communication processes. Some says its reliance on symmetrical communication obscures the networks of power and influence and assumes that PR practitioners are the only and most effective communicators. Another critique is that PR practitioners must adopt a managerial stance in order to succeed. However, it remains the primary theory which can be applied to the organization and management of public relations operations. It has been very influential upon corporate communication and communication management practice and theory, which will be noted in the development of communication performance management models discussed in later chapters.

Grunig's primacy

Grunig's four models of practice and his situational theory of public relations have been in development for over two decades. In that time, there has been little competition to these models, although some elements, notably his reliance on the symmetrical model as the 'excellent' form of public relations practice, are increasingly debated. Grunig's four models do not in themselves add up to a theory of public relations because they are essentially observations which have been processed into a classification of practitioner behaviour and attitudes.

From this base, however, Grunig has developed his situational theory, using the symmetrical model of public relations (Grunig, 1994). This theory seeks to explain why people communicate and when they are most likely to communicate. He says it explains how predicted communication behaviour can be used to analyse the mass population into publics. Grunig says this theory provides a means of segmenting publics in a manner similar to theories of market segmentation. It aims to predict the differential responses which are most relevant to the planning of public relations activity: namely, responsiveness to issues; amount of and nature of communication behaviour; effects of communication on cognition, attitudes and behaviour; and the likelihood of participation in collective behaviour to pressure organizations. Grunig continues to develop this theory and it is also used by others to study other concepts such as the interaction of publics, the media and public relations practitioners.

In this first chapter, we have considered the valuable role of theory, the evolution of public relations mainly in the past century, its definition, modes of practice, two-way symmetrical theory and Excellence Theory. Combined, these all give a platform for the discussion and exploration of the measurement and evaluation of public relations activity.

Questions to discuss

- What is the difference between one-way and two-way communication, as defined by Grunig and Hunt? Consider the benefits and problems with them.
- When would it be appropriate to use one-way communication? Think of examples that you have observed.
- From the various definitions of public relations discussed, choose one that you consider is most appropriate for most forms of public relations activity? Is it suitable for strategic communications, as well?
- How has public relations developed over the past century?
- What are the benefits of theory in relation to public relations practice?
- What is 'excellent', according to Excellence Theory, when it comes to organizing PR operations and departments?

02
Evaluation and communication psychology

As early as 1920, US public relations practitioners were discussing the role of evaluation of public relations activity. Forty years ago, writers predicted that evaluation practices would move from informal judgement to scientifically derived knowledge. Now, in the 21st century, evaluation is still earnestly discussed. This chapter looks at evaluation theory and its link with psychology.

Like most studies of humans, there is considerable and continuing debate among psychologists on behaviour. The causes and responses are never simple and often unpredictable. Yet for the purposes of communication public relations practitioners seek some characteristics or something upon which they can base their campaigns.

Because of the continuing discussion of behavioural and mass communication theory, it is not possible to offer simple verities. However, this chapter will review the main themes among theorists and then link them with evaluation theories.

In the 1930s, there were studies that argued that the mass media had a powerful and continuing ability to influence public behaviour. The reasons put forward were based on rising literacy, the immediate impact of radio broadcasting and the rise of mass movements in many European countries. During the next two decades, there was a swing to the reverse argument that mass media did not have a persuasive impact, the so-called 'minimal effects' theories. From these theories, the genesis of many current attitudes and public relations practices can be found.

Some of the key concepts, outlined by McCoy and Hargie (2003), are:

- Interpersonal influence is very strong and opinion leaders play a vital role in spreading and interpreting information (Lazarsfeld *et al*, 1948).

- Among the barriers that limit campaign effectiveness are: selective exposure – the tendency to attend to messages that are consistent with prior attitudes and experience; selective perception – the tendency to interpret a message in terms of prior attitudes and experiences; and selective retention – the tendency to remember messages that are consistent with prior attitudes and experience (Hyman and Sheatsley, 1947).

- Contrasting with this 'cognitive consistency' was Festinger's theory of cognitive dissonance, which said that attitudes can be changed if they are contrasted with a dissonant attitude that is inconsistent with the existing viewpoint (Festinger, 1957).

- While Festinger's theory said that changes in attitudes could come via dissonance, it has become evident over time that people select information because it is relevant to them, rather than because it reinforces existing attitudes (McCoy and Hargie, 2003).

- Discussion moved from the impact of mass media to the influence of interpersonal networks. Social learning theorists have pointed out that we create, modify and retain attitudes in discussion with other people in all the social networks. For example, we may see a story in the media but our attitudes towards an issue, ethical stance or product may be formed when discussing it with others in our family, workplace or other social environment.

There have been many theories and models to explain attitude and the ways in which we receive, retain and act upon information. There are domino models that show that step A leads to step B and so on until the message recipient acts in a predictable way. The domino model is often found in communication strategy documents which propose that a particular approach will almost certainly result in a specific outcome. We humans, however, don't think and act in a mechanistic manner. If we accept that models are only illustrative and not predictive, they can be of assistance for the development of public relations campaigns.

The dominant paradigm of practice is the equation of public relations with persuasion and influence. In order to discuss models of evaluation, the nature of persuasion should be reviewed. From communications psychology, there are models that offer processes which public relations practitioners can apply to the evaluation of their own models. Among the frameworks that have been proposed, McGuire's output analysis of the communication/persuasion process has attributes that can be considered for persuasion-based public relations evaluation (McGuire, 1984). It can be summarized in six steps as:

- *Presentation:* Getting the message to the target.

- *Attention:* Target pays attention.

- *Comprehension:* Target processes messages. [The target does not necessarily understand the message or understand it correctly or as intended, but does acquire an understanding.]

- *Acceptance:* Target incorporates message as understood and cognitive/affective state is changed as a result. [This can include boomerang effects.]

- *Retention:* Target retains message for a specified time. [The message may, however, be changed as a result of retention and is not therefore the same as acceptance.]

- *Action:* Target behaves in the manner desired by the originating communicator.

McGuire's model is not a domino model, as he outlines the likely problems at each stage that may result in attitudes that are not the ones sought. It does show, however, that distribution of information, the most evaluated element of public relations activity, is only the first presentation step in a communication process. To concentrate on that step only is of little value to monitoring the campaign's progress and judging its outcomes.

This six-step process of the model can be further condensed into three major stages of *output* (presentation), *impact* (attention, comprehension, acceptance and retention) and *effect* (action). The implication for public relations evaluation arising from this stepped process is that judgements should encompass the full range of the communication process from output to effect.

It can be argued that models or evaluation actions which measure output only are ignoring the full (and sometimes difficult to judge) persuasion process. They view only the first major stage and omit impact and effect. Yet it is in the interest of the client/employer to assess whether public relations effort (expressed in terms of time, budget and staff resources) has been effective in attaining the desired goals of acceptance or action.

In academic discussion of current public relation practice, there is often criticism that campaigns propose unattainable behavioural change. McCoy and Hargie (2003: 309–10) argue that:

> PR practitioners must first break away from reliance on behaviouristic domino models, secondly accept more conservative expectations of effects and, thirdly, aim for alternative potential outcome. Even researchers who have investigated the communications effects of campaigns and have found positive results acknowledged it is simplistic to believe that PR creates awareness which in turn leads to knowledge, which in turn leads to the formation of a favourable attitude, which results in a behaviour change.

US researchers Dozier and Ehling (1992) comment that PR campaigns have a 0.04 per cent chance of achieving behaviour change. So McCoy and Hargie (2003: 311) propose that practitioners should set more realistic objectives which could include agenda setting and the stimulation of interpersonal discussion, which as we noted earlier, is one of the most likely sources of attitudinal and behavioural change.

As Australian commentator Jim Macnamara (2007: 9) says: 'Public relations executives should note that results are less likely the further one moves from cognition to behaviour. If overly optimistic objectives are set, evaluation of public relations will be a difficult and frequently disappointing experience.'

Number one practitioner topic

In Delphi studies among practitioners and academics of research priorities conducted by White and Blamphin (1994), McElreath and Blamphin (1994), Synnott and McKie (1997) and Watson (2008), the topic of evaluation was always ranked in the top two or three topics (and often number one) for the development of public relations practice and research. It was important for self-esteem and reputation that methods of evaluation were devised to measure the effectiveness of campaigns.

Yet what is evaluation of public relations? Is it measuring output or monitoring progress against defined objectives? Is it giving a numerical value to the results of programmes and campaigns? Is it the final step in the public relations process or a continuing activity?

When discussing the topic of evaluation, there is considerable confusion as to what it means. For budget-holders, whether employers or clients, the judgements have a 'bottom line' profit-related significance. Grunig and Hunt wrote of a practitioner who justified the budgetary expenditure on public relations by the large volume of press coverage generated. He was flummoxed by a senior executive's question: 'What's all this worth to us?' In the United Kingdom, articles in the public relations and marketing press refer to evaluation in terms of 'justifying expenditure', which is similar to Grunig and Hunt's example. White (1991) suggests that company managers have a special interest in the evaluation of public relations: 'Evaluation helps to answer the questions about the time, effort and resources to be invested in public relations activities: can the investment, and the costs involved, be justified?' More than 20 years ago, an Australian business commentator said: 'For public relations to be widely accepted as a serious marketing tool, it needs to develop new ways to prove its worth and make its actions accountable, pointing to a pile of press clippings is not enough' (Shoebridge, 1989). Although public relations is seen in a limited marketing context, the reference to un-analysed collations of press clippings or any other media, including social media, as inadequate proof of performance is still valid decades later.

Defining evaluation

Evaluation as a practice is firmly rooted in social scientific research methods. As Noble (1994) points out: 'Evaluation as a means of assessing communications effectiveness is nothing new'. Rossi and Freeman (1982: 23) traced the origins of evaluation as a social scientific practice back to attempts in the 1930s to evaluate Roosevelt's New Deal social programmes. However, Patton (1982: 15) argues that evaluation did not emerge as a 'distinctive field of professional social scientific practice' until the late 1960s, about the same time as evaluation began to emerge as an issue in public relations. Public relations evaluation and evaluation, as an identifiable social scientific activity – separately – came under scrutiny over at about the same time and thus have been able inform each other's development.

For example, Patton (1982: 15) confirms the broad nature of evaluation with his definition:

> The practice of evaluation involves the systematic collection of information about the activities, characteristics, and outcomes of programs, personnel, and products for use by specific people to reduce uncertainties, improve effectiveness, and make decisions with regard to what those programs, personnel, or products are doing and affecting.

In commenting on this rather convoluted definition Patton makes the important point that: 'the central focus is on evaluation studies and consulting processes that aim to improve program effectiveness'. This places emphasis on evaluation as a formative activity: that is, obtaining feedback to enhance programme management.

The definitions by many experts emphasize effectiveness, for example: Broom and Sha (2013) – 'measure program impact', Pavlik (1987) – 'evaluation research is used to determine effectiveness', Blissland (cited in Wilcox *et al*, 2000) – 'the systematic assessment of a program and its results' and Lindenmann (1993) – 'measure public relations effectiveness'. Developments of these definitions are those which are related to programme or campaign objectives, a reflection on the management-by-objectives influence on public relations practice in the United States. Wylie (cited in Wilcox *et al*, 2000) says, 'we are talking about an orderly evaluation of progress in attaining the specific objectives of our public relations plan'.

The term 'evaluation' is a broad one and this breadth gives the potential for confusion. Public relations uses research for a variety of purposes. Dozier and Repper (1992: 186) argue that a distinction needs to be drawn between research designed to analyse the situation at the beginning of the planning process and research designed to evaluate the planning, implementation and impact of the programme. However, they themselves blur this distinction by stressing that the first type of research acts as the benchmark for programme evaluation. In short, a research-based culture is an evaluative culture and vice versa.

Public relations, in particular, frequently embraces evaluation in a defensive, summative guise: assessing final programme outcome. For example, Blissland (cited in Wilcox *et al*, 2000: 191) defines evaluation in summative terms: 'the systematic assessment of a programme and its results. It is a means for practitioners to offer accountability to clients – and to themselves.' Broom and Dozier (1990: 17) criticize this style of public relations evaluation because research is not seen as essential for planning, but limited to tracking and assessing impact. It encourages the view of evaluation as a separate activity undertaken at a distinct, late stage in the programme. The implication, frequently made, is therefore that programmes can be implemented without evaluation. Wylie (as cited in Wilcox *et al*, 2000: 192) reverts to Patton's emphasis on formative evaluation, but without excluding summative thinking: 'We are talking about an orderly evaluation of our progress in attaining the specific objectives of our public relations plan. We are learning what we did right, what we did wrong, how much progress we've made and, most importantly, how we can do it better next time.'

Watson (1997: 284) confirms that there is indeed 'considerable confusion'. He asserts that definitions of evaluation fall into three groups: 'the commercial, which is a justification of budget spend; simple-effectiveness, which asks whether the programme has worked in terms of output; and objectives-effectiveness, which judges programmes in terms of meeting objectives and creation of desired effects'.

While all these three groups of definitions display a summative ('evaluation only') focus, at least the third group introduces the concept of relating evaluation to the objectives set and therefore – by integrating evaluation into the planning process – at least establishes a formative foundation. It is also possible to argue that an evaluation process that establishes that the public relations programme has achieved the objective(s) set, by definition justifies the budget spent.

The most recent and authoritative definition comes from the Commission on Measurement and Evaluation of Public Relations, whose *Dictionary of Public Relations Measurement and Research* defines evaluation research as:

> A form of research that determines the relative effectiveness of a public relations campaign or program by measuring program outcomes (changes in the level of awareness, understanding, attitudes, opinions and/or behaviours of a targeted audience of public) against a predetermined set of objectives that initially established the level or degree of change desired. (Stacks, 2006: 7)

This definition shows that evaluation is a key element of planned public relations activity as outcomes should be measured against the objectives the campaign or activity has been set to achieve.

Objectives of evaluation

For effective evaluation to be undertaken, starting points have to be set out, a basis of comparison researched, and specific objectives established. Dozier (1985) has commented that 'measurement of programs without goals is form without substance; true evaluation is impossible'. Weiss (1977) says the 'purpose [of evaluation] should be clearly stated and measurable goals must be formulated before the questions can be devised and the evaluation design chosen'. This is an argument endorsed by many commentators.

The starting point and the objective must be defined as part of the programme design; then waypoints can be measured and the effectiveness or impact assessed. White (1991) argues that 'setting precise and measurable objectives at the outset of a programme is a prerequisite for later evaluation'. Swinehart (1979) says that the objectives of a campaign or programme should be closely related to the research design and data collection as well as the campaign methods and strategy used.

He says that there are five areas of questioning that should be applied to objectives:

1 What is the content of the objective?
2 What is the target population?
3 When should the intended change occur?
4 Are the intended changes unitary or multiple?
5 How much effect is desired?

By posing these questions, it can be seen that simplistic media measurement or reader response analysis only considers output – volume of mentions – and not effects. Objectives of, say, more mentions in the *Financial Times*, which may be sought by a quoted industrial company, or 'Likes' on Facebook or retweets on Twitter are little more than a stick with which to beat the public relations practitioner. Dozier (1985) refers to this approach as 'pseudo-planning' and 'pseudo-evaluation'. Pseudo-planning is the allocation of resources to communications activities, where the goal is communication itself, and pseudo-evaluation is 'simply counting news release placements, and other communications'.

Swinehart (1979) divides evaluation into four categories: process, quality, intermediate objectives and ultimate objectives. He suggests that there is more to evaluation than impact:

1 Process is 'the nature of the activities involved in the preparation and dissemination of material'.

2 Quality is 'the assessment of materials or programs in terms of accuracy, clarity, design, production values'.

3 Intermediate objectives are 'sub-objectives necessary for a goal to be achieved', eg placement of information.

4 Ultimate objectives are 'changes in the target audience's knowledge, attitudes and behaviour'.

This analysis points out the need for planning and evaluation to be linked. The simpler approaches such as those undertaken by 'media mentions' calculators separate planning from the campaign and subsequent evaluation.

Complexity of evaluation

Patton (1982: 17) makes the same point in the context of evaluation in general when he describes the move towards situational evaluation which requires that evaluators deal with different people operating in different situations. This is challenging because: 'in most areas of decision-making and judgement, when faced with complex choices and multiple possibilities, we fall back on a set of deeply embedded rules and standard operating procedures that predetermine what we do, thereby effectively short circuiting situational adaptability'. The natural inclination of the human mind is to make sense of new experiences and situations by focusing on those aspects that are familiar, and selectively ignoring evidence that does not fit stereotypes. Thus the tendency is to use existing techniques and explanations, selectively ignoring evidence that indicates a fresh approach might be required.

Situational evaluation not only takes into account the environment in which the programme to be evaluated is operating, but also considers the audience for whom the evaluation is being undertaken. FitzGibbon and Morris (1978: 13–14) explain: 'The critical characteristic of any one evaluation study is that it provides the best possible information that could have been collected under the circumstances, and that this information *meets the credibility requirements of its evaluation audience*' [italics added]. Evaluation is not undertaken for its own sake, but for a purpose, and that purpose requires the audience for whom the evaluation is being undertaken to regard the evaluation process and methodology as relevant and reasonable.

Another aspect of the complexity associated with public relations evaluation is the large number of variables with which public relations practice is concerned. White (1991: 106) explains the point when comparing the disciplines of public relations and marketing: 'Marketing is a more precise practice, which is able to draw on research as it manipulates a small number of variables to aim for predicted results, such as sales targets and measurable market share'. However, public relations remains a more complex activity: 'Public relations is concerned with a far larger number of variables'.

A further dimension of public relations' complexity, which is associated with all forms of mediated communication, is the introduction of an additional step and/or a third party. 'But appraising communication becomes more complicated as soon as the media steps in' (Tixier, 1995: 17). However, when public relations is used in its principal tactical incarnation of media relations, then the lack of control over this mediated communication muddies the waters even further. For example, when comparing publicity-generating media relations with advertising, one market researcher (Sennott, 1990: 63) explains: 'I just saw a press kit from which nobody wrote a story. Good kit. Looked good. Nothing happened.' So in public relations, and unlike advertising, there is an extra phase of passing through media gateways to consider.

Methodology problems

There are some intrinsic methodological problems that make the evaluation process difficult. These include:

- Campaigns are unique and are planned for very specific purposes. It is therefore difficult to evaluate the reliability of a unique event or process.

- Comparison groups are difficult. A client would not be sympathetic to leaving out half of the target population so that one could compare 'intentions' with control groups.

- Control of other variables, such as those outside the control of the public relations practitioner. These may impact on the campaign's target publics and may include campaigns run by competitors, the clutter of messages on the same subject from advertising, direct mail, word of mouth etc.

- Timescale can affect the process and the results. For methodologically sound evaluation, a 'before' sample is needed as well as 'after' data. This, however, means implementing the evaluation process before the campaign.

- The probity of the person or organization managing the campaign also being responsible for audit or evaluation. There is a danger of subjective judgement or distortion of result.

- The plethora of techniques for evaluation of varying effectiveness.

Effects-based planning

Developing a more complete approach to planning (and subsequent evaluation) is the purpose of the 'effects-based planning' theories put forward by VanLeuven *et al* (1988). Underlying this approach is the premise that a programme's intended communication and behavioural effects serve as the basis from which all other planning decisions can be made.

The process involves setting separate objectives and sub-objectives for each public. Planning thus becomes more consistent by having to justify programme and creative decisions on the basis of their intended communication and behavioural effects. It also acts as a continuing evaluation process because the search for consistency means that monitoring is continuous and so provides valid, contemporaneous evidence on which to reach decisions. Effects-based planning means that programmes can be compared without the need for isolated case studies. The search for consistency is one of the most difficult practical issues faced by the public relations professional. A more disciplined approach will allow the parameters of the programme to be more closely defined and for continuous monitoring to replace a single post-intervention evaluation. It will also bolster the objectivity of the evaluation process.

Principles of evaluation

In summarizing thinking on public relations evaluation, Noble (1999: 19–20) set out seven principles of evaluation:

1 *Evaluation is research*. Evaluation is a research-based discipline. Its purpose is to inform and clarify and it operates to high standards of rigour and logic. As the orbit of public relations extends from publicity-seeking media relations to issues management and corporate reputation, research will play an increasingly important role in the planning, execution and measurement of public relations programmes.

2 *Evaluation looks both ways*. Evaluation is a proactive, forward-looking and formative activity that provides feedback to enhance programme management. It is also a reviewing, backward-looking summative activity that assesses the final outcome of the campaign/ programme. By so doing it proves public relations' worth to the organization and justifies the budget allocated to it. Formative evaluation is an integral part of day-to-day professional public relations practice and aids the achievement of the ultimate impact with which summative evaluation is concerned. However, public relations loses credibility – and evaluation loses value – if formative techniques are substituted for measurement and assessment of the ultimate impact of public relations programmes.

3 *Evaluation is user and situation dependent*. Evaluation should be undertaken according to the objectives and criteria that are relevant to the organization and campaign concerned. It is a function of public relations management to understand the organization's expectations of public relations activity. Having managed those expectations, the activity then needs to be evaluated in the context of them. It is also a management function to assess the objectives level appropriate to the campaign concerned and to implement it accordingly.

4 *Evaluation is short-term*. Short-term evaluation is usually campaign or project based. Such campaigns are frequently concerned with raising awareness through the use of media relations techniques. There is not usually sufficient time for results to feed back and fine-tune the current project. They will, however, add to the pool of experience to enhance the effectiveness of future campaigns. Short-term in this context definitely means less than 12 months.

5 *Evaluation is long-term*. Long-term evaluation operates at a broader, strategic level and usually concerns issues management, corporate reputation, and/or brand positioning. It is here that there is maximum opportunity for (or threat of) the substitution of impact evaluation methodologies with process evaluation. The key issue is to ensure that evaluation is undertaken against the criteria established in the objectives. Direct measurement, possibly in the form of market research, is likely to form part of the range of evaluation methodologies employed. Because the communications programme is continuous and long-term, regular feedback from evaluation research

can help fine-tune planning and implementation as well as measuring results.

6 *Evaluation is comparative.* Evaluation frequently makes no absolute judgements but instead draws comparative conclusions. For example, media evaluation frequently makes historical and/or competitive comparisons, as well as comparing the messages transmitted by the media against those directed at journalists. The purpose of process evaluation is frequently to encourage a positive trend rather than hit arbitrary – and therefore meaningless – targets.

7 *Evaluation is multifaceted.* Public relations has been established as a multi-step process, if only because of the additional stepping stone represented by the media. A range of different evaluation methodologies are required at each step (or level), with process evaluation, for example, being used to enhance the effectiveness of impact effects. The concept of using a selection of different techniques in different circumstances has prompted the use of the term 'toolkit' to describe the range of methodologies available to the communications practitioner.

The reaction of practitioners to the evaluation debate has included emphasis on the role that the setting of appropriate objectives plays in enabling effective evaluation. Theorists, who have long argued in favour of careful objective setting, echo these exhortations. They have also called for public relations to become more of a research-based discipline. In an ideal world, the setting of specific, quantified and measurable objectives would indeed be the panacea for effective evaluation. However, public relations is rarely – if ever – able to achieve substantive objectives by itself, certainly in the marketing environment where the evaluation spotlight shines brightest.

Questions to discuss

- How do psychological concepts relate to public relations?
- How would you define 'evaluation' when it is related to public relations activity?
- McCoy and Hargie (2003) argue that practitioners should avoid domino models of communication. How would you map out the communication path from the proposal of an idea to its implementation? How could progress on that path be measured?
- Five 'areas of questioning' are proposed for the setting of objectives. Can you add to them?
- The chapter sets out seven principles of evaluation. Which would be the three most important principles?

03
The history and culture of PR measurement and evaluation

There has long been a considerable gap between the academic desire for a social science-based approach to public relations evaluation and the informal, 'seat of the pants' methods used by the vast majority of practitioners. The culture of public relations practitioners is a fundamental issue when considering attitudes towards evaluation and the methodology used. In text-books and articles about public relations, writers and academics are almost unanimous in their advice that programmes must be researched during preparation and evaluated during and after implementation. Many research-ers, however, have found that a minority of practitioners used scientific evaluation methods.

Although some research claims that practitioners are becoming more sophisticated, there appear to be barriers to widespread acceptance of systematic evaluation and its techniques across the world. More recently, as budgets have tightened in tough economic times, there has been greater interest in proving the value of public relations activities. This has led to a sharpening of interest in various forms of 'valuation' which will be explored later in the chapter. Before recent developments in PR measurement and evaluation are discussed, the history of PR measurement and evaluation will be set out as it demonstrates the cultural directions of practice development and how it has, until recently, separated from academic discussion and research.

The evolution of public relations measurement started more than two centuries ago, with some suggesting that media monitoring practices can be identified from the late 18th century onwards, even involving staff of the first US president, George Washington (Lamme and Miller, 2010). The measurement and evaluation of public relations activity has long been an important practice discussion and debate.

From the beginning of the 20th century, when 'public relations' began to be widely used as the description for a set of communication activities, measurement practices can be identified. Some methods used in the first decade of the 20th century would be familiar to practitioners over a century later. One of these, 'The Barometer', was used by the first known publicity agency in the United States, The Publicity Bureau of Boston (Cutlip, 1994). It was a card index of the attitudes of editors and media usage of publicity material. This allowed the agency to judge 'whether a paper is 'Good' or 'Bad' from the standpoint (of its clients)' (Cutlip, 1994: 21). Cutlip commented on The Barometer, with considerable irony, that 'public relations research is not as new as some think' (1994: 21).

In many ways this evolution has similarities to the development of public relations itself as an emerging and then extensive communications practice. Like public relations, it started with elements of both social science research, especially opinion polling, and of a practice emphasis on publicity through media channels. By the mid-20th century, this moved more towards a publicity-led practice with the use of media analytics becoming far more important than social science methods. However, by the beginning of the current century, the balance was moving back towards more sophistication in measurement and the wider alignment of public relations communication objectives with organizational objectives, especially in corporate public relations where new techniques such as scorecards (Zerfass, 2005) are being used.

Early influences

Although Ivy Lee and Edward Bernays are often cited as influential fathers of public relations practice, it was Arthur W Page who introduced systematic opinion research into corporate public relations and organizational communication at AT&T. He championed the use of surveys, which were to be an important factor in developing a customer-facing culture at the telecommunications giant. 'He deserves credit for recognizing the need for feedback and encouraging development of systems to gauge the moods of AT&T's publics. Integration of formal feedback systems into the public relations function is one of his contributions to public relations practise' (Griese, 2001: 122).

By the late 1930s and early 1940s in North America, two methods of measurement were being established that are still widely used. Batchelor

(1938) provided two examples of the monitoring and interpretation of media coverage. The first was that the Roosevelt Administration gave close attention to both publicity dissemination and its reception. 'In other words, it watches carefully all changes in the political attitudes of a community' (212). He also referred to the extensive media monitoring operation of the city of Toledo, Ohio in the Great Depression. It measured some 72,000 media clippings from newspapers and found 91 per cent favourable to the city's interests. So it can be seen that at high levels of national and city government, measurement and evaluation were taking place using methods that are still in place today.

At the same time, the connection between advertising costs and editorial space gained by press agents and publicists came into practice (Tedlow, 1979). This was later exemplified by Plackard and Blackmon (1947) who offered a fully worked example of advertising value equivalence (AVE), many decades before it became a common (if dubious) practice.

Mid-century

In the 1950s and 1960s, there was a world-wide growth in public relations activity. In the United Kingdom, whose Institute of Public Relations was founded in 1948, there was discussion of evaluation in its *Journal* from the outset, mainly proposing analysis of clippings and documents. However, the increasing number of 'how to' books on public relations produced in the United Kingdom and North America rarely touched the topic. Analysis of the 'program research and evaluation' sub-section of Cutlip's bibliography of public relations research (Cutlip, 1965) finds that there was little discussion of the methodology of measuring public relations activity or programmes, with the main emphasis on objective setting based on opinion research.

Evaluation remained an elusive topic. Institute of Public Relations (IPR) President Alan Eden-Green, writing the foreword in the *Handbook of Public Relations* (1963), positioned PR as being 'primarily concerned with communication' (Ellis and Bowman, 1963, foreword). Other texts at the time also focused on processes, but not planning, measurement or outcomes. In Germany, Albert Oeckl (1964) proposed three methods of research – publics and how they use media, content analysis and research on media effects. He was much more linked to the Bernaysian social science of PR than were UK and US practitioners.

Increasing discussion

The 1970s was the decade when books and articles addressing public relations evaluation started to appear. *Measuring and Evaluating Public Relations*

Activities was published by the American Management Association in 1968 with seven articles on methods of measuring public relations results. Soon after, Robinson's *Public Relations and Survey Research* (1969) was published. Pavlik says that '[Robinson] predicted that PR evaluation would move away from seat-of-the-pants approaches and towards 'scientific derived knowledge' (1987: 66). Academics then began taking the lead. A conference in 1977 at the University of Maryland chaired by James E Grunig, partnering with AT&T, was followed by the first scholarly special issue, 'Measuring the Effectiveness of Public Relations,' in *Public Relations Review's* Winter 1977 edition, which featured papers from the conference.

The 1980s and 1990s – debate widens

Following on from the initial conference and academic journal discussion late in the previous decade, US journals came alive in the 1980s with papers from leading academics such as Glenn Broom, David Dozier, James Grunig, Douglass Newsom and Donald Wright. From the consultancy side, Lloyd Kirban of Burson-Marsteller and Walter Lindenmann of Ketchum were prolific and drove the subject higher on the practitioner agenda.

James Grunig (1983) has a *cri de coeur* about practitioner attitudes to measurement and evaluation:

> I have begun to feel more and more like a fundamentalist preacher railing against sin; the difference being that I have railed for evaluation in public relations practice; just as everyone is against sin, so most public relations people I talk to are for evaluation. People keep on sinning, however, and PR people continue not to do evaluation research.

In 1990 *Public Relations Review* had another special edition on evaluation, 'Using research to plan and evaluate public relations' (Summer 1990). Widely cited, it showed that measurement and evaluation were consistently part of academic and professional discourse. All these authors emphasized the need for public relations to be researched, planned and evaluated using robust social science techniques. It was particularly fostered by Broom and Dozier's seminal *Using Research in Public Relations* (1990).

John Pavlik (1987) has commented that measuring the effectiveness of public relations has proved almost as elusive as finding the Holy Grail. Until the mid-1990s, most studies found that public relations practitioners and their employers/clients had ignored evaluation.

By the final decade of the 20th century, public relations measurement and evaluation was a leading research and professional practice topic (McElreath, 1989; White and Blamphin, 1994; Synnott and McKie, 1997). There were major practitioner education initiatives in several developed countries, many linked closely to the Excellence Theory expression of public relations as communication management. In the United States, the Institute for Public Relations Research and Education (now the IPR), harnessing Walter Lindenmann's enthusiasm, published research and commentaries on establishing objectives and assessing results. The International Public Relations Association published its Gold Paper No 11: *Public Relations Evaluation: Professional Accountability*. In 1996, the Swedish PR body, Svenska Informationsförening, moved ahead of the debate at the time to report on Return on Communication, a form of Return on Investment (ROI) that considered the creation of non-financial value through communications.

Tom Watson's studies of UK practitioners in the 1990s showed movement on attitudes. By the latter part of the decade, the attitude in the profession towards evaluation and its integration into campaign and programme planning had changed. Nonetheless, there remains work to be done. The IPR/CDF (2004) study included this statement among its recommendations: 'A significant change in the culture of the PR industry is required towards more sophisticated PR'.

New century

In the first decade of the 21st century, other influences came upon PR planning, research and evaluation. Approaches based on scorecards (Zerfass, 2005) have moved the emphasis of evaluation of corporate communication away from the effects of media towards the development of communication strategies more closely related to organizational objectives where key performance indicators are measured, rather than outputs from communication activity.

In 2008, an international study of PR research priorities (Watson, 2008) found the top three topics were all closely related to the creation and demonstration of value for organizations:

1 public relations' role in contributing to strategic decision-making, strategy development and realization and organizational functioning;

2 the value that public relations creates for organizations through building social capital; managing key relationships and realizing organizational advantage;

3 the measurement and evaluation of public relations both offline and online.

The first two are related to the setting of measurable objectives and their measurement, while the third is related to methods of measurement. Following on from other studies starting as long ago as 1980, this research showed that measurement and evaluation remained as a leading issue for practitioners, researchers and teachers of public relations.

Two important factors in the increased development of interest in measurement and evaluation were the formation in the United Kingdom of the Association of Media Evaluation Companies (AMEC) which was the trade body for the media analysis sector and the second was the commencement of annual conferences on the subjects, first in the United States and then, from 2009 onwards, in Europe. AMEC has been renamed as the International Association for the Measurement and Evaluation of Communication and has members in over 30 countries. Its annual European Summit on Measurement is now the main international event, from which major statements on PR measurement and evaluation have resulted, such as the Barcelona Declaration of Measurement Principles which was adopted at the European Measurement Summit in June 2010 (AMEC, 2010).

This declaration, which was adopted by many PR professional and trade bodies also demonstrated that PR measurement and evaluation is a major service business and greatly developed from the cuttings agencies of 50 to 100 years ago.

Among the practice topics to be discussed in this chapter are the use of financial metrics such as AVE and the Barcelona Principles and follow-on actions, including the valid metrics model.

As the most headline-catching of the Barcelona Principles was the statement effectively barring AVE, 'Principle 5 – AVEs are not the Value of Public Relations', this metric will be discussed first before moving on to all seven Principles and their impact. On page 27, it was stated that the connection between advertising space costs and publicity activity can be traced to the years between the World Wars in the United States. There, it was often stated by press agents and publicists that they could get coverage for clients in newspapers for one-third of the cost of equivalent advertising space. From these claims, the practice of measurement by AVE arose and may have led to the often-cited (but never proven) assertion that editorial is worth three times more than advertising. By the late 1940s, there were examples in books and PR trade publications of AVE in operation.

In the increasing number of books on PR and later in academic research, AVE was ignored or criticized but was widely applied by practitioners, especially in relation to product publicity. By 2009, a study of international PR practitioners presented at the first European Summit on Measurement showed that 35 per cent of respondents were satisfied with using AVE, despite almost universal criticism. UK evaluation pioneer Dermot McKeown described it as 'an early attempt to assign spurious monetary values to media relations activities' (1995: 149) while social media expert David Phillips refers to it as 'voodoo', 'make-believe' and 'inventive nonsense' (2001: 227).

In July 2010, the public relations industry began the process of barring future use of AVE as a methodology for the measurement of public relations effectiveness with the adoption of the Barcelona Principles for PR Measurement (AMEC, 2010). In the following year, AMEC used the term 'outlawed' (AMEC, 2011). In this set of seven principles supported by delegates at the Second European Summit on Measurement held in Barcelona (June 2010), principle 5 was that 'AVEs are not the value of public relations'. The statement supporting this principle said:

> Advertising Value Equivalents (AVEs) do not measure the value of public relations and do not inform future activity; they measure the cost of media space and are rejected as a concept to value public relations. (AMEC, 2010)

Shortly after the event, Robert W Grupp writing a commentary about the Barcelona Principles for the IPR commented that: 'The legitimate intent here is not to debate the validity of AVEs (which simply measure the cost of media space) but to move beyond this measure once and for all' (Grupp, 2010). During the second half of 2010, other PR organizations moved quickly to support the Barcelona Principles, especially in regard to AVE. The Public Relations Society of America (PRSA) supported the initiative (PRSA, 2010). In the United Kingdom, the Chartered Institute of Public Relations (CIPR), which represents individual members, and the Public Relations Consultants Association (PRCA), the trade body for PR consultancies and in-house communication departments, both decided on new policy to cease recognizing AVE as a valid measurement technique. In November 2010, CIPR's CEO Jane Wilson gave strong organizational support:

> AVEs cannot be a part of serious business communication because they have no relevance to the value, financial or otherwise, of an organization. They don't reflect what has actually been achieved. With any successful communications campaign there has to be a tangible result if it is to be deemed successful. Whether it's a product or a perception, something has to have shifted. (CIPR, 2010)

CIPR undertook to lead policy on measurement and evaluation. It identified entries to its annual Excellence Awards programme as the route to enforce its policy by stating that 'AVEs will no longer be deemed an acceptable form of measurement and evaluation, and judges will be briefed to this effect when shortlisting each category's entries' (CIPR, 2010). PRCA's chair Sally Costerton also announced that evaluation would be at the heart of best practices. In addition to these national public relations organizations, the Global Alliance for Public Relations and Communication Management, the umbrella body for national public relations professional bodies, described the Barcelona Principles as a new 'global measurement standard' in April 2011 (Global Alliance, 2011). The impact of the decision was not, however, immediate as one of this book's authors when judging regional public relations awards in the United Kingdom found the vast majority of entries were setting objectives and measuring results in terms of AVE.

The remainder of the Barcelona Principles was less headline-grabbing, and offered a benchmark of existing attitudes, many derived from academic research and best practice:

- importance of goal setting and measurement;
- measuring the effect on outcomes is preferred to measuring outputs;
- the effect on business results can and should be measured where possible;
- media measurement requires quantity and quality;
- AVEs are not the value of public relations;
- social media can and should be measured;

- transparency and replicability are paramount to sound measurement.

Let's consider the principles in detail:

Importance of goal setting and measurement

The setting of goals and the selection of measurement criteria are 'fundamental aspects' of PR programmes. They should be as quantitative as possible and link to the 'who, what, when and how much' the PR programme is intended to affect.

Measurement should take an holistic approach, including traditional and social media; changes in awareness among key stakeholders; comprehension, attitude, and behaviour as applicable; and effect on business results.

Measuring the effect on outcomes is preferred to measuring results

Although measurement of outcomes has long been the topic of academic discussion, this principle makes the point to practitioners. It recommends measurement of awareness changes, audience comprehension, attitude and behaviour related to purchase, corporate reputation, donations, employee engagement, public policy decisions and other changes in stakeholders' views of an organization. It does mix up out-take judgement with outcomes but the broad point is that measurement should be linked to the business/organizational objectives of the PR activities. Quantitative measures such as benchmarking and tracking surveys are commended but can be supplemented with qualitative methods (interviews, focus groups, content analysis).

The effect on business results can and should be measured where possible

Methods that determine the quantity and quality of PR outputs (activity, collateral) upon sales and other business metrics are preferred for measuring business results from consumer or brand marketing. This principle recommends the use of market mix models to evaluate the effect of PR upon consumer marketing and calls for the sector to 'develop PR measures that can provide reliable input into market mix models' in order to isolate the impact of PR methods from other marketing, advertising and promotional inputs. It adds that survey research can be applied to identify changes in purchasing, purchase preference and attitude change brought about by PR.

Media measurement requires quantity and quality

Clip counts and general impression are usually meaningless, says this principle. Instead measurement of media, either in traditional media or online, should account for the impressions among the stakeholder or target audience. It proposes that long-standing measures such as tone, credibility and relevance of the medium to stakeholders or audiences, message delivery, inclusion of third-party comment or company spokesperson and prominence that is relevant to the medium are all used. The tonality of coverage can range from negative to neutral and positive. (As noted earlier in the historical introduction to this chapter, these measures date back a century or more.)

AVEs are not the value of public relations

AVE was discussed earlier in this chapter, with the role of AMEC noted as strongly opposing its use. The principle also states clearly that multipliers, which seek to show that earned media has a greater media cost value than equivalent paid media space, 'should never be applied unless proven to exist in the specific case'.

Social media can and should be measured

Social media measurement, says this principle, 'is a discipline, not a tool' adding 'there is no single metric'. It aligns aspects of measurement of social media with conventional techniques – goal and outcomes to be set; quality and quantity to be evaluated; understanding reach and influence is important (but methods are not yet reliable). In terms of social media specialist measurement, content analysis can be supplemented by web and search analytics, sales and customer relationship management data and surveys. Measurement, it adds, 'must focus on conversation and communities, not just coverage'.

Transparency and replicability are paramount to sound measurement

'PR measurement should be done in a manner that is transparent and replicable for all steps in the process', says the final principle reminding evaluators and practitioners that it is a research process, not a justification technique. There is strong emphasis on transparency of methods so that clients and employers know where the data has come from and how it has been analysed. AMEC's stance was to remove the 'dark arts' approach of some evaluators. The principle recommends that media measurement should state the sources of the content and the criteria used for collection, along with the analysis methodology (human or computer, tone scale, reach to target, content analysis parameters). Surveys need methodology to be clearly stated along with sample size, margin of error and whether they are probability or non-probability design. All questions and the statistical methodology should be disclosed.

The Barcelona Principles have been widely seen as 'a good thing' and supported by the PR industry. They are not a great leap forwards, although it is claimed that there was a 'light bulb moment' from AMEC's executive director that led to their creation as a universal framework for PR measurement. Richard Bagnall, a leading media evaluator, says that there was 'a new era in the PR and measurement industry – one where the industry had agreed to turn away from spurious scores and weighted outputs and to focus on measuring outcomes based on objectives of campaigns' (Bagnall, 2012: 165–66). Others considered that the principles did no more than state some good practices clearly to practitioners. British commentator Philip Sheldrake defended their simplicity, 'these principles have been criticized by some as being too simple, too basic, but that, I think is their value. Absent consensus on the basics, the foundations and building anything grander becomes a dicey endeavour' (Sheldrake, 2011: 46).

Reaction from practitioners themselves, when told that AVEs were not considered valid, was to ask 'what will replace them?' Which was missing the point that there is no (and never was) single metric for the range and complexity of public relations activity. AMEC's response has been to develop the valid metrics matrix of measurement methods, which will be discussed in Chapter 11. It aims to offer all practitioners a menu of measurement and evaluation methods to be applied to a range of campaign types and methods.

The Barcelona Principles and the subsequent valid metrics matrix aren't the only recent developments in PR measurement and evaluation. In later chapters, the debate about the application of the ROI concept to PR and the development of a communications performance management system in Germany and Austria called communication controlling will also be reviewed.

Questions to discuss

- Does the history of PR measurement and evaluation help current practitioners understand the culture in which they work?
- What do you consider were the most influential developments in PR measurement and evaluation?
- The Barcelona Principles were introduced in mid-2010. Are they well known and respected by PR practitioners? What might be barriers to their widespread adoption?
- Can you rank the seven principles in order of their importance for development of best practice in PR? What are the reasons for your ranking?
- Is there an eighth or ninth measurement principle that you would propose?
- Richard Bagnall has stated there is 'a new era in the PR and measurement industry' following the devising of the Barcelona Principles. What's your view?

04
Gathering and interpreting information

Stacks (2013) effectively summarizes the role that research plays in public relations:

> So basic research begins before a public relations campaign or program begins. It establishes what has been done in the past that might impact on the future, it establishes a baseline against which to evaluate success, and it has planned benchmarks against which to evaluate objectives. Data gathered across the campaign or program should be measured so that can be inputted into whatever decision-making process is being employed by the client or business. Finally, the data gathered must be used to demonstrate an impact or correlation with other business units to demonstrate a return of investment in the public relations function.

Evaluation is a research-based activity, so any progress in evaluation practice has to be underpinned by an understanding of research methods. This is not to say that public relations practitioners have to become experts in research methodology. It does, however, mean that a basic understanding of research methods is part of the professional practitioner's toolkit and that there is a role for research specialists in public relations consultancies and departments. Anyone managing public relations campaigns and activities therefore needs to be an effective commissioner and user of research.

Broom and Sha (2013: 265) expand on this point: 'Even though it cannot answer all the questions or sway all decisions, methodical, systematic research is the foundation of effective public relations'. Without research, public relations practitioners are restricted to asserting that they understand the situation and can provide a solution, while, with research (followed by analysis of the data gathered), they can put forward proposals clearly backed up with evidence to support them. Research is the 'scientific alternative to tenacity, authority and intuition'. While lack of resources and time are often the reasons proffered for not doing more research, a better explanation might be a combination of practitioners lacking an understanding of research methods and clients/employers regarding research as unnecessary.

Importantly, research does not have to mean wide-ranging, expensive and highly technical exercises. McElreath (1997: 203) makes the point that research may range from the informal to the formal. While formal research will have advantages such as the ability to be replicated, all types of research have the potential to yield useful results: 'One insightful revelation from one focus group can be as telling as the key result from a massive opinion poll'. Similarly, Smith (2005: 9) suggests: 'Research begins with informal and often simple methods of gathering relevant information'.

All types of research, however informal and anecdotal, can be useful. All too often, practitioners ignore the 'free' research available within many (particularly large) organizations. Two related topics are the use of 'piggy-back' research (eg adding questions to an existing survey), or an 'omnibus' survey where questions – and therefore costs – are shared with others.

The UK's Chartered Institute of Public Relations has long advocated research as an integral part of public relations planning and implementation. Its *Evaluation Toolkit* (2011: 8) outlines the importance of research, planning and measurement:

- to demonstrate the value of PR and the attainment of both PR and business objectives;
- to facilitate more effective audience engagement and to feed into PR planning;
- to help build the credibility and influence of PR within organizations, and demonstrate the contribution of [PR] to strategic business decision-making and organizational success;
- to analyse key message pick-up, adaption and reproduction among publics and those who influence publics;
- to gather intelligence about a sector, trends and issues (historic and future), and how an organization and its peers and competitors are regarded;
- to provide a benchmark against which to measure the effectiveness of a PR programme;
- to provide a 'hard' measure of success to reinforce the case for PR.

So, evaluation is both a research-based discipline and intimately involved with (if not actually a prerequisite for) professional public relations practice. Its purpose is to inform and clarify and it operates to high standards of rigour and logic. As the orbit of public relations extends from publicity-seeking media relations to issues management and corporate reputation, research will play an increasingly important role in the planning, execution and measurement of public relations programmes.

Similarly, Smith (2005: 9) confirms the integration of research and planning with his 'nine steps of strategic public relations'.

Phase One: Formative Research
Step 1: Analysing the Situation
Step 2: Analysing the Organization
Step 3: Analysing the Publics

Phase Two: Strategy
Step 4: Establishing Goals and Objectives
Step 5: Formulating Action and Response Strategies
Step 6: Using Effective Communications

Phase Three: Tactics
Step 7: Choosing Communication Tactics
Step 8: Implementing the Strategic Plan

Phase Four: Evaluative Research
Step 9: Evaluating the Strategic Plan

Research and a strategic perspective on public relations are intimately connected. Most texts which claim to address strategic public relations planning and practice will – quite appropriately – have significant sections on research methods. Why is this? The thinking that lies behind a public relations strategy has echoes of Smith's (2005) nine steps and could be listed as the following:

- analysing the problem;
- establishing objectives;
- building the creative theme;
- segmenting target publics;
- positioning the organization;
- evaluating the results.

A cursory glance at any of these elements confirms the linkage between research and developing a public relations strategy. Analysis (of a problem) requires the gathering of extensive data, for example. Similarly, if 'the big idea' proves elusive you need more information: on the organization, market, environment, competitors, product/service, and so on.

Here, we have a broader view of public relations evaluation than just research undertaken at the end of the programme to establish effectiveness (important as this is). We extend evaluation to encompass formative research and use the term 'summative' to describe the final research phase. This is aligned with McElreath's (1997: 203) terminology: formative evaluation research and summative evaluative research: 'Research conducted to help a manager better formulate plans for implementing a program is called formative evaluative research. Research designed to help summarize the overall impact of a program is called summative evaluative research.'

Elsewhere (see Chapter 5), we discuss the concepts of outputs, out-takes and outcomes to classify the different categories of results that flow from public relations activities. The point is made (Lindenmann, 2003: 7) that the measurement of PR outputs is relatively simple: 'usually counting, tracking and observing'. In contrast, for PR out-takes and PR outcomes, 'it is a matter of asking and carrying out extensive review and analysis of what was said and what was done'. The latter often requires the use of research techniques, so the nature of evaluation activity will determine how extensive the research activity to support it needs to be.

The scope of research

When evaluation was defined in Chapter 2, the role of evaluation as a proactive, forward-looking activity was confirmed. Naturally the collection of historical data is a prerequisite, but evaluation is not restricted to making conclusions on past activity. The emphasis on improving programme effectiveness strongly indicates that the information collected on previous activity is used as feedback to adapt the nature of future activities, and therefore argues for a formative (as well as summative) perspective on public relations evaluation. McCoy and Hargie (2003: 305) confirm this orientation and also link formative evaluation into a strategic role for public relations practitioners: 'If practitioners engage in formative evaluation and environmental monitoring it is suggested that this will help them to manage relationships, link PR to organizational goals and make PR more strategic than tactical'.

Professional practitioners base their activities on a body of knowledge as well as techniques. They see public relations operating at a strategic level within organizations: managing relationships with the publics that are key to the success of the organization. This implies an out-take/outcome orientation to public relations research and evaluation.

The current momentum for evaluation in public relations is predicated on the assumption that social scientific methods can be applied to public relations. Broom and Dozier (1990: 14) established the foundations on which much modern thinking associated with research and public relations is based. They identified five major approaches to the management of public relations programmes, based on the role of research in that management. These range from the no-research approach in which 'public relations technicians operate on the basis of their intuition and artistic judgement' through the informal approach, media-event approach and evaluation-only approach to the scientific management approach.

The informal approach uses research but only so-called informal, 'pre-scientific' research that is then misappropriated as the basis for strategic planning. The media-event approach is the province of the visibility study where research (which is usually internally rigorous) is used not in a scientific, knowledge-seeking manner, but rather to create newsworthy, attention-attracting information.

The evaluation-only approach consigns research to an impact-measuring role only, as opposed to a planning tool. This is a common theme, with, for example, McCoy and Hargie (2003: 305) arguing that the focus of public relations evaluation remains on output measures and that, anyway, these tend to be subjective, ad hoc and informal: 'evaluation should include formative evaluation and environmental monitoring rather than just the summative output evaluation that is common in PR'. It is symptomatic of the problems of terminology surrounding public relations in general and evaluation in particular that, while media coverage is often described as the 'output' of public relations activity, many others would argue that media evaluation is at best formative as it focuses on the process of public relations rather than being summative by examining any impact that the PR campaign in question has.

The scientific management approach sees research threaded through every stage of the management of public relations programmes: research is undertaken to analyse the starting point, monitor the programme as it unfolds and ascertain whether objectives have been met.

Earlier research by Dozier (1984) to test whether public relations had adopted 'scientifically derived knowledge' revealed three major approaches to evaluation. Seat-of-the-pants evaluation is a subjective and intuitive method of evaluation which uses casual observation by the practitioner to judge the output of the campaign. It is the traditional approach used by public relations practitioners, particularly those concerned with the process of public relations rather than outcomes, thereby displaying the no-research intuitive approach to the management of public relations programmes.

Scientific dissemination evaluation is another process-oriented approach but with particular emphasis on distribution. It rests on the assumption that wider dissemination means higher impact. It is usually based on numerical analysis of press clippings or broadcast transcripts, the circulation/readership of media used, or analysis of the content achieved. It almost goes without saying that media evaluation falls into this category.

In contrast to scientific dissemination, scientific impact evaluation primarily uses quantitative, social scientific methods of data collection to determine the public relations campaign impact directly. Frequently, practitioners rely upon experimental or quasi-experimental research designs in which measures are taken both before and after a new programme is implemented. This design allows one to determine whether the programme 'caused' the observed change.

Broom and Dozier (1990: 26) mirror the frequent three-step/stage analysis of public relations evaluation (see Chapter 5) when they discuss using research to plan programmes, to monitor programmes and to evaluate programmes. The first stage in programme planning is indeed to analyse the situation, which is effectively an analysis of the public relations 'problem'. This problem concerns the mismatch between the situation as it is and the situation as the organization would ideally like it to be. The public relations programme is designed to align this dichotomy. The key here is to use a cycle of formal and informal, quantitative and qualitative approaches first to confirm and delineate the 'problem', and then to understand and explain it. This approach can be exemplified in this way:

> Somebody tells you that there is a rumour going around that redundancies are in the offing and that staff are worried. Senior management confirm that the rumour is completely unfounded. Informal discussions with opinion formers in the staff canteen confirm that there is indeed such a rumour doing the rounds and 'a lot of people are worried'. You poll a systematic sample of employees to check how widespread the concern is and then talk to a random sample of nine employees to see why they think layoffs are imminent and get a feel as to how the rumour started in the first place.

Once the programme has been launched, research is used to monitor its effectiveness (or otherwise). This can be challenging, but it is essential to avoid wasting resources on pointless activity. The key point is that it is the process that is being examined, but not the ultimate impact (yet). It is worth monitoring process activity because effective processes are more likely to lead to successful results. But, however good the process, this is no guarantee of successful results (see the substitution game, Chapter 5).

When moving on to assessment of the impact of the public relations programme, the outcomes stated in the programme's objectives must be examined. Broom and Dozier (1990: 77) divide these programme outcomes into three categories: change or maintenance of a public's knowledge (including awareness and understanding); predispositions (opinions and attitudes); and behaviour. This is where direct measurement is required, frequently using formal research techniques, but sometimes using more easily available quantitative data such as sales enquiries (or even sales).

The operational management of public relations is centred on the planning of public relations programmes or campaigns. A common theme of public relations planning models is that they start with a research phase designed to analyse the current situation; the starting point needs to be defined if the correct strategy to reach the end point (objectives/goals) is to be identified.

Primary and secondary research

Formal research is divided into primary and secondary. Secondary research (also known as desk research) refers to information that has already been published in some form, ranging from information on the internet to internal reports. Secondary research is frequently quick to obtain and is usually – but not always – free. Stacks and Michaelson (2010: 51) state that:

'All research methods begin with the gathering of information or data on a given topic or problem'. They go on to suggest that it is widely overlooked by public relations practitioners.

In contrast to secondary research, primary research (also known as field research) is undertaken to meet a specific need – frequently, to fill a gap identified by secondary research. Primary research can be time-consuming, technical and resource intensive. Primary research methods are frequently described as either quantitative or qualitative. The former is associated with statistics/numbers and tends to answer the question 'what is happening?' Associated with questionnaires and surveys, quantitative research normally involves relatively large numbers and is regarded as relatively objective. Sampling and piloting are issues that quantitative research needs to address. In contrast, qualitative research tends to answer the question 'why is it happening?' and involves more in-depth enquiry among relatively small numbers of respondents.

Research methods

So, primary research is usually either qualitative or quantitative in form. Qualitative research usually refers to studies that are somewhat subjective, but nevertheless in-depth, using a probing, open-end, free response format. Quantitative research usually refers to studies that are highly objective and projectable, using closed-end, forced-choice questionnaires. These studies tend to rely heavily on statistics and numerical measures.

Denscombe comprehensively defines and distinguishes the quantitative and the qualitative (2010: 237–39); see Table 4.1.

TABLE 4.1   Research families, approaches and techniques

Quantitative research tends to be associated with:	<ul><li>numbers as the unit of analysis;</li><li>analysis;</li><li>large-scale studies;</li><li>a specific focus;</li><li>researcher detachment;</li><li>a predetermined research design.</li></ul>
Qualitative research tends to be associated with:	<ul><li>words as the unit of analysis;</li><li>description;</li><li>small-scale studies;</li><li>holistic perspective;</li><li>researcher involvement;</li><li>an emergent research design.</li></ul>

Action research

There is much discussion among social scientists about the concept of action research. Its distinguishing feature is that it avoids any two-stage approach: specialist researchers generating some research findings as one stage, and then after consideration and reflection a separate body of practitioners taking some action as a result of those findings as a separate stage. Closer examination indicates that, rather than a research strategy, in a public relations context action research is more a planning and management framework that accepts a rigorous research orientation.

The parallels with public relations practice are reinforced (and become almost uncanny) wherever action research is discussed. For example, Blaxter, Hughes and Tight (2010: 69–70), discussing action research, state:

> It is well suited to the needs of people conducting research in their workplaces, and who have a focus on improving aspects of their own and their colleagues' practices. ... It offers a research design which links the research process closely to its context, and is predicated on the idea of research having a practical purpose in view and leading to change. ... It also fits well with the idea of the research process as a spiral activity, going through repeated cycles and changing each time.

Three parallels immediately appear. First, the focus on improving practice links to the thinking behind formative evaluation. Second, public relations is frequently associated with the management of change. Finally, there is wide agreement that the public relations planning process is necessarily a cyclical one and action research is clearly cyclical as well (see Figure 4.1). Denscombe (2010: 129) adds: 'The crucial points about the cycle of enquiry in action research are: (1) that *research feeds back directly into practice*; and (2) that the *process is ongoing*'. He continues by suggesting that action research is not only about 'improving practice' but 'can also involve an evaluation of changes just instigated'.

Case studies

The use of case studies (single or multiple) is increasingly popular among social science researchers. By looking in depth at a single instance (or a few instances) it may be possible to derive understandings that are more widely applicable than the single case being studied. For example, a detailed investigation into the organizational behaviour of one complex company may give us an insight into how large companies in general behave. In public relations, case studies are not so much a research technique as a useful means of demonstrating the efficacy of a company's/client's products or services as well as generating third-party endorsement. Case studies sacrifice breadth of study for depth of study: 'Case studies focus on one instance (or just a few) of a particular phenomenon with a view to providing an in-depth account

FIGURE 4.1 Action research parallels the cyclical nature of PR planning

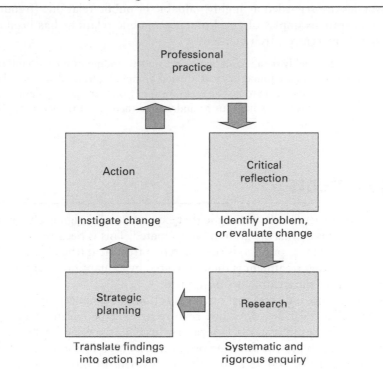

of events, relationships, experiences or processes occurring in that particular instance' (Denscombe, 2010: 52).

Daymon and Holloway (2011) have examined the role of (qualitative) research methods in the context of public relations and marketing communications. They point out that a case study is a distinctive approach because it focuses specifically on the case as an end in itself:

A case study is an extensive examination, using multiple sources of evidence (which may be qualitative, quantitative or both), of a single entity which is bounded by time and place. Usually it is associated with a location. The 'case' may be an organization, a set of people such as a social or work group, a community, an event, a process, an issue or a campaign.

Many PR and marcomms (marketing communications) people prefer quantitative survey research. The term case study is used to refer to slightly different concepts, indeed not restricted to a research context.

In public relations consultancies and advertising agencies, for example, 'case studies' are compiled to illustrate good practice, such as award-winning campaigns, and used for promotional purposes or competitive purposes ... to generate new business. In education, 'case studies' act as a teaching tool to stimulate discussion, debate and practical solutions. Used in this way, they are examples of professional practices within industry or professional contexts (Daymon and Holloway, 2011: 117).

Stacks (2002: 71–72) is one of the few other writers to have examined research issues in a public relations context. He points out that, although case studies are regarded as highly valuable in public relations (frequently to demonstrate examples of good practice), public relations has been slow to adopt them as a research method:

> They provide a richly detailed and complete understanding of the case under study. Case studies are found in most applied disciplines, from business to law to advertising to medicine to public relations. They offer insight into good and bad practice. A case study helps us to understand theory, but theory as applied to specific situations.

Experiments

Broom and Dozier (1990: 99) argue that experimental design is always used when a public relations programme is evaluated. This is because a group of subjects (one or more publics) is subjected to a treatment (the PR campaign). The impact of that treatment is then measured by a quantitative comparison before and after the treatment was applied.

Common sense indicates that any application of the concept of an experiment to public relations does not revolve around people in white coats wielding test tubes in a sterile laboratory. Instead, the experimental design predicates field studies, such as the pre-testing of messages among naturally occurring groups of people before the deployment of those messages in a planned campaign. The true scientific experiment seeks to control all the variables associated with the experiment. This becomes increasingly difficult as the experiment moves out of the laboratory and into the field. The latter can only really be described as 'quasi-experimental' in that: 'The quasi (as if) experimental approach is conducted in the spirit of the classic laboratory experiment, but recognizes that the researcher cannot dictate circumstances and needs to take the role of observing events "as they naturally occur"' (Denscombe, 2010: 73).

Surveys

A field survey should only be used when secondary sources are exhausted, otherwise you will be wasting time and money finding out what you already know. Unfortunately, however, desk research is not always going to provide all the information that is required. In this case, primary or field research will be required. This is an area fraught with difficulty, theoretically requiring a great deal of technical competence as well as resources in terms of both time and money.

However, in practice a surprising amount of information can be obtained by 'gifted amateurs' and fairly limited surveys, provided no more emphasis is placed on the results than they deserve. All research is subject to error and, in general, the less detailed the research and the smaller the sample size the wider the margin of error. There is no harm in undertaking a brief survey among a small number of people provided that these limitations are taken into account when interpreting the results. Asking six randomly selected people what car they drive cannot be used to calculate Ford's UK market share, although it might indicate that Ford is a popular brand. This is the province of 'informal research', theoretically a contradiction in terms, but nevertheless, thought-provoking feedback from a few unsystematically polled but influential opinion formers could hardly be ignored.

Denscombe (2010: 11/12) suggests that the three key characteristics of a survey are: wide and inclusive coverage; at a specific point in time; and empirical research. Surveys imply a broad perspective, are a snapshot (allowing the possibility of tracking changes over time), and involve getting out into the field to see what is happening 'out there'. He also stresses that although there are research methods associated with surveys (such as questionnaires), together with case studies and a number of other approaches to social research, a survey is a research strategy that can be implemented through a variety of research methods.

The traditional postal survey is being overtaken by postal and internet surveys; cost, turnaround times and response rates all militate against them. E-mail and web-based surveys overcome many of these drawbacks while still providing good quality of data. The telephone allows for interviews as well as surveys but increasing reliance on mobiles poses its own challenges such as – in the United Kingdom, at least – not having 'prior knowledge about the social background or geographical location' (Denscombe, 2010: 15).

Westminster Council (2011: 30) outlines the key considerations associated with website surveys:

- Focus on quantitative scale questions with some open-ended qualitative questions. The former 'helps find pockets of discontent' but the latter 'add depth'.

- Random sampling can seem the most obvious approach, but it may be better to survey people who have had some specific engagement with the site.

- There is no need to survey every visitor, a random sample is fine if the traffic on the website is at a reasonable level.

- Continuous surveys can be more useful than a series of ad hoc ones – accounting for seasonality and other variations.

- Surveys can be undertaken on entry, during the session, or on exit. The latter is frequently preferable.

- Feedback from surveys should be sent to the relevant people/ department in the organization.

Interviews

One of the main techniques when undertaking field research is the interview (administered by telephone or face-to-face). Interviews can vary from being highly structured where a questionnaire has to be strictly followed, while others are completely unstructured and the topic is examined in depth, with the respondent being allowed to lead the discussion in virtually any direction they wish. The less structured the interview, the more skill is required by the researcher in both conducting the interview and interpreting its results.

Because of the cost and time involved, it is normally impractical to carry out a significant number of personal interviews. However, if there are a small number of people with valuable information that requires intricate and detailed questions then this approach might well be appropriate.

The advantages of a personal interview include a low refusal rate by respondents, and the sample is usually less distorted (postal enquiries have an erratic response rate and with the telephone you will not be able to get hold of everybody in the sample). Also, a rapport can be established between respondent and interviewer that breaks down any initial suspicion associated with surveys, and also a wider range of questions can be asked. Dr Kevin Moloney of Bournemouth University has developed a set of rules of thumb for doing research-based interviews which we have adapted (with permission):

Before the interview, ensure that you:

- understand that you are doing qualitative research which may or may not be backed up by survey data;
- can justify how you have chosen your interview sample: randomly, representatively or purposively;
- have a master research question which breaks down into sub-questions.

During the interview, ensure that you:

- either ask the questions in a tightly structured way, or go with the flow of the responses;
- ensure by the end of the interview that you have asked all the questions on your research agenda;
- tape the interview;
- do not take notes (more than a few key words) – concentrate on what is being said;
- note body language, repetitions and omissions;
- don't ask leading questions;
- don't expect respondents to be overly self-critical;
- realize you may have to get at critical points obliquely.

After the interview, ensure that you:

- write up observation notes on leaving the interview and listen to the tape right through twice;
- are on the look-out for topics emerging that you may have missed;
- transcribe everything and do so within two days of the interview;
- remember that a 20-minute interview takes three hours to transcribe (so consider paying somebody else to do it!).

Telephone interviews are cheaper than personal interviews in terms of use of time. They also enable interviews to be completed faster. A wide geographical spread can be covered, the interviewer can take copious notes and is able to study reference or confidential material. Compared with postal questionnaires, the interviewer is able to explain the survey in some detail, even using semi-structured questionnaires that would be totally inappropriate by post. The principal problem is that the length of the interview tends to be restricted compared with a personal interview, and the lack of eye contact makes the relationship between respondent and interviewer less relaxed.

The key benefit of the in-depth interview is the opportunity to probe, to encourage people to expand on their answers. Kane and O'Reilly-de Brun (2001: 206) offer useful advice on probing techniques for interviews:

- Ask questions that allow people to develop their answers, not questions that can simply be answered by 'yes' or 'no'.

- Pursue information further by asking questions that will tell you 'Who?', 'What?', 'Where?', 'Why?' and 'How?', as appropriate.

- Encourage people to expand on an answer by pausing after the reply, and perhaps giving some sign of encouragement.

- Encourage people to clarify their answers.

- Cross-check the answers by phrasing the question slightly differently.

Focus groups

A focus group can be regarded as a group interview but the interaction between group members gives it particular richness, as well as requiring skill to moderate. Focus groups are undoubtedly a powerful research tool and can provide a useful complement to quantitative approaches to get a deep understanding of the opinions and attitudes of particular publics. However, they do need to be moderated by trained researchers and are not really the province of the 'gifted amateur'. Therefore, the likely need to outsource their operation has implications in terms of cost.

Daymon and Holloway (2011: 242) suggest that the key features of a focus group are:

- they provide evidence from many voices on the same topic;
- they are interactive and dynamic;
- they allow participants to socially construct their views, which in turn can result in attitude change;
- they provide a supportive forum for expressing suppressed views;
- they allow you to collect a large amount of data fairly quickly;
- they are often used in conjunction with other methods, including those which are quantitative.

The interactive nature of the focus group is important, as one person's comments motivate others to expand upon and develop their own views. They are also useful for involving participants who are suspicious of research-ing and hesitant to articulate their own views, opinions and perspectives. Typically, focus groups can be used to examine issues that vary from the micro to the macro:

- advertising or concept testing;
- understanding behaviours and attitudes;
- exploring strategic policies and issues;
- developing and understanding brands, products and services;
- exploring organizational and industry issues.

The length of a focus group session varies, but typically is two hours. Similarly, the size of the group varies, with smaller groups preferred for detailed discussions of contentious issues, and larger groups for less intensive discussions of less controversial topics. The facilitator moves from introduc-ing the session, through putting members at ease and outlining the scope of the topic, to the main discussion, with questioning moving from the general to the particular. Note that while contrasting views can be illuminating, an important role for the facilitator is to diffuse any potential hostility:

> The qualities of an effective moderator are the same as those of an in-depth interviewer: flexibility, open-mindedness, skills in eliciting information, and the ability to both listen and interpret. In addition, because you take on a leadership role when moderating, you must have excellent social and refereeing skills. These allow you, first, to guide participants towards effective interaction. Then they enable you to focus and control the discussion without coercing participants or directing the debate.
>
> (Daymon and Holloway, 2011: 254)

Questionnaires

While it has already been mentioned that a questionnaire can be administered face-to-face, particularly in a market research context, the use of the questionnaire is normally considered when it is administered by post, or increasingly by e-mail where many of the same considerations apply. Denscombe (2010: 156) outlines those situations when this type of questionnaire is at its most effective:

- when used with *large numbers* of respondents in many locations, eg the postal questionnaire;

- when what is required tends to be fairly *straightforward information –* relatively brief and uncontroversial;

- when there is a need for *standardized data* from identical questions – without requiring personal, face-to-face interaction;

- when the respondents can be expected to be *able to read and understand the question*s – the implications of age, intellect and eyesight need to be considered;

- when the *social climate is open* enough to allow full and honest answers.

Questionnaires are generally reckoned to be a relatively cost-effective form of research, and certainly postal and internet surveys can be carried out at reasonable cost. The net can be spread wide geographically and speed is another advantage. Usually, if people are to respond to a questionnaire they do so immediately and, although you will find the odd straggler coming in some time after issue, the bulk of response will come back within a few days. Internet and postal questionnaires also eliminates interviewer bias, which is a major problem associated with telephone and face-to-face interviewers.

The main problem of postal questionnaires specifically is lack of response. The principal factor governing response is the degree of interest the questionnaire generates among respondents. Providing some sort of incentive to respond (prize draw or free gift) can increase response rate but does add cost. Another problem is getting a representative mailing list in the first place. Another restricting factor is the length of the questionnaire. Once it gets beyond two sides of A4, the length of the questionnaire is going to deter postal and e-mail respondents. This restriction naturally limits the amount of information that can be obtained.

Lindenmann (2006: 8) confirms that 'conducting surveys via e-mail or through websites is growing in popularity'. The major advantage of self-administered questionnaires distributed electronically is speed of response, but there can be problems with formatting and incomplete data. Web-based surveys are rather different, 'in that a specialized software program or system is needed to construct a questionnaire and to collect and eventually process the results' (Lindenmann, 2006: 8). One advantage is that survey responses are automatically collected, removing the need for manual entry. However, they are relatively passive as they rely on respondents seeking out the online questionnaire. This has issues for the eligibility of respondents and the representative nature of the sample.

Denscombe (2010: 159) identifies three different forms of delivery for internet questionnaires. An e-mail questionnaire (where the questionnaire is part of the e-mail) is simple to design and respond to but 'cannot be made to look very attractive' as well as the problems identified by Lindenmann. A questionnaire as an attachment addresses design drawbacks but is relatively laborious to respond to. Finally, the web-based questionnaire has the advantages outlined above, there may be a need to e-mail a link to the website to encourage response.

Sampling methods

Survey research is based on the idea that to obtain representative views from a body of people, it is not normally necessary to talk to them all. The problem is to derive a sample that is large enough and broad enough to be representative of the group as a whole. The sample size is usually a compromise between the resources available to devote to the survey and the accuracy required. There is almost no limit to the statistical knots that some researchers will tie themselves up in trying to perfect sampling techniques. However, much useful information can be gathered using low-cost, small-sample research and, although sample selection should always be approached very carefully, this care should be based on common sense rather than academic statistical theory.

Denscombe (2010: 45) points out that: 'In practice, social research frequently involves surveys with relatively small numbers – *between 30 and 250* – and when estimating the required sample size such surveys tend to depend on non-probability sampling techniques'.

Briefly, there are two major types of sampling procedures: probability or random sampling, and non-probability or quota sampling. With random sampling, each member of the population to be sampled has an equal chance of being selected. This is not as simple as it sounds, since random does not mean haphazard. For example, picking 20 names in no particular order from a telephone directory does not produce a random sample. There will be some bias in the sample selection (the eye being drawn to familiar or short names, for example). Instead, a preferable approach is to use random number tables.

An alternative approach is quota sampling. Here, those who should be interviewed are specified in terms of specific variables. A simple example would be a decision to poll equal numbers of females and males. They may well be randomly selected initially but once a quota of 50 per cent (of males, for example) is reached, then recruitment of males is abandoned and only females accepted until the sample is complete.

Macnamara (2011) sings the praises of a census where all the population is surveyed. Clearly this is only appropriate with groups that are relatively small but does avoid the complexities associated with sampling. If sampling is required, Macnamara (2011: 46) suggests a third method in addition to random and quota:

- *Random* – relatively simple as it selects every nth person in a population, but may not yield a sample that is representative of a group and sub-groups in it.

- *Representative or quota* – a more sophisticated method where particular groups can be segregated and samples drawn from each to ensure the total survey base represents the population.

- *Purposive* – a technique for use where there is a defined purpose or objective. Denscombe (2010: 34) describes it as 'hand-picked for the topic'.

Questionnaire design

Crucial to the whole issue of public relations research is questionnaire design. It is the vehicle for collecting the information required. One golden rule with questionnaires is to pilot them by doing a pre-test with two or three potential or typical respondents. Before tackling the questions themselves, two quick points. First, the length of the questionnaire: as a guideline, a postal questionnaire should be limited to 20 questions, a telephone survey to 15 minutes and a face-to-face interview either 30 minutes (in the home or office) or three minutes (in the street). The other vital consideration is to ensure that the instructions to both the respondent and interviewer (if applicable) are clear and unambiguous.

Dichotomous questions are the simplest type of questions to ask since, theoretically, there are only two possible answers. Questions such as these are easy to ask and analyse but make sure that in the circumstances in which you use them they truly are a two-way choice. Sometimes, 'don't know' could well be a response, while on other occasions 'neither' or 'both' are possibilities.

With multiple-choice questions, respondents are able to choose from a range of possible answers. Again, these questions are very easy to analyse but it is important to list all possible options and always include an answer 'other (please specify)' in case an option you had not considered emerges.

Scaling questions are an attempt to identify attitudes and strength of feeling. The most common means of attempting to gauge strength of feeling is the so-called 'Likert' scale. A respondent is asked to what extent they agree or disagree with a particular statement, indicating whether he or she strongly agrees, agrees, is uncertain, disagrees or strongly disagrees.

Macnamara (2011: 46) confirms that Likert scales 'most commonly use a five-point scale' and lists other common types of research question as multiple choice, rankings, semantic differentials and yes/no choices.

The exact form and phrasing of questions will vary according to the particular research exercise being undertaken. However, there are a number of points to consider:

- Given the subject matter, make it as simple and easy as possible.

- Do not digress: keep to the subject and ask only relevant questions.

- Bear in mind that you will have to analyse the results afterwards.

- Each question should cover one point at a time.

- Questions should be unambiguous.

- Avoid leading and misleading questions.

- Ensure good sequencing and question flow.

- Do not ask unanswerable questions.

- Do not offend or embarrass.

- Introduce some variety; don't be monotonous.

- Use positive questions; try to avoid negatives.

Content analysis

Content analysis is an established research method of particular relevance to communications evaluation. Denscombe (2010) suggests that content analysis is useful for analysing documents when they are being used as an alternative to questionnaires, interviews, or observation. There is a consensus (Denscombe, 2010 and Stacks, 2002) that content analysis can be applied to a wide range of 'texts', including written, oral, and video content. Stacks (2002: 107) clarifies matters: 'Content analysis enables us to look at qualitative data in a quantitative manner'. And later, 'Content analysis *is a systematic, objective, and quantitative method for researching messages*'.

Denscombe (2010: 282) states clearly that 'The main strength of content analysis is that it provides a means for quantifying the contents of text', and that it does so in a fashion that is clear and repeatable. From a public relations perspective, Stacks (2002: 107) confirms that: 'Content analysis enables us to look at qualitative data in a quantitative manner'. Indeed, although the phrase is rarely used, content analysis is commonly applied to communications, as much media evaluation would be better referred to as content analysis. And Stacks (2002) adds that public relations has long employed content analysis to examine media coverage.

Denscombe (2010) argues that content analysis identifies the presence of relevant words or ideas (for example), frequency and whether views are positive or negative. And there is a broadly standard approach to how content analysis is undertaken (Denscombe, 2010; Stacks, 2002; and Smith, 2005). It involves identifying the content to be analysed (eg key messages), what is to be analysed (eg media coverage), the approach to categorization (eg positive, negative and neutral), and then the coding, counting and recording. In some circumstances, sampling may be employed so that not every artefact needs to be examined.

Broom and Sha (2013: 282) confirm the definition of content analysis, reinforce its role in analysing media coverage, and outline its limitations.

Content analysis is the application of systematic procedures for objectively determining what is being reported in the media. Press clippings and broadcast monitor reports, all available from commercial services, have long been used as the bases for content analysis. They indicate only what is being printed or broadcast, *not* what is read or heard. And they *do not* measure whether or not the audiences learned or believed message content.

Macnamara (2005a: 1) confirms that: 'Media content analysis is a specialized sub-set of content analysis, a well-established research methodology'. Note that media content analysis is a more accurate term for what is generally referred to as media evaluation. He distinguishes between quantitative and qualitative content analysis: 'Quantitative content analysis collects data about media content such a topics or issues, volume of mentions, "messages" ... circulation of the media (audience reach) and frequency' (2005a: 4).

Qualitative content analysis appreciates that different readers will interpret texts differently and takes into account wider considerations than just the text itself. It depends on interpretation of the text by the researcher and is resource intensive so is usually based on small samples – factors which Macnamara suggest has resulted in criticism of qualitative content analysis. He summarizes the situation in these terms (2005a: 5):

Quantitative content analysis can conform to the scientific method and produce reliable findings. Qualitative content analysis is difficult and maybe impossible to do with scientific reliability. But qualitative analysis of texts is necessary to understand their deeper meanings and likely interpretations by audiences – surely the ultimate goal of analysing media content. So a combination of the two seems to be the ideal approach.

Questions to discuss

- Why is it that many public relations practitioners are uncomfortable with understanding and applying research methods?
- What role does research play in the planning and management of public relations programmes?
- Does a case study research strategy have any relevance to public relations?
- What are the benefits in using mixed methods (combining qualitative and quantitative approaches) in primary research?
- Is there more to content analysis than underpinning media evaluation (media content analysis)?

05
Evaluation structures and processes

A number of well-proven evaluation structures and models have been available to practitioners for many years in order to help them define and implement evaluation strategies. They have not been universally adopted; the reasons for this are discussed and, together with practitioner research, this discussion is used as the basis of developing more accessible alternatives.

When practitioners undertake evaluation, they tend to take a narrow view of the methods used and concentrate on simplistic methodologies. However, there are structures and models which outline processes for public relations evaluation. This chapter considers those structures and proposes two more based on research among (and feedback from) practitioners.

It is increasingly recognized that the evaluation of public relations programmes/activities requires a mix of techniques. This is confirmed by experienced practitioner Walter Lindenmann (1993: 9): 'it is important to recognize that there is no one simplistic method for measuring PR effectiveness. Depending on which level of measurement is required, an array of different tools and techniques is needed to properly assess PR impact.'

Frequently a triple-layered or three-stage model is established as a framework for this 'combination of methods'. Typical is Cutlip, Center and Broom's long-taught 'Phases and Levels for Evaluating Public Relations Programs' model, which has three levels of programme evaluation: preparation, implementation, and impact (Broom and Sha, 2013: 343).

Preparation, Implementation, Impact (PII)

PII (Preparation, Implementation, Impact) is a step model that offers levels of evaluation for differing demands. It does not prescribe methodology, but accepts that 'evaluation means different things to different practitioners' (see Figure 5.1).

FIGURE 5.1   The PII model

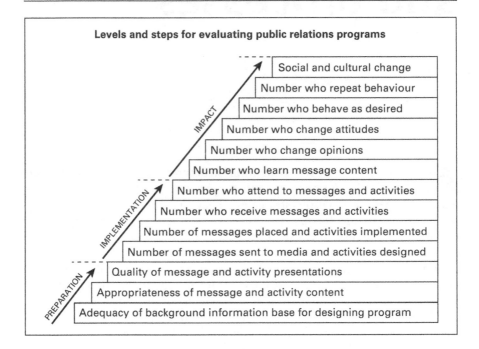

Each step in the PII model contributes to increased understanding and adds information for assessing effectiveness. The bottom rung of preparation evaluation examines whether adequate background information has been gathered in order to plan the programme effectively.

Next, the content of materials produced is examined to ensure it matches the plan (does the press release carry one or more of the campaign's key messages, for example?). Finally, at this level, the presentation of materials is examined – a professionally produced annual report does not guarantee effective investor relations but it contributes towards it.

At the second level, implementation evaluation considers how tactics and effort have been applied. The starting point is distribution (of materials) and attendance (at events), moving on to opportunities for exposing members of the target audience to organizational messages. This type of evaluation can identify flaws: a professionally written press release will not be effective unless distributed to the right contacts. Although significant numbers can be quoted for Opportunities to See (OTS), these figures are just that – opportunities to see – and give no indication of the extent to which messages were attended to. As an aside, therefore, OTS and similar constructs play a role in media planning, but have limited use in any sort of measurement of campaign effectiveness.

Although public relations evaluation is frequently centred around the implementation phase, Broom and Sha (2013: 348) sound a warning note: 'The ease with which practitioners can amass large numbers of column inches, broadcast minutes, readers, viewers, attendees, and gross impressions probably accounts for widespread use – and misuse – of evaluations at this level'.

The discussion to date has been concerned with 'process' evaluation. However, at the impact level, the emphasis switches to examining the extent to which the outcomes specified in the objectives and overall goals for the programme have been achieved. Impact evaluation is based on measuring the same variables that formed the benchmark for the campaign to establish whether the quantified changes spelled out in the objectives have been achieved – or not. Direct measurement using research techniques from surveys to observation (direct and indirect) is required here and requires both an understanding of research techniques and some ingenuity in establishing indicators of attitude and behavioural changes.

The PII model is valuable for its separation of output and impact and for counselling against the confusion of these different measures. It acts as a checklist and a reminder when planning evaluation. Its most important message (Broom and Sha, 2013: 344) bears reiteration as it is a point returned to several times in this text:

> **The most common error in program evaluation is substituting measures from one level for those at another level.** This is most clearly illustrated when practitioners use the number of news releases sent, websites visited or pages viewed, brochures distributed, or meetings held (implementation efforts) to document alleged program effectiveness (impact). These are not measures of the changes in target publics' knowledge, predisposition, and behaviour spelled out in program objectives. Evaluation researchers refer to this as the 'substitution game'. Somewhat analogously, magicians talk of 'misdirecting' audience attention from what is really happening on order to create an illusion.

Macnamara's Pyramid Model

Since the early 1990s, Australian evaluation specialist Jim Macnamara has developed a model (similar to PII), initially called the 'Macro Model' and now titled the 'Pyramid Model of PR Research'. The Pyramid Model has a 'bottom-up' structure, with the base showing the start-point of the strategy and the peak being the desired outcome of the campaign. Macnamara (2005b: 264) says:

> The pyramid metaphor is useful in conveying that, at the base when communication planning begins, practitioners have a large amount of information to assemble and a wide range of options in terms or media and activities. Selection and choices are made to direct certain messages at certain target audiences through certain media, and ultimately, achieve specific defined objectives (the peak of the program or project).

In the Pyramid Model, inputs are the components of communication programmes or projects and include the choice of medium, content of communication tools and format. Outputs are the materials and activities produced (such as media publicity, events, and promotional materials) and the processes to produce them, while outcomes are the impacts and effects of communication. A comprehensive menu of evaluation techniques for most public relations situations – from desk research (secondary sources) through media content analysis to observation and quantitative research – is offered.

Macnamara (2005b: 266–67) writes that the key steps in the communication process are shown, having been derived from the PII model, but the Pyramid Model offers extra value by listing the measurement methodologies for each of the three stages. Feedback loops are not shown on the model, but 'it is implicit in this model that findings from each stage of research are constantly looped back into planning'. The model includes formative and summative research methods in order to allow data to be integrated into the continued monitoring and development of communication programmes and so 'work as a continuum of information gathering and feedback on the communication process, not as separate discrete functions'.

Public Relations Effectiveness Yardstick

The Public Relations Yardstick model, developed by Walter Lindenmann, differs from the other models because its staging does not progress from planning to objectives. It could therefore be criticized for not reinforcing the role of evaluation right at the beginning of the planning process when the situation is analysed and benchmarks established. Instead, it is another three-stage model but the three stages encompass the latter two stages (implementation and preparation) of the PII model and final two stages of the Macro model (outputs and results/outcomes).

Lindenmann (1993: 7) argues that it is possible to measure public relations effectiveness and that there is growing pressure from clients and employers to be more accountable. He adds: 'measuring public relations effectiveness does not have to be either unbelievably expensive or laboriously time-consuming. PR measurement studies can be done at relatively modest cost and in a matter of only a few weeks.' (See Figure 5.3.)

FIGURE 5.2 Pyramid model of PR research

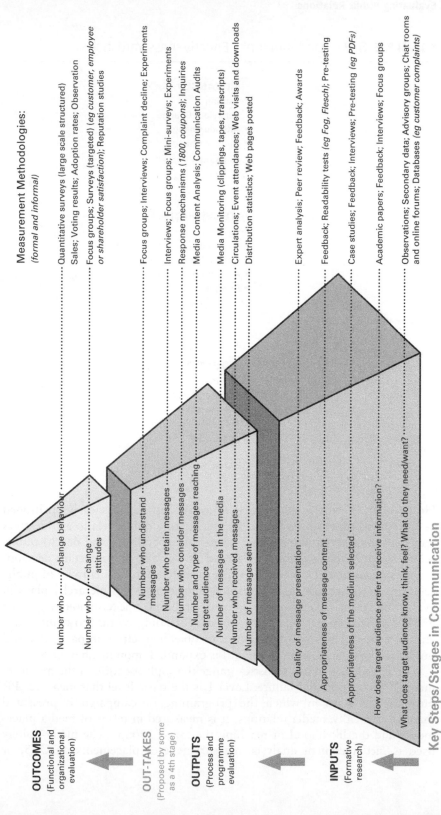

© Copyright Jim R Macnamara, 1992 and 2001

FIGURE 5.3   Lindenmann' s Effectiveness Yardstick

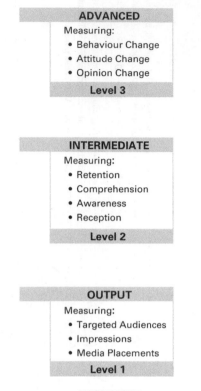

However, the Yardstick is rooted in objective setting and clearly positioned as the second of a two-step process: first, setting public relations objectives and, second, determining at what levels (of expenditure and depth) public relations effectiveness is to be measured. It was also an important development as it was one of the first attempts to sketch out the hierarchy of public relations objective setting, establishing the key role this hierarchy plays in evaluation. At the same time, Lindenmann established the terminology – which has become the de facto standard – of outputs, outgrowths (now out-takes) and outcomes. This important aspect of objective setting in particular and public relations evaluation in general is expanded upon in Chapter 8.

The three levels of the Yardstick gauge the sophistication of the measurement of PR success and failure. Level 1 is the basic level that measures PR outputs: the ways in which the programme or campaign is presented through, typically, media relations. It is measured in terms of media placements and the likelihood of reaching the target groups. The methodology used is media content analysis, measurement of placements or OTS, or simple surveys measuring awareness change among target groups. It is essentially the low-cost approach but is more detailed than counting up cuttings or using 'gut reactions', which are informal judgements lacking any rigour in terms of methodology.

Level 2 is termed by Lindenmann as the intermediate level as it uses outgrowth (or out-take) measures. These judge whether or not the target audience actually received the messages and so evaluates retention, comprehension and awareness. Practitioners will use a mix of qualitative and quantitative data collection techniques such as focus groups, interviews with opinion leaders and polling of target groups. This stage is more sophisticated than Level 1 and for programmes and campaigns that do not rely solely on media relations for their tactics, this stage will produce data that will be valuable for feedback on strategy and tactics. The data collection methods may not give evidence that attitudes have changed but for practical public relations purposes, it is a lower-cost evaluation strategy.

Outcomes are measured in Level 3. These include opinion, attitudes and behavioural changes. This is where the role of pre- and post-testing comes into its own, with the use of before and after polling, observational methods, psychographic analysis and other social science techniques. It is more complete, takes a longer period to undertake and is more expensive, but for a long-term campaign gives a clear-cut understanding of target audience awareness, comprehension levels and behavioural patterns. It is the comprehensive and valid test of effectiveness and success.

The Yardstick may not be strictly comparable to the other models as it offers a vertical progression of techniques rather than a horizontal movement from inputs to results (Macro) or preparation, implementation, impact (PII). It does emphasize the setting of objectives and choosing evaluation methods before starting public relations activity. These are important factors that should be included in any model of evaluation. However, the Yardstick is largely an educational (or promotional) device to encourage practitioners to use evaluation techniques. Its role is to make selection of methodology more accessible to practitioners whose knowledge and understanding of research techniques is poor and to help them bid more accurately for budget in order to undertake evaluation.

Research and planning

The three models discussed above have varying provenances. PII is well known, the Pyramid model less so. Lindenmann's Yardstick has been publicized in the United States and United Kingdom. They have, however, had considerable exposure in the public relations media of their countries of origin and in other countries. That they have not been adopted by practitioners as appropriate methods can be a result of several factors: practitioners' lack of knowledge, a base of dissemination that is too narrow and academic, or that they lack a practical and universal appeal.

Existing models may be too complex; without an integral relationship with effects creation and lacking dynamic feedback. They are static, step-by-step processes seen as the final stage in the public relations campaign. Yet public relations is not a 'start/stop' communications process where an organization stops interactions with publics while results of a media relations programme are measured. All through the programme, activities will be informally monitored and tactics adjusted. At the completion of a particular tactical stage, effectiveness may be formally measured, but there will be continuing parallel actions and the public relations team will not stop working while the evaluation judgements take place. The Pyramid model, with its pinnacle of 'objective achieved or problem solved', is an exemplar of the problem of practical application. In the real world of public relations, nothing stops and activity continues – any valid model must reflect the dynamic, progressive and continuous nature of this process.

The Chartered Institute of Public Relations (CIPR) (2011) has published several editions of its *Evaluation Toolkit* in an attempt to give practitioners practical tools to undertake evaluation. They have focused on the concept of research, planning and measurement. This concept establishes evaluation as an integral part of public relations planning (not to be tacked on afterwards) and reinforces the close linkage between evaluation and research. Indeed, the original author, Michael Fairchild's (2002: 36) list of the particular shortcomings related to development of planned, measurable campaigns could be mistaken for the challenges facing public relations in general:

- failure to tap into existing, and often free, sources of research, or to appreciate the value of developing a working relationship with the client's professional market research providers;

- failure to align communications objectives with the business or public sector goals of the client or internal customer;

- the tendency to go into creative mode before constructing a robust planning, research and evaluation framework;

- using terminology for effect rather than for clarity, eg regarding 'objectives', 'strategy' and 'tactics' as interchangeable terms;

- focusing too heavily on the value of media publicity or failing to assess its value in a broader context.

The CIPR's recommended process is outlined as a five-step circular process: audit, setting objectives, strategy and plan, ongoing measurement, and results and evaluation (CIPR, 2011: 9). Importantly, it is portrayed as a dynamic process (see Figure 5.4).

FIGURE 5.4 The Planning, Research and Evaluation (PRE) process

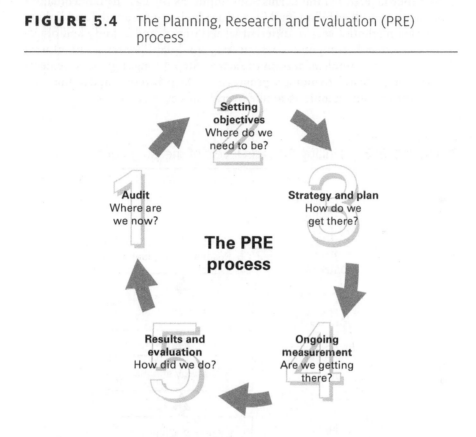

Step 1 (audit) is concerned with conducting research and gathering information to form a foundation on which the programme or campaign is based. Then objectives are set (step 2) and the point is made that as well as being SMART (specific, measurable, achievable, realistic and timely), they should not be set in a vacuum: public relations objectives need to be aligned with organizational goals and objectives. Next, the strategy and its implementation are established (step 3) but even here, research and evaluation are to the forefront, with decisions made about selecting the type of measurement to be used and pre-testing of PR techniques/messages to be employed. Formative evaluation is the province of the fourth step (ongoing measurement), when checks are made as to whether the programme is on track and decisions are made about any adjustments required (or even whether the programme needs to be abandoned).

Step 5 (results and evaluation) examines to what degree the objectives set for the campaign or programme have been achieved. While this step is very much summative in nature, there is still a learning perspective, such as what can be fed back into the planning process for the future?

Finally, the dynamic, circular, feedback-oriented process can be mapped onto a four-layered pyramid. This adds 'input' as the base to Lindenmann's three steps, as well as following Macnamara by being pyramidal and linking evaluation methodologies to different levels. Steps 1 and 2 (audit and objectives) use research as input: Step 3 (strategy and plan) pre-tests and informs the choice of and implementation of tactics; Step 4 (ongoing measurement) uses tracking research to monitor progress; and Step 5 (results and evaluation) uses direct measurement to examine overall success (see Figure 5.5).

FIGURE 5.5   Linking PRE and levels of measurement

The Unified model

An analysis of the four existing three-level or three-stage models indicates that, together, they actually describe four steps (as indicated by the Measurement Pyramid) and use a variety of terminology to describe very similar stages in the public relations process. Lindenmann does well to separate cognitive and behavioural (also referred to as informational and motivational) effects but maintains three levels by omitting a preparation/input stage. The PII and Macro models feature the latter but fail to make this important distinction at the impact/results stage. The CIPR's five-step process uses slightly different terms for Lindenmann's three levels but separately recognizes the necessity for an input stage as a benchmark. But it also introduces a dynamic perspective compared with the other – static – models.

However, these approaches remain a useful concept. The first stage to evaluation 'wisdom' in public relations is an understanding that public relations is a multi-step process and that different evaluation methodologies are probably appropriate at these different steps. This is the principle behind all these models. Grasping this concept leads to an understanding of the pitfalls of the substitution game. But, the substitution game continues to be played and therefore the models have not been able to do their job in even this simple respect. The suggestion is that their complexity, allied with confusing terminology, prevents them completing this task. Consequently, the Unified model first takes a relatively simple approach. Second, it is expanded to five levels so that it can accept both an input stage and split out the evaluation of public relations programmes or activities with objectives at the three different levels of the hierarchy.

The integral part of situational analysis in a research and evaluation framework has already been argued. With objective setting such an integral part of a professional evaluation culture, it is a final criticism of the established models that they do not recognize this hierarchy, nor that objectives at different levels will almost certainly require different evaluation methodologies. For both these reasons, a truly representative evaluation structure needs to separate out these three different levels of objective-setting. Consequently, the term 'outcome' is abandoned in favour of a family of outcomes labelled 'impact', 'effect' and 'result' according to whether the objective(s) set are knowledge/awareness, predisposition or behaviour, respectively. Naturally, as the objectives are hierarchical, impact and effect have to be achieved before result (and, indeed, impact before effect). (See Figure 5.6 and Table 5.1.)

No methodologies are spelt out in the Unified model. Although it is natural that different methodologies will be required at different levels, the research methodology required should be governed by the particular research problem in the particular circumstances that apply. Consequently, any listing would simply be a collection of likely approaches rather than something of universal applicability. Also, given that an evaluation culture is a research culture, as an evaluation culture develops then so should an appreciation of research methods. As well as accepting the hierarchy of objectives, the Unified model takes account of the lack of dynamic feedback for which its predecessors have been criticized. This is done in the formative spirit of public relations evaluation but operates at two levels. At one level, there is likely to be formative feedback from one stage to the preceding stage as a means of fine-tuning the current campaign. At another level, there is likely to be lessons learned from one campaign that will feed back into the planning of future campaigns.

FIGURE 5.6   The Unified model

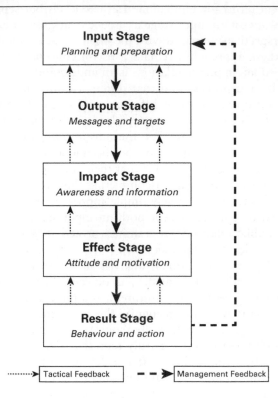

TABLE 5.1   Mapping terminology

	Unified model	PII model	Pyramid model	Lindenmann	PRE
Level/Stage	(S)	(L/S)	(S)	(L)	(L)
A	Input	Preparation	Inputs	–	Inputs
B	Output	Implementation	Outputs	Outputs	Outputs
C (awareness)	Impact	Impact	Results	Outgrowths	Out-takes
D (predisposition)	Effect	Impact	Results	Outcomes	Outcomes
E (behavioural)	Results	Impact	Results/Outcomes	Outcomes	Outcomes

Practitioner-derived models

Watson (1995) used four case studies to investigate the real-life constraints and practical difficulties of systematic evaluation. In two case studies, a major industrial redevelopment and a proposal for a new town, it was found that the environmental and development issues embodied in the two projects were so sensitive that it was not practical for pre-testing of attitudes to be undertaken. In the industrial redevelopment programme, research was used to validate the community relations programme and modify it for the future. An iterative loop was used to sustain the public relations process.

In a third case study – an intensive three-month-long lobbying campaign – there was only one opportunity to make an impact. The proof of performance (ie indication of success) came when the UK government found new money for a project and the threat to the organization receded. Unlike the longer-term campaigns, this intensive campaign had an outcome that was quickly visible and could be expressed as a Yes or No result. The methodology to evaluate the results did not need an iterative loop.

The fourth case study was a community public relations campaign against a new coal-fired power station in an environmentally sensitive area. The results were measured by failure of the public utility's proposals. The campaign's effectiveness demonstrated the value of effects-based planning and the manner in which it creates feedback to review tactics.

The case studies demonstrated different structures of public relations actions, ranging from the short, sharp lobbying activities to the long-running industrial development and new community programmes. Thus different implications for evaluation theory have emerged. The lobbying campaign pointed to the need for simple models to overcome the barriers to evaluation of lack of time and money (budget/cost factors). It also indicated that a simple Yes/No or Win/Lose outcome from the evaluation process was needed in a short time span.

Evaluation models designed for short-term public relations action must answer the Win/Lose dichotomy. The nature of these types of public relations campaigns is a call to action. Effects are not being created because the objectives are usually concerned with awareness. As a result of these short time spans, practitioners are unlikely to be creating attitudinal or behavioural effects.

The longer-term programmes have different characteristics. They segment audiences and aim to create a range of effects among target groups by a variety of strategies and tactics. The effects can be judged through continuing, consistent research. They also operate at varying speeds, compared with a short, intense awareness campaign. Indeed, their pace can vary quite considerably over the years. Awareness campaigns largely feature media relations strategies and evaluate the communication of messages through the media filter. Long-term programmes may have minimal use of media relations, preferring lobbying and direct communication with target groups.

Evaluation based on media analysis is thus less relevant for these programmes and so a model suitable for continuing, long-term actions needs to take account of the desired effects and whether these and the objectives are being achieved. It should also offer answers to the Win/Lose dichotomy and to the 'staying alive' factor in mid-campaign. Another factor is that a long-term programme will use a greater variety of strategy and tactics and these will need to be monitored, formally or informally, as the programme progresses.

In summary, the case studies indicated that two different evaluation models are needed to judge two very different scenarios: the common short-term awareness campaign based heavily on media relations and the longer-term programme which has a variety of strategies and tactics.

The evidence of practitioner surveys and the case studies supports the assertion that simpler approaches to evaluation are called for to bring down the barriers hindering the widespread study of impact of public relations activity. Existing models were mostly static step-by-step models that relied on the public relations activity stopping while evaluation was undertaken. No in-house or consultancy public relations operation can stop and take stock in such a leisurely way. Public relations evaluation models must reflect the dynamic nature of communications in a pressurized world.

The International Public Relations Association's Gold Paper No 11 proposed a circular model which links planning with evaluation in much the same way that the CIPR's process attempts to. While descriptive of a process of planning and subsequent evaluation for long-term activity, it does not appear to have been developed empirically and practitioner acceptance and understanding are limited. Thus it does not address the barriers and practitioner perceptions that have been identified by so many studies.

Short term and continuing programmes

Taking into account the need for accessible, dynamic models of evaluation, two models are proposed: the Short Term model for short time span, largely media-relations-based campaigns and activities which seek a rapid result, and the Continuing model for long-term activities where the consistent promotion of messages is a central strategy and the outcome may occur after a long period (a year or more) of continuous activity. These models link with Grunig's four summations of public relations activity. The Short Term model is similar to the press agentry and public information one-way summations as it does not seek a dialogue or feedback. The Continuing model fits with the two-way asymmetrical and two-way symmetrical models that cover a broader band of communication methods and rely on feedback for campaign monitoring and modification of messages. These models can be expressed graphically (see Figures 5.7 and 5.8).

FIGURE 5.7   Watson's Short Term model

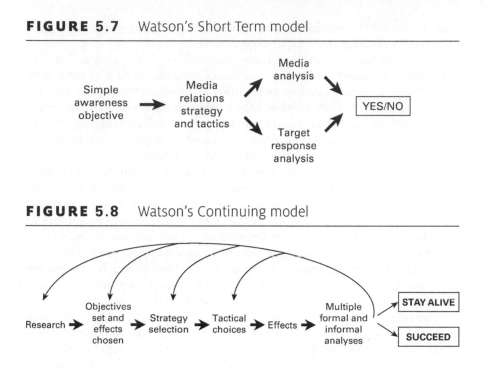

FIGURE 5.8   Watson's Continuing model

The Short Term model has a single track, linear process with an outcome. It does not set out to measure effects and because it does not have a continuing existence, there is no feedback mechanism. Typically, a public relations campaign has a simple awareness objective with one or two strategies. A common example of public relations practice in the Public Information summation is the distribution of news releases about products or services to the media. This is a technician skill of assembling information and photographs or drawings in the manner most acceptable to the media. Measuring achievement of the objectives can be by media analysis, sales response or phone research among the target market.

Using the Short Term model, the objectives could be set on the basis of obtaining coverage in specific media (chosen for its relevance to target audiences), the number of sales responses (realistically set according to the appropriateness of the media and the attractions of the product or service) or quantitative techniques such as phone research or mail surveys. The judgement of success or failure is thus made on whether or not the targets are reached.

This simple model can be applied in different cultures because the accent is on setting realistic awareness objectives and choosing relevant strategies. The terminology can be translated and the model structure is straightforward. If the client or employer sets unrealistic objectives, the model will be as irrelevant as a step-by-step model or informal 'seat of the pants' judgement.

The quality of the model's results depends on the professionalism of the practitioner in designing the campaign.

This continuing model has been designed for long-term activity. In reviewing the case studies, the need for a dynamic model to cope with ever-changing circumstances was identified. A programme such as that for the new settlement, with multiple long-term corporate and planning objectives, or for the industrial redevelopment, with a medium-term objective of planning permission and a long-term objective of improved relations with the local community, needed a flexible evaluation model.

The Continuing model offers elements that have not been included in step-by-step models. It has an iterative loop and takes into account the effects that are being created by the programme. An additional element is that it offers an opportunity to make a judgement on 'staying alive' – the important stage in a long-term, issues-centred programme when keeping the issue in the decision frame is important. The Continuing model epitomizes VanLeuven's effects-based planning approach. By adopting these principles within the Continuing model, a dynamic and continuing evaluation process is created because the search for consistency means that monitoring is continuous.

The evidence from the long-term case studies reviewed in the research shows that the search for consistency is one of the most difficult practical issues facing public relations practitioners. The Continuing model, using effects-based planning, offers a more disciplined approach that allows the parameters of the programme to be more closely defined and enables continuous monitoring to replace after-the-event evaluation. The consistency of effects-based planning also aids validity and reliability of data.

The elements of the Continuing model are an initial stage of research, the setting of objectives and choice of programme effects; from these follow the strategy selection and tactical choices. As the programme continues, there are multiple levels of Formal and Informal Analysis from which judgements can be made on progress in terms of success or 'staying alive'. The judgements are fed back through iterative loops to each of the programme elements. The loops assist the practitioners in validating the initial research and adding new data, adjusting the objectives and strategy, monitoring the progress to create the desired attitudinal or behavioural effects and helping with the adjustment or variation of tactics. This model is a continuing process that can be applied to a specific programme or to the overall public relations activities of an organization.

Universality of application

The research into practitioner attitudes since the early 1990s has found many similarities: barriers, reliance on output measures, technician activities and lack of knowledge. The recognition of these similarities has been important in the design of the two models of evaluation and will encourage their use by practitioners in many countries. Their simplicity and accessibility go beyond anglophone public relations. There is no rigidity in the evaluation methodology. Whereas a British practitioner may use a market research approach to analysing response to a campaign among target audiences, a European practitioner may, typically, adopt sociological methodology.

The Continuing model, with its iterative loop, provides the response element that both of Grunig's two-way models require. It is suited to the two-way asymmetrical model as it accepts that the proponent determines the objectives and strategy but this can be equally acceptable for the two-way symmetrical model because the research and objectives setting can be part of a negotiation process in a bilateral or multilateral situation.

With the exception of Lindenmann's Yardstick, which is not strictly comparable with the other models, the models discussed in this chapter have 'summative' methods of seeking to answer questions of effectiveness at the end of a programme or campaign. They lack a dynamic element that could offer the formative research to feed back and improve the effectiveness of the continuing campaign or future programmes.

Leaving aside practitioner issues such as setting objectives properly and agreeing evaluation methodology before the start of the activity, evaluation models should provide both formative and summative information. Their role should not be the last stage in a public relations programme, but the springboard to the next stage or, in a campaign, to help adjust strategy and tactics.

The Short Term and Continuing models do not provide answers as to which single method of evaluation gives the universal solution. There is, of course, no single answer to this because each public relations programme or campaign has different objectives and client/employer imperatives. Different methods of data collection and analysis are called for. By using the two models, practitioners can apply an integrated planning and evaluation framework to all public relations activity, and thus test whether objectives have been reached and the desired effects have been created.

VanLeuven's effects-based approach to public relations (see Chapter 2) was a valuable addition to applied theory. The inclusion of effects elements in the Continuing model was a direct result of testing this approach against real-life practice. These elements strengthen the integrated planning and evaluation style of the Continuing model with its characteristic iterative loop design.

These two evaluation models proposed give clearly expressed dynamic frameworks for evaluation to practitioners in all cultures. They are based on empirical research and reside in the mainstream of public relations theory and practice. By highlighting the relative simplicity of short-term, awareness-based, public relations activity, and the complexity of continuing programmes probably associated with attitude and/or behaviour change, the models can clarify thinking on evaluation. However, they complement, rather than replace, the various three-stage linear models. For example, the Short Term model sits comfortably with Lindenmann's Level 2 and the more complex tasks associated with the Continuing model are appropriate to Level 3.

Modelling evaluation as a continuing activity formalizes and reinforces evaluation as a formative – as well as summative – process. The evaluation of a short-term campaign necessarily means that it cannot provide direct feedback as the particular campaign in question has been implemented by the time the evaluation process has been completed. However, by adding to the body of knowledge and experience of running campaigns it does act in a formative role: providing feedback to the communications management process in general, and thereby increasing the effectiveness of similar campaigns in the future.

Indeed, the Unified and Short Term/Continuing models are complementary rather than competitive, providing different perspectives on the same reality. For example, the Short Term model is exclusively concerned with cognitive awareness objectives (represented by the impact stage in the Unified model) and the Continuing model is likely to be concerned with higher-level motivational and behavioural objectives, represented by the effect and result stages of the Unified model. These models are not detailed prescriptions for undertaking evaluation of public relations programmes. This is a complex problem that does not lend itself to simple, straightforward solutions; nor is a long list of potential evaluation techniques useful for similar reasons. The role of the structures and approaches outlined and discussed in this chapter is to provide a framework that enables the practitioner to apply the sophisticated level of analysis that will lead to some sort of answer to the challenges promoted by this complex issue.

Dashboards and scorecards

The dashboard is an increasingly used tool for the measurement and evaluation of public relations activity, especially in relation to corporate communications strategy. The term arises from the dashboard of a car in which there are several gauges of performance, such as speed, rpm, fuel, engine temperature and battery charge. Taking the analogy further, these instruments tell you how fast you are going, how the engine (campaign) is performing and whether there are any threats (low fuel, high engine temperature or battery discharge).

This tool has arisen from corporate information systems that brought together various performance data into a single, easily read document for senior management. They were endowed with metrics on sales, revenue and overhead costs. They pushed managers into setting performance targets and continually managing them. Having begun in finance departments, they have been introduced into sales, marketing and more recently communications departments.

Paine (2006) says that their usefulness depends on professionals articulating their definitions of excellence. She says they need to be persuaded to look beyond the easy measures of clips and hits and 'to design metrics tied to business performance and organisational mission' (Paine, 2006: 1).

There are six steps to design and implement dashboards (Paine, 2006: 1–5):

1 Ensure that all those who will be operating the communications programmes measured by the dashboard develop it together. Don't have it imposed by others.

2 Identify the measurement priorities by ranking audiences in order of importance.

3 Choose the measures of effectiveness for each of the audiences.

4 Set benchmarks by comparing current year performance with previous years and against similar organizations. (Paine writes of a county in New York state, comparing itself against a similar county by measuring media coverage for both.)

5 Choose the tools for measurement and seek integration between the tools.

6 Make the dashboard report simple and short, no more than a page or two.

Communication scorecards have similarities to dashboards but are more integrated with the organizational operations and strategy. In public relations, they have evolved along two related streams. In 1997, Fleisher and Mahaffy proposed a scorecard for the measurement of public relations activity. Others have come from Vos and Schoemaker (2004), who proposed criteria for the communication management elements of a business scorecard; and German consultants Hering, Schuppener and Sommerhalder (2004), who introduced a Communications Scorecard in their market. They have also been used in the form of a Communication Matrix in South Africa for communications in the mining sector, and reported by Putt and van der Waldt (2005).

The main push for them has come from the Balanced Scorecard (BSC) management tool that was first introduced in the mid-1990s by Robert Kaplan and David Norton (1996). The initial premise was that businesses and other organizations should not be managed on a basis where profit and loss and Return on Investment were the sole criteria for success. The BSC was a more extensive control system that tied strategy more closely to performance, but also took account of the human and reputational issues that make businesses excellent. Since then they have developed the BSC further.

Ansgar Zerfass, who has written extensively on the concept and delivery of a BSC-linked Corporate Communication Scorecard, says that the BSC is developed by a process in which managers and staff can identify their own performance's effect on business success, 'including interdependencies to other units and goals' (Zerfass, 2005: 4). When units' goals and key performance indicators are brought together into the scorecard (sometimes presented as a dashboard), performance can be measured 'across different units as well as continuously adjusting the scorecard for the company and its (other) business units'. In this way communication activity is integrated into the business strategy and operations, rather than remaining separate.

The value of dashboards and scorecards are questioned by some. Macnamara (2005b: 311–12) says, 'they are simply ways of collecting measurement data and presenting it in an organization-wide format' and that the research methodologies are those already used widely in measuring public relations. However, as a tool that aligns communication strategy with business objectives and presents data in a concise and readable manner, they have a lot to offer in creating and monitoring highly effective communication programmes. Chapter 11's discussion of the 'communication controlling' performance management system shows how dashboards can be used to considerable effect.

Questions to discuss

- What is the value of models of PR evaluation?
- Which model or structure of PR evaluation would be most relevant to your work?
- How do you research and plan PR campaigns? Apply the CIPR's five-step process to a recent campaign.
- Can you create your own model of evaluation? Would you include long-term and short-term elements or a single structure?
- Dashboards and scorecards have been promoted as methods to engage management in the measurement and evaluation of communication: What elements would be included in your typical dashboard?

06
Developing a media evaluation system

This chapter focuses on practical steps towards establishing media evaluation systems: the first part proposes a simple media monitoring system while the second proposes a more detailed analysis. Both are achievable by consultancies and in-house practitioners and offer usable feedback and data for short-term and continuing public relations activity. The simple system has methodological limitations and may lack social science purity, but it can be set up quickly and at low cost. This could be a major advantage for practitioners who have identified cost as an important barrier to evaluation. The more complex system can threaten to be too time-consuming for manual implementation. However, it can form the basis of a customized in-house system (implemented by a specialist) or a specification for an external media evaluation bureau.

Setting up a simple media monitoring system

The traditional method of measuring public relations success was amassing a collection of media clippings and transcriptions. Mounted on sturdy paper to give added bulk, the clippings were seen as the 'deliverable' of the process and programme. To borrow an analogy from flying, this was like flying on one instrument and ignoring all the others. Kaplan and Norton (1996: 1–2) describe a pilot who uses only an airspeed indicator and ignores fuel gauges, altimeters and other instruments. They conclude that 'we suspect that you would not board the plane after this discussion'. The point for practitioners is that they would not pilot a programme without checking the progress against objectives, yet many rely on a collection of clippings as the sole indicator of so-called success. Sadly, clients and employers often use the same judgement, too.

PR people are communicators, analysts, strategists and tacticians who are always making judgements in fluid and often complex environments. So how can they deduce whether the programme is flying fast or heading straight for a mountain of problems? 'Gut feel' and informal feedback are sometimes useful, but often misleading. To make accurate judgements, solid planning and valid, reliable information are needed.

This helps us decide whether we are 'doing well', but first we must set measurable public relations objectives. These are the four most important words for the development of both simple and complex evaluation. They tell us where we are starting from and where the programme is heading. 'Measurable' gives the basis of planning and aids validity of feedback data.

The definitions of public relations discussed in Chapter 1 mostly typify PR as a 'management function' and so this is a planned, structured and reviewed process which means more than scoring mentions in the media or online. Objectives are the reasons behind the programme in terms of audiences to be reached, messages communicated, channels of communication used and the reactions and responses sought. As a persuasive process, public relations needs measurable objectives or it becomes a random information dissemination activity.

Lindenmann's Public Relations Yardstick (Chapter 5) has proposed three increasingly complex stages of evaluation entitled output, outgrowth or out-take and outcomes. For a simple media monitoring system the appropriate Yardstick is Output, which measures production of the PR effort, as opposed to audience response and attitudinal change, which are covered by the others. Output analysis judges where the message was received in the various types of media, the manner and tone of its interpretation and quantitative dimensions of its appearance. At this point, it is important to note the limitations of media analysis because it cannot judge the message(s) impact upon non-media target groups. This needs an additional level of research among those groups, although in practice response to articles via letters, phone calls, sales, literature uptake or visits do give an informal (but partial) measure. Measuring media coverage should be systematic, continuous, part of an overall evaluation process and related to objectives.

Creating a simple media monitoring system is essentially a clerical process in which more time is spent on the initial set-up than continuing regular analysis. The raw material is media clippings and transcripts, which can be generated through monitoring of the media by the practitioner or through agencies and broadcast monitoring bureaux. These can be supplemented by word and topic searches by online information organizations and scanning of the internet through search engines.

Gathering data is now much easier and inexpensive than previous times when clipping agencies delivered physical 'cuttings' snipped from the pages of the media, or transcripts were laboriously typed from recordings. Both authors have been both using and teaching hundreds of students to use the News search facility on Google to track coverage of organizations, events and people. This has vastly improved the ability of quite junior staff to spend a limited time each day or once a week to gather all types of media coverage for analysis.

Google News searches can be tailored by the search name, type of report and editions. Experimentation helps find the best search combination. Microsoft's Bing search engine has fewer options, however, and is less flexible for basic media monitoring.

When using these search engines, the emphasis moves away from detailed placement of reports and information offered when dissecting placements in print media towards the size of article and its placement in the hierarchy of websites. For example, news reports on BBC News websites can start on the home page (Tier 1) but can then be moved to specialist areas (Tiers 2 or 3). For example, an organization may be referred to in a single introductory sentence on the home page, with the main report on the specialist page, such as Business (Tier 2). Or they can start their published existence on a specialist page, such as Companies in the Business section (Tier 3).

Experiments with simple media monitoring systems applied to internet news coverage have also led to a simplified system of coding the size of reports as large, medium or small. Greater granularity of data has not been found to offer higher levels of insights.

Now for an example: At the time of writing this chapter, the BBC ran a UK home page news introduction about Google which clicked through to another introductory paragraph which was the lead news item in the Tier 2 Business section and was reported in detail as the lead story in the Tier 3 Companies section. It would remain there for longer than the two higher tier introductions would. As it was the lead story on Tier 3 with a photo and 18 sentences, it would be classified as large coverage. The content could be interrogated for Google's messages and counter-messages, the name of the spokesperson, the tone of the article, the media in which it appeared, etc. In many ways, the same processes for analysis of old (print and broadcast) media could be applied.

There are six steps to set up the system and fully utilize the information drawn from it:

1 define objectives;
2 determine criteria;
3 choose a benchmark;
4 select a measurement tool;
5 compare results with objectives;
6 modify campaign.

The objectives can include exposure of message, dissemination, education of target publics, sales lead generation, share of voice (vis-à-vis competitors or issues) or others that have been set out in the programme. When selecting criteria for judgement, there is a mnemonic called IMPACT; it sets out these criteria:

Influence or tone
Message communicated

Prominence

Audience reached

Consultant/spokesman quoted

Type of article

In order of importance, the letters could be reorganized as M (Message communicated), A (Audience reached), T (Type of article), C (Consultant/spokesman quoted), I (Influence or Tone) and P (Prominence). Sadly, MATCIP is not as catchy as IMPACT. The most questionable of factors is Prominence. As McGuire's output analysis of the communication/persuasion flow showed (Chapter 2), the way that we awkward humans scan and retain information is not linear. So it follows that we do not necessarily retain the information offered by the largest article on a prominent page, the first report in a broadcast or online news programme, or the picture with the most 'Likes' or retweets. Some of the best-read sections of print media are 'fillers' and diary pages that have terse, compressed information.

Having chosen criteria, the next stage is to benchmark media coverage and then choose the period by which the analysis will be undertaken. Practically, establishing an effective benchmark is best achieved by reviewing the previous 12 months' media coverage and then repeating the process monthly or quarterly. In a crisis or a very active situation, coverage can be monitored in real time, daily or weekly. Once the hard work in setting up the benchmark has been done the period-on-period comparisons take much less time and use frequent repetitions.

Analysing media coverage: the key questions

1   Where has it appeared and how often? (Which media?)

2   Which journalists have by-lines?

3   What is the tone of coverage? 0 to 10 ranking for each item.
    0 is completely negative. 5 is neutral. 10 is completely positive.
    (Other variations are 0 to 100 for a granular assessment, and
    −5 (completely negative) to +5 (completely positive).

4   Which products/services/issues have had coverage? (Where and
    frequency?)

5   Coverage of major competitors; where and how often?

6   Classify the coverage as filler, medium or large. Indicate when photos
    have been used.

7   What are the key messages carried in the press coverage?

In order to get valid information, the project or programme manager should avoid personally judging the 'tone' or favourability of coverage and interpreting the messages carried by the media. If the manager or a close colleague undertakes the analysis role, there is a strong likelihood of 'observer bias', ie they will scan for the positive messages that support their advice and hoped-for results and bypass the negative feedback. The most effective route to take is to establish a panel of independent readers who scan the clippings and transcripts and give their objective opinion. This panel of readers should not be colleagues in the same organization or consultancy but come from outside the business. The media material is circulated among them (at least three people) for analysis using a pro forma. In this way, the level of subjective interpretation is reduced, the analysis is undertaken on a common basis and the practitioner benefits through valid feedback.

There are varying ways of organizing the reader panel. It can manage itself with one of its members preparing reports, the material can be returned to

TABLE 6.1   A typical form used in a simple media analysis system

Factors to judge	Data and answers
Which publications have articles appeared in and how often? Use initials for frequently quoted publications.	
List names of by-lined journalists and the publications.	
On a scale of 1 to 10, make a judgement on the tone of the article. 0 = completely negative; 10 = completely positive; 5 = neutral.	
Write a one-sentence summary of what you see as the key message contained in the article.	Use a separate sheet
Identify if it was a small (filler), medium (average of 5 paragraphs) or large (sizeable) article.	F M L
Name any client company spokespeople referred to within the story.	
If competitors or opponents are mentioned in the same story, list them and how often they appear.	

the practitioner for collation or it can be sent to an independent expert for interpretation. Usually, the panel members are part-time and operate from home, but this is a matter of convenience rather than of methodological importance.

When it comes to interpreting and implementing the information from simple media analysis, a pitfall to be avoided is the 'substitution game'. These analyses only describe the dissemination of messages and their reception and interpretation in the media (the output phase), but they don't tell of the impact upon the audiences. To ascribe impact to the output analyses will lead to inaccurate modifications of programmes and preparation for new ones. As indicated above and in earlier chapters, impact must be judged by research among the target audiences, not in the channels of communication to them.

In summary, simple media analysis should be continuous and objective. It need not be expensive to undertake and can be operated with in-house resources, with the exception of the reader panel. The information is limited to the programme's output, but it can be linked with other measures on impact to give an overall picture of 'doing well?' or not.

A media analysis report based on a real financial services organization. Names have been changed to protect client confidentiality.

CLIENT MEDIA ANALYSIS

'THE SOCIETY'

(12 MONTHS TO THE END OF PERIOD)

1   Publications in which articles referring to The Society have appeared
    National newspapers – named (5)
    Regional daily and weekly newspapers; business magazines – named (48)
    Financial publications – named (4)
    TOTAL 57

2   By-lined journalists – named (8)

3   Tone of coverage (0 = very negative, 10 = very positive. 5 = neutral)
    6.6/10, which is more positive than neutral and well ahead of average scores, which are usually around 5/10. There were three exceptionally high scores of 10/10 given to coverage in the regional media. The lowest scores of 4/10 went to coverage in a national daily and a financial publication.

    The strongest tone of coverage came in regional media at 6.8/10, which was a positive score when set against the sample of 48 stories upon which it was drawn. Tone scores ranged from 5/10 to 10/10, with no scores lower than neutral.

Coverage in the nationals averaged 5.8/10, with four out of five articles ranking between 5/10 and 8/10. In the small number of financial press articles, the tone ranking was marginally above neutral at 5.25/10. The four articles were scored tightly between 4/10 and 6/10.

4 Volume of coverage
Fillers 39 per cent
Medium 39 per cent
Large 22 per cent

5 Client spokespeople – named (6)

6 Competitors mentioned in the same story as The Society (four named, in a total of 17 mentions)

7 Messages carried in the media about The Society
Products and industry comment
The Society has a lot to offer in the world of friendly societies.
Funeral plan launched by The Society.
Society discusses its pre-paid funeral plan.
Family Income Plan outlined by The Society.
Family Income Benefit described (three separate articles).
Chief Executive says products will fit into government plans.
Chairman talks of the major role of friendly societies in welfare provision
Low-cost sickness plan offered
Investors can contribute up to £5,760 a year for cash ISAs.
A parent can be valued at more than £30,000 a year, so insurance cover
    is needed.
Community
£500 donated to school for wheelchair access.
The Society investing in revival of property market.
Society replaces doctor's equipment destroyed in an arson attack.
£500 donated to Salvation Army.
Medical Trust has received £100.
Scout group saved from closure.
Conference to be held at Cathedral.
Surgery has new equipment, thanks to The Society.
Football team gets new strip from The Society.
Cheque presented to emergency doctors group.

While a manual clerical media evaluation system is simple, very low cost and can be operated in situations of low-volume coverage, it is clumsy to manage for medium- to high-volume coverage where frequent reports are needed. There are commercial software packages which can offer turnkey solutions. Alternatives can be developed using spreadsheet software, notably Microsoft Excel, which is easy to tailor for different employer/client needs and campaign situations. The main skill is creating and manipulating the macros (mathematical formulae) to relevant data. One example is the apPRaise system originally developed by UK consultancy Hallmark Public Relations over a decade ago. It has been used for clients such as professional services firms, government agencies and commercial property agents.

The essence of apPRaise is that the consultancy and the client jointly choose up to six messages that they want to disseminate through the media. (Any number of messages can be chosen, but it is considered difficult for audiences to comprehend or retain more than three to six messages during a campaign.) These messages can be linked to corporate objectives, product promotion, key contact information (such as websites or phone numbers), etc.

The media targets are set and then monitored by regular scanning of publications, broadcast and internet media. While the data entry is essentially a clerical task, it is the analysis of the data that provides value.

The apPRaise system allows the collection of alternative messages, such as negative comment and competitor response. It also collects data on the PR activity that generated the media coverage, journalists who are writing about the client organization, corporate spokespeople quoted by the media and the placement of the articles in the media by position.

A typical apPRaise analysis form (see Figure 6.1) will cover date, headline, media title, media type, section, Opportunities to See (OTS), messages 1 to 6, alternative messages, media activity, spokespeople, reporter/author, target audience, placement of article, and visual impact, and have a space for comments by the analyst.

From this data, charts and text can be developed to provide information on:

- number of articles per target media;
- OTS received per message;
- OTS per media activity;
- number of times that key messages are featured;
- tone of coverage for each message on a +5 to −5 scale;
- section in which articles appeared;

- number of articles per media title;
- position of articles;
- visual impact of articles.

The apPRaise system gives a width of information that helps monitor the progress of a campaign or short-term project. Former Hallmark PR director Steve Osborne-Brown says:

> With regular production of reports, we knew whether the messages that clients wanted to express were reaching their media targets. If they weren't, decisions could be made to modify them or put in additional effort. Conversely, if messages were being accepted in the media, the campaign team could move on to new challenges.

This low-cost system monitors placement of articles but does not allocate a value to them. This requires the development of sophisticated algorithms and that there is still debate as to whether a story on page 1 or page 10 has a differential value. The psychology of communication shows that every reader comprehends and retains information in a different manner. A short filler story of one or two sentences can have just as big an impact as the page one lead report in print or online. It all depends on what the reader's information need is at the time. A media analysis system cannot demonstrate that.

Another approach developed by the Canadian Public Relations Society (**www.cprs.ca**) is the 'Media Relations Rating Points' (MR^{2}P). CPRS says: 'the primary objective of creating the MR^{2}P system was the development of a simple, standardized reporting system that can be widely accepted and utilized with ease to measure any type of editorial coverage (ie print, broadcast, online) stemming from proactive media relations campaigns, crisis communications or unplanned media attention. The MR^{2}P system includes a media report template, rating system and tool for obtaining up-to-date accurate reach numbers. The MR^{2}P system analyses editorial media coverage by tone, customized criteria and cost-per-contact.'

Each piece of media coverage generated proactively can score up to 10 points. Up to five are awarded for tone (five for positive, three for neutral and none for negative). Predetermined criteria make up the other five possible points to give a rating score. Five criteria are chosen to include in the system. While this is an effort to ensure that the evaluation is undertaken in the context of goals for the campaign, the fact that different campaigns are evaluated according to different criteria weakens the claim for standardization. Criteria suggested by the designers are given on page 89.

FIGURE 6.1 Sample of apPRaise evaluation report

Client name/period

Date	Headline	Media title	Media type	Section	OTS

FIGURE 6.1 *continued*

Client name/period

Headline	Message 1	Message 2	Message 3	Message 4	Message 5	Message 6

FIGURE 6.1 *continued*

Client name/period

Headline	Alternative messages	Media activity	Spokespeople	Reporter/author

FIGURE 6.1 *continued*

Client name/period

Headline	Target audience	Placement of article	Visual impact	Comments

TABLE 6.2   apPRaise – key to analysis

Media type	Refers to whether broadcast, press, national, regional, trade, consumer, etc
Section	Where was the story found? – news, features, health, business, letters, classifieds, etc
OTS	The circulation of a publication or number of viewers/ listeners of a programme multiplied by 2.5 (to indicate average readership or audience)
Messages	Indicate the tone of a message in each piece of coverage on a scale from –5 to +5: those messages not featured within a piece of coverage leave blank
Alternative messages	Indicate messages that appear that are not one of your key messages
Media activity	Indicate which activity generated the coverage – press release, launch event, phone call, etc
Spokespeople	Who was quoted?
Reporter/author	Any by-line?
Target audience	Who did it reach?
Placement of article	Its position, using the code below: 10: Front page, DPS (double-page spread), centre pages 9: Pages 2 and 3, feature (article) 8: Pages 4–9 7: Pages 10-centre 6: Back page, columnist's comments 5: Editor's comments, centre-mid-back 4: Letters 3: Neighbourhood/community news 2: Mid-late back 1: Filler

TABLE 6.2   *continued*

Visual impact	Use the key below
	A – full page/DPS
	B – 3/4 page
	C – 1/2 page
	D – 1/3 page
	E – 1/4 page
	F – 1 column
	G – 1/2 column
	H – 1/3 column
	I – 1/4 column
	J – couple of lines

Suggested MR²P Criteria

Company/brand mention	Key message(s)
Photo/image	Exclusivity
Colour (photo)	Headline/newscast positioning
Spokesperson quote	Tier 1 vs Tier 2 media outlets
Prominence/position	Competitive/peer inclusion
Target audience	Inclusion of website
Credibility of spokesperson/expert	Call to action

An optional bonus/demerit point can be awarded (outside of the 10 point rating system) for coverage that is either exceptionally positive or negative. With the inclusion of media data, cost per contact can also be calculated by dividing campaign cost by OTS/impressions.

Hill+Knowlton reported a case study of a 'very successful product launch' for one of the consultancy's larger clients. A total of 624 articles were rated using the following five criteria (as well as up to five points for tone):

1 Company/brand mention.

2 Spokesperson quote.

3 Call to action.

4 Key messages/product mention.

5 Fifty+ words on broadcast segment/print/online.

The results were:

Total articles/stories: 624

Total impressions (OTS): 123,461,315

Budget: $149,050.00

Average Tone: 4.9 out of 5

Average Rating: 3.5 out of 5

Total Score: 84 per cent (tone plus rating expressed as a percentage)

Cost per contact: $0.00121 (budget divided by impressions).

The principal drawback from Hill+Knowlton's perspectives was the time and effort to load 624 articles into the system, described as 'considerable', and – by implication – costly. However, the client was 'thrilled' as the numbers 'satisfied the requirements and expectations of the executives to which that person [client contact] reported'.

A more complex system than MR²P is based on the same principles but adds more flexibility in the choice of criteria/variables to be analysed. The additional complexity – such that it is – comes from the need to go through a 'pre-definition' stage to arrive at the outputs required. These outputs are quantitative in nature in the form of bar charts, line graphs, pie charts and the like.

The 'dimensional' methodology outlined below can be implemented manually, but is ideally suited to automation using database software. There is always a trade-off between the time taken to process the analyses and their usefulness. The key issue here would be to find a balance between capturing all the information that might possibly be useful, and making the process so time-consuming and tedious that it becomes self-defeating.

The health warnings that apply to media evaluation outlined below and elsewhere in this book to do with the 'substitution game' – output not impact – and the like apply equally to the dimensional methodology. Even though the dimensional methodology claims to be relatively sophisticated, it remains concerned with media monitoring and therefore still addresses output only and has nothing directly to do with the impact of the programme, campaign or activity.

The case study shows the type of data captured and outputs produced for a customized in-house media evaluation system developed using the dimensional methodology. In this anonymous (owing to client confidentiality) example, the emphasis is very much on formative – rather than summative – evaluation, a role in which media evaluation provides valuable insights.

The ability to design a truly customized approach was of central importance to enable the organization to derive maximum benefit from media evaluation. It was not seeking to use media evaluation to justify the worth of its activities to the organization as a whole. Instead, it was seeking feedback from the public relations process in order to improve and fine-tune the day-to-day management of its media relations efforts.

So, for example, a key output (see below) is the relative volume of coverage generated by different activities (eg press release). Linking this with the known resources (time and additional costs) required to support this activity would then enable the department to establish which types of activity were most cost-effective. Similarly, feedback on the relative favourability of comment from different media could influence where the emphasis of media relations effort would be placed.

A dimensional model of media evaluation

Media evaluation is concerned with evaluating outputs, specifically the number of messages placed in the media, the number of messages supporting objectives, and the number of people who receive (or have the opportunity to receive) the message. In spite of our repeated concerns expressed here about the limitations of media evaluation, particularly with respect to the substitution game, we enthusiastically accept that media evaluation has an important role to play.

It is equally important to understand the limitations that media evaluation has in fulfilling this role. Media evaluation is concerned with the outputs – not the results – of a public relations programme so it can be used as feedback to improve the quality of those results and – if we accept a link between outputs and results – can be used to make cautious, limited inferences about results where direct measurement is impossible or impractical.

There is an important point to be made about the use of reader panels. They are important if media evaluation is being used in a summative, judgemental – 'how did we do?' – manner for the reasons already outlined. However, it can be acceptable for the practitioners running the programme to undertake the media analysis themselves if the purpose is formative, that is, feedback is being sought in order to fine-tune continuing implementation.

The types of questions that media evaluation seeks to answer are:

- Is the coverage beneficial, neutral or adverse?
- Are the media reporting our key corporate messages?

- Which journalists/publications are reporting us favourably?
- What is the source of the press coverage we are achieving?
- How are we doing compared to our competitors?
- Is our media coverage getting better or worse?
- What are the emerging issues affecting our organization?

The type of analyses that are useful to a particular public relations department will vary according to the organization/client concerned. The dimensional model sets out a media evaluation methodology that first specifies a customized set of reports and then defines how they are produced.

So, in contrast to the media monitoring system outlined above, the dimensional methodology is an approach within which practitioners can develop their own system or systems. It is a structure within which a customized system can be developed rather than being itself a customized step-by-step procedure. The case study gives an example of a system developed using the dimensional methodology. Indeed, both the simple and more complex systems outlined in this chapter are eminently compatible with some of the specific tools (eg pro formas) developed as part of the generalized monitoring system able to be used for an individual system developed under the dimensional methodology. The latter is essentially a framework for practitioners to develop their own system, customized according to the specific needs of different clients or organizations. It complements research which indicates that the way forward for media evaluation may well be the development of externally designed, but internally operated, systems.

Quantitative axes

The dimensional media evaluation model has four sets of four axes: quantitative axes, qualitative axes, focus axes, and time axes. The quantitative axes relate to the output 'layers' of Macnamara's Pyramid model (similarly they can be converted into equivalent levels as outlined by other authors, see Chapter 5).

TABLE 6.3

Dimensional model – quantitative axes	Pyramid model layer
Number of clippings	Number who receive messages
Volume of coverage	Number who receive messages
Name checks	Number of messages placed
Number of key messages	Number of messages supporting objectives

The number of clippings is self-explanatory, but note that the term clippings is taken to incorporate broadcast media transcripts. It is highly desirable to handle press and broadcast coverage in an integrated manner. This is done by monitoring broadcast coverage through transcripts which then allow the volume of broadcast coverage to be converted into equivalent column centimetres through a conversion based on word counts. Similarly, readership and viewing figures would be considered comparable. Volume of coverage refers to the number of words or can be expressed as column centimetres. Name checks simply refers to the number of mentions of the company or brand name, and number of key messages refers to the number of occasions on which specified key messages appear.

Qualitative axes

The qualitative axes start to put some flesh on the bare bones of the quantitative axes.

Different media will have different raw circulation and readership figures, and it may be appropriate to adjust for these variances. It may be appropriate to account for the proportion of readership or audience that fall into the target market. Attribution concerns the extent to which volume can be attributed to one name check; for example, can the whole clipping be attributed to a company or brand name when there is one name check in a two-page article? Normal practice might be to leave the decision to the practitioner but to have a default value of, say, 50 column centimetres. BNA (beneficial, neutral, and adverse) refers to the extent that editorial coverage is positive, negative or neutral.

The impact of an article and the strength with which any messages within it are transmitted are determined by a wide range of factors, many of which are peculiar to particular media or sectors of media. Factors which can affect impact include headlines, photographs, position on the page, position of the page, solus, length and many others.

TABLE 6.4

Dimensional model – qualitative axes
Circulation/readership
Attribution
Beneficial/neutral/adverse (BNA)
Impact or message strength

Focus axes

The focus axes determine how focused the media evaluation exercise needs to be.

TABLE 6.5

Dimensional model – focus axes
Source
Medium
Media sector
Total media

The source can either be a particular journalist or third-party commentator. The medium is a particular publication or broadcast programme, while media sector is a classification such as national press, local media, trade press, etc.

The fourth dimension

Science regards time as the fourth dimension and this gives the dimensional model its name.

TABLE 6.6

Dimensional model – time axes
Historical comparison
Competitive comparison
Objectives comparison
Benchmarking

Specifying a working model

With four sets of four variables, the dimensional model theoretically gives us 256 separate analyses that can be performed. In practice, not all possible combinations are meaningful but, nonetheless, there is a requirement to select a small number of meaningful analyses, from the vast number available, for each evaluation exercise. The process is as follows. First, decide which combinations of time and focus dimensions are required.

TABLE 6.7

	Source	Media	Sector	Total
Historical				
Competitive				
Objectives				
Benchmarking				

Then, for each of these combinations, select a further combination of quantitative and qualitative analyses (see Table 6.8).

TABLE 6.8

	Circulation	Attribution	BNA	Impact
Clippings				
Volume				
Name checks				
Key messages				

One example might be a competitive analysis in the trade press, using volume adjusted for impact, tone and attribution. In this way, it is possible to arrive at an evaluation approach, customized for the brand, company or client in question.

Case study: in-house media evaluation system

Background

XYZ's Public Affairs department has used a media evaluation bureau in the past but the reports provided were of limited use and the service was discontinued. More recently, one staff member has begun to undertake a manual analysis of media coverage. Time constraints mean that any manual approach to media evaluation is going to be limited in scope.

It is anticipated that the software issues associated with a simple computerized media evaluation system are relatively trivial. The aim, therefore, was to design an in-house, computerized media evaluation system customized to the planning and management requirements of the department. A limited range of specific reports would be produced but more detailed and broader in scope than those able to be produced manually at present.

Input

Central to the process would be the electronic coding sheet completed for each press cutting, transcript or online mention. Note that the scanning in of press cuttings and broadcast transcripts (the latter may well be available electronically anyway) is an attractive proposition. It would allow simple automatic content analysis such as the identification of key words and/or messages, as well as being an efficient means of storing press coverage. Finally, internal electronic distribution of key items of media coverage internally via intranet is likely to happen soon anyway. However, the feeling is that the project should be implemented one step at a time so that, initially anyway, cuttings and transcripts will remain paper based.

The design of the coding sheet (actually a screen rather than a physical piece of paper) would be part of the next phase of the project. Its precise content would be dependent on the specific outputs required from the system. However, capture of the following data should enable all likely outputs required to be generated:

- Publication/programme and date plus time of transmission (if appropriate).
- Publisher/broadcaster plus circulation, readership and viewership/ listenership (this might be imported from a media directory or entered manually but once only in each case; there would have to be the facility for periodic update of media data).
- Journalist (if known) and position within publication/ programme.
- Presence or absence of a photograph (print media only) and whether the photograph is branded.

- Presence or absence of name in headline.
- Campaign coding (to enable specific campaigns to be tracked).
- Genre (eg documentary, travel section, etc).
- Media sector (automatically prompted from a look-up list).
- Importance of publication/programme (1 = key, 2 = important, 3 = the rest).
- Raw volume in column centimetres (for broadcast coverage either number of lines [transcript] or transmission time [tape] would be entered and a constant used to produce an 'equivalent column centimetre').
- Number of company/product mentions.
- Attributed volume if appropriate, ie only 10 column centimetres would be attributed to each mention up to a maximum equivalent to the length of the item.
- Whether the coverage is beneficial, neutral or adverse (BNA). In the case of beneficial or adverse, a score might be added to indicate slightly, fairly or very.
- The presence of a small range of specified key corporate messages and an indication of the strength (1–5) of those messages. If those messages were directly contradicted, a negative score would be entered. Occasionally, key messages might change so the user would need the facility to update key messages.
- Mention of a small specified selection of key issues. From time to time particular issues would go away and new issues arise.
- A yes/no indication of whether the coverage was generated proactively. If yes, an indication of which type of action from a range (eg press release, facility trip, launch event, video news release, product placement, etc, and which particular release, event, etc).
- Name of any spokesperson quoted.

The key issue here would be to find a balance between capturing all the information that might possibly be useful, and making the process so time-consuming and tedious that it becomes self-defeating.

Reports

A large number of report outputs would be available from the system: the precise range and their nature would be identified as part of the next phase of the project (if appropriate). It is, however, possible to give a broad indication of the type of outputs sought and some specific examples. The output will be quantitative and therefore tabular or graphical (frequently multi-coloured to assist interpretation) in the form of bar charts, line graphs and pie charts. Written commentaries will be added by public affairs staff as a post-report activity.

Normally there will be a measure of volume of coverage. This may be expressed as column centimetres, circulation/readership, or OTS. Readership figures are available for national media (not always for local or trade publications) and could probably be sourced through the advertising or media agency. These figures (particularly when aggregated, and duplication/overlap cannot be taken into account) are frequently meaningless in absolute terms, but can be useful to indicate trends and make comparisons. They may also provide information on target groups' relationship/audience within the total circulation or audience.

There are several ways in which figures for raw volume of coverage can be adjusted. Media coverage can be classified as beneficial, neutral or adverse (or rated on a numerical scale) and also adjusted for impact. Subject to confirmation, the sort of factors that might be taken into account when assessing the impact of media coverage are whether the article is accompanied by a photograph, whether that photograph is branded, the position of that article within the publication, and whether the brand name is in the headline. Attribution is a further factor to be considered: is it appropriate to attribute the full volume (say, 100 column centimetres) of a long article when there is only a single, passing mention?

Two types of report are of particular interest: first, the presence (or absence) in the media and strength of a limited number of key messages directed at the media; and second, whether or not the coverage had been directly prompted by the public relations department and, if so, what type of activity had acted as the prompt (press release, launch event, facility trip, telephone contact, product placement, etc).

These reports would also be subject to varying degrees of focus. It may be desirable to analyse the coverage prompted by one particular journalist or emanating from one particular publication or programme. More likely, coverage might well be broken down into media sectors: national, consumer, trade, local, etc. Coverage could also be analysed according to target media, important media, and the rest.

It would be highly desirable to handle press and broadcast coverage in an integrated manner. This would be done by monitoring broadcast coverage through transcripts, which would then allow the volume of broadcast coverage to be converted into equivalent column centimetres through a conversion based on word counts. Similarly, readership and viewing figures would be considered comparable.

Sample outputs

This is a list of possible outputs to give an indication of the type of outputs that are envisaged. Their precise nature and scope would need to be discussed/examined in more detail. The absence of a particular output does not necessarily mean it could not be generated. Also given is some indication of the perceived management benefits:

1 Raw (unadjusted) volume of coverage in column centimetres or number of mentions by month (bar chart). A crude indication of presence in the media and how it compares with previous periods.

2 Weighted volume (adjusted for readership/viewership, attribution, BNA and impact [position of page, name in headline, photograph, branded photograph]) of coverage in column centimetres per month for a) target/important/other and b) media sectors (two bar charts with multiple bars per month). Media presence taking into account nature of coverage and where it appears; again allowing historical comparison.

3 Relative volume of coverage (percentage) for a specified period (eg three months, six months, 12 months) according to activity that prompted the coverage. This volume could be weighted and the analysis carried out for different media sectors (pie charts). An indication of the effectiveness of different activities which could then be compared with the time/resources devoted to those activities.

4 Number of mentions of specified key issues in national media over time (number of mentions against month/week with a line for each issue). Inevitably historical, but past trends might give early indication of those issues which will dominate media interest in the future.

5 Volume of coverage attributed to key messages (adjusted for strength) per month in target media (bar chart with multiple bars per month, each bar representing a specified key issue). Success or otherwise of persuading the media to report the organization's key messages.

6 Separate rankings of journalists and publications/programmes according to the beneficial, neutral and adverse comment (table). A clear indication of those journalists or media who report the organization's particularly positively or negatively.

7 A campaign analysis listing the volume of coverage (column centimetres for press, time for broadcast, and a combined figure using equivalent column centimetres), both raw and adjusted, including OTS, for a particular campaign. This could be split by media category and/or genre if required (probably a table according to complexity). Quantitative data to support reporting on and analysis of a specific campaign.

8 An activity analysis listing the volume of coverage (column centimetres for press, time for broadcast, and a combined figure using equivalent column centimetres), both raw and adjusted, OTS, and advertising value equivalence for a particular activity such as a press trip (table). Quantitative data to support reporting on and analysis of a specific activity.

International media analysis

Mike Daniels, former chair of the International Association for the Measurement and Evaluation of Communication, with Angela Jeffrey has produced an excellent guide to international media analysis (Daniels and Jeffrey, 2012). They suggest that when designing an international media measurement system, the first step is initial research to understand the communications environment and wider situation. This then enables appropriate communications planning: defining PR objectives and audiences in the context of what the organization concerned is attempting to achieve in an international context. They suggest that the measurement of objectives is based on selecting tools that relate to PR outputs, PR out-takes, PR outcomes and organizational outcomes.

When thinking about the options for media monitoring and analysis, the focus is on finding a balance between resources and cost-effectiveness. For example, it may be preferable to focus on the most important countries and languages (initially, at least) rather than go for comprehensive coverage and be forced to use automated analysis to save costs. Similarly, careful selection of media sources might be more cost-effective than trying to capture and analyse every clip. Another potential area of cost saving can be to 'start an international program with aggregated coverage, and then fill in critical title gaps with traditional media monitoring' (Daniels and Jeffrey, 2012: 17).

The presentation of the data is going to require some thought. The options outlined by (Daniels and Jeffrey, 2012: 20–21) are as follows:

- **Narrative analysis reports** – all monitoring and (full) analysis is outsourced; costs can be reduced if reports only (not clips) are required. How reporting is organized in terms of geography, frequency and product breakdown will be important considerations.

- **Online dashboards** – all clips provided in real-time (or near real-time) with clients running searches and generating reports themselves. Real-time clip delivery backed up by automated analysis can be inexpensive but with the penalty of analysis inaccuracies. There are added problems for international use as automated translation lacks accuracy. Near real-time is less common but can be effective. Greater accuracy is provided through screening by human analysts – but at a cost.

- **Combinations** – an effort to get the best of both worlds can be made by using a low cost, real-time tool for daily reports and overviews, with either of the two approaches above being used for detailed analysis of selected media titles.

Unsurprisingly, translation is a major challenge in an international pro-gramme – in terms of cost if nothing else. One suggested approach is to use native speakers to analyse each clip and this to be reported alongside a brief English summary. 'In this way, the subtle messages hidden in each clip are identified and coded accurately for analysis without having to go through the costly full translation step' (Daniels and Jeffrey, 2012: 23).

Frequently, scorecards are developed that draw on both qualitative and quantitative elements – frequently tone and message delivery are stressed. The Canadian media relations rating points system discussed earlier in this chapter and the Philips case study (in Chapter 7) both feature aspects of such an approach.

Questions to discuss

- What are the important criteria for measurement of PR activity in your workplace?
- What resources are needed to establish a basic media analysis system?
- Using these methods and structures in this chapter, could you set up a media analysis system in your organization? What elements would you include or add?
- How would you plan to gather online information and discussion and measure it? Would it be related to campaign or organization objectives or would it monitor the environment around your workplace or clients?
- If you have experience of operating internationally, what particular challenges does this offer for the monitoring and analysis of media coverage?
- What challenges are social media presenting to the practice of media evaluation/media content analysis?

07
Evaluation in practice – case studies

Philips: strategic use of measurement

In March 2009, Philips appointed OneVoice (an Omnicom multi-agency team including Fleishman-Hillard and Ketchum Pleon) to provide global communication counsel and support. Key to the appointment was a focus on unified global measurement as part of Philips' strategy of repositioning itself from a consumer electronics company to one associated with health and well-being. The existing network of disparate monitoring and measurement services was replaced by a new integrated global system to evaluate the organization's diverse public relations activities. The new OneVoice measurement system (developed by Report International) delivered cost savings, but also provides an effective, accurate, and consistent measure of progress: 'We needed our communication measurement to look forward rather than backward, to focus on outcomes and effects, rather than quantifying mere output' (Andre Manning, VP and Global Head of Corporate Communications, Royal Philips Electronics).

The standard metric used across all Philips' management functions to evaluate communications is Net Promoter Score (NPS). As well as being widely used – and understood – within Philips, NPS is an established industry-wide metric. Customers are asked one simple question: 'How likely is it that you would recommend Philips to a friend or colleague?' Customers respond on scale of 0 to 10:

- those scoring 9–10 are *promoters*: loyal enthusiasts who will keep buying and refer others;

- those scoring 7–8 are *passives*: satisfied but unenthusiastic, vulnerable to competitive offerings;
- those scoring 0–6 are *detractors*: unhappy, can damage the brand and impede growth through word-of-mouth.

The requirement was to develop a media impact score that would be compatible with Philips' NPS scoring. And to ensure best practice, the approach to measurement was required to meet the standards set by the Barcelona Principles as well as the valid metrics framework developed from them.

The system operates across 42 countries in 17 regions. It tracks Philips' coverage and that of five key competitors across business and sector media, and across Philips' three business units (healthcare, lighting and consumer lifestyle). At a corporate level, the top 250 global business publications are monitored. These key drivers of reputation represent media sentiment but enable global coverage to be monitored by looking at between 300 and 600 clippings per month; avoiding the need to track every piece of coverage makes a significant contribution to the cost effectiveness of the system.

In addition to this monitoring at a corporate level, 250 specialist publications relevant to the three business areas where Philips operates are also tracked. And the five competitors tracked are adjusted according to what is appropriate in each sector.

The system evaluates all global and sectoral coverage against a small number of key performance indicators (KPIs) informed by the key corporate issues that Philips prioritizes. Each clipping is assessed according to a compound metric known as the media score: reach (by tiered media list); presence and alignment of messages; prominence in relation to competition; spokesperson quote; third party quote; and tone (positive/negative).

The media score of each clipping is then aggregated to produce an average media score (AMS). This compound score is then converted to an NPS which acts as the basis of all reporting. A media score ranges from −100 to + 100. A simple algorithm converts the AMS into a media NPS: NPS = (AMS + 100)/20. The equivalence between NPS and AMS is based on both indicators deriving from consumers or commentators making the case for Philips.

The KPIs are calculated for each message and reputation driver, business unit, market and region, and against defined competitors, as well as for product launches, media events and campaigns. Importantly, the analysis is undertaken by in-country, native language analysts.

The bespoke online portal enables immediate on-demand access to data and continuously updates in 'near real-time'. It allows users to drill KPIs down to the level of specific messages, campaigns, or actors. Social media content and data is also integrated into performance overviews. Additionally, regular monthly reports and ad-hoc reports covering breaking news, events, campaigns, and product launches are provided. 'Media events, product launches and campaigns require quick turn-around measurement and reporting as the client wants to know how it worked, ideally in real time' (Ben Levine, European Lead, OneVoice Measurement).

FIGURE 7.1   Philips case study: online portal

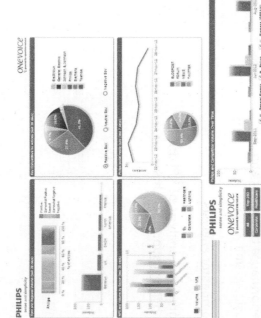

The Online Portal

- Interactive online dashboard.

- Historical data available.

- Data viewable by business unit and by market.

- Data available on the type of coverage generated by journalists.

FIGURE 7.2 Philips case study: reporting

Reporting

- Snap-shot of KPIs:
  - traditional media;
  - key blogs.

- Month-on-month perspective.

- Performance by market and business unit.

- Competitor analysis.

- Contextual analysis of KPI drivers and implications/insights.

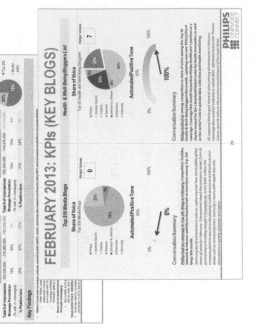

The dashboards look at how different messages affect coverage, feedback on performance in different sectors, help understand what drives coverage, and identify which messages resonate most. 'This consistent measurement-led approach has raised the perception of PR within the organization. It will serve as an example for the industry to move beyond transactional practices, to a much more strategic level where activities are judged by their impact on business results' (Andre Manning).

The Pepsi Refresh Project: evaluating the outcomes

The Pepsi Refresh Project (PRP) was set up in 2009 to encourage Americans to Do Good by participating on a digitally-led community relations project funded by the major soft drinks company. In 2010, it led to 12,000 projects being funded to the tune of $20 million in grants, following 76 million online votes by Americans. The communications were managed by PepsiCo and two major PR consultancies, Edelman and Weber Shandwick. It was based on the premise of 'that's a good idea' – a simple statement that recognized the potential value of community-based projects. This campaign offered consumers the opportunity to vote for projects and see them put into action.

The background to the campaign included studies into consumer attitudes to personal and corporate giving: 84 per cent want to select their own causes; 83 per cent say personal relevance is important (Cone Cause Evolution Study); 95 per cent of Millennials (born from early 1980s onwards) are very optimistic about their lives; the best ideas come from 'normal people' (66 per cent) versus public figures (2009 Pepsi Optimism Project).

Based on this scan, Pepsi chose to develop online and offline forums 'where social innovation could become personal' and help ideas progress to implementation in a 'worthwhile, fun and contagious concept'.

The objectives were:

1 raise awareness and interest in PRP; position Pepsi as the optimistic catalyst for idea creation;

2 generate a steady stream of national, local and online media buzz to support business and brand goals;

3 drive Americans to the campaign website, RefreshEverything.com.

The audiences targeted were Millennials and Boomer (born 1946 to 1964), for whom research found that positive change was a priority. Over two-thirds (71 per cent) believed brands spend too much on marketing and should invest more in good causes (philanthropy). The 2009 Good Purpose Study found that 64 per cent of consumers would recommend brands that support good causes and that 59 per cent will then help that brand promote its products.

Strategy

- Position Pepsi as a credible motivator to empower ordinary Americans as 'the next social entrepreneur', with a national spotlight on the implementation of ideas.
- Collaborate with employees and business partners to generate local news and drive awareness.
- The website to be promoted as the online destination to Do Good; encourage individuals to submit ideas and vote.
- Encourage online engagement with PRP on Facebook and Twitter.
- Develop national partnerships that enable stories to be told of PRP's impact and reach.

Campaign execution

There was extensive media coverage based on milestone events, including the Super Bowl, and presentations to grant recipients; a launch event was held at the New York Stock Exchange; partnerships were built with celebrities and performing artists to encourage participation by youth; specific actions were targeted at the Gulf states of the southern United States after the Deepwater Horizon oil spill; thought leader events were created; and digital engagement was monitored and given real-time responses.

Evaluation

- Raise awareness and interest in PRP: the results were that 37 per cent of Americans were aware of PRP, compared with 12–21 per cent for similar cause marketing programmes.
- Generate a steady stream of media buzz: the media impressions goal was exceeded nearly 12-fold; PRP received 140,000 tweets and over 2 million Facebook 'likes', both well above target; interaction with the campaign website increased brand attributes (favourability, intent, and trust) significantly, as well as intent to purchase Pepsi among Millennials.
- Drive Americans to RefreshEverything.com: there were 18 million unique visitors over 11 months in 2011 resulting in 76 million votes on 12,000 projects, with 2 million online comments.

PRP was a 2011 Public Relations Society of America Silver Anvil winner for Community Relations – Business Products.

Crime fighting PR: success on a low budget

One of the most successful recent public relations campaigns in the United Kingdom was carried out in 2011 by Lothian & Borders Police, now part of Police Scotland. It targeted assets that had been acquired by criminal activity such as drug-dealing and money laundering.

The campaign, 'Made from Crime?' was developed by the force's communications team. It was targeted at internal audiences, who were mainly police officers, and external audiences including the media and the public in its region, which includes the capital of Edinburgh and the south-east of Scotland.

The objectives were:

1 internal – increase financial intelligence reports by officers by 50 per cent;

2 external – increase the public's reports on criminal assets to the Crimestoppers phone and online service by 10 per cent;

3 supporting objectives – 65 per cent positive or neutral coverage in Scottish media;

4 demonstrate to the public that the police force would act on information received about people making money illegally.

The budget allocated, above the costs for staff and existing services, was £4,500.

Planning

Research was undertaken to ensure the campaign would target 'the right people, in the right way'. There was consultation with partner agencies including the nationally-operating Serious Organised Crime Agency, as well as focus groups and in-depth interviews. It found:

● the public often don't know what to do when they see suspicious activity;

● a barrier to people reporting crime was a 'perceived lack of anonymity';

● the public were most likely to consider reporting suspicious activity where they were alone; and

● police officers believed financial investigation was the responsibility of the detectives, but not themselves.

Strategy

- Reach the public when they are on their own.
- Remind the public that they can report anonymously via Crimestoppers (an anonymous phone-reporting facility).
- Educate police officers that financial intelligence is every officer's responsibility.

Campaign execution

Before the campaign was launched, all officers were briefed about their powers to report suspicious activities that generate illegal income and about the forthcoming campaign. This was followed in summer 2011 with a media launch event, including a government minister, at which the campaign and its materials were presented. This was also put forward on the Force's website and intranet and distributed on social media. The 'Made from Crime?' campaign also used Facebook advertisements, Bluetooth messages, outdoor posters and direct mail targeted to areas where known criminals resided. All aimed at prompting anonymous reports to Crimestoppers with a message of 'Suspect someone of making cash illegally? Don't stand for it'.

Evaluation

Campaign output

- 4 million 'page impressions' on Facebook over a five-week period.
- Extensive coverage in national (Scottish) and local print, broadcast and online media.

Campaign outcomes

- Internal – 137 per cent rise in financial intelligence reports by police staff.
- External – 17 per cent in Crimestoppers reports by the public; 63 online reports to Crimestoppers and 882 visits to its website, which had been influenced by the Facebook campaign.

As a result of the intelligence gained from the 'Made from Crime?' campaign, the police force launched Operation Opulent, a 48-hour 'period of enforcement action' which involved over 280 officers and staff. It led to:

- 25 house searches;
- 44 people arrested and charged;
- £68,000 in cash seized;

- £22,000 worth of drugs and £13,000 worth of counterfeit goods confiscated;
- 77 vehicle offences detected;
- £6.4 million worth of restraint reports sent to prosecutors for future action.

The 'Made from Crime?' campaign won the Chartered Institute of Public Relations (CIPR) Excellence Awards for Best Low Budget campaign and Best Use of Measurement and Evaluation in 2012. It is also used as a best communications practice case by UK police forces.

St John Ambulance: promoting first aid training

This campaign was developed in 2010 by the St John Ambulance and its PR adviser Golin Harris to rebuild the importance of first aid training and to develop the charity's brand in the United Kingdom. It sought to train more people through free guides, website pages, an iPhone app and courses. There was a subsidiary aim of building support for St John Ambulance and to increase donations.

Research had found that many people lacked basic first aid skills, with a claim that 150,000 people died each year in the United Kingdom 'in situations where first aid could have given the chance to live'. YouGov survey results showed the public lacked knowledge in responding to five severe, life-threatening situations: choking, heart not beating, severe bleeding, heart attack and blocked airway.

Objectives for an eight-week campaign included:

- increase the number of people learning first aid by encouraging 50,000 people to request a free first aid guide; sell £1 million worth of training courses;
- sell 10,000 iPhone apps;
- increase 'awareness, understanding and positive feeling towards the brand by 20 per cent';
- increase visits to St John Ambulance website by 20 per cent and Facebook fans by 10 per cent;
- increase doorstep donations by 10 per cent and obtain 2,000 new donors' telephone numbers.

Strategy

- Establish first aid as a life and death matter; stress importance of learning the skill.
- Create a call to action to request a first aid guide or buy an app (now available free).
- Target influential media.
- Redevelop the charity's website to carry the campaign message.
- Relaunch Facebook and Twitter channels to increase engagement.

Campaign execution

The tactical approach was to place the 'life and death' angle in the media through case studies, personal advocates and free first aid training for the media. The charity's CEO and its lead first aid trainer were placed as commentators with the media, supported by a Q&A document for spokespeople and the public relations team. The messages and the campaign were also communicated to staff and volunteers to encourage advocacy. The first aid guide was used as a pocket guide to handling the five critical situations.

As well as media relations, the campaign placed comments and discussion on the charity's Facebook site, which also had three first aid 'vox pops'. There were also pavement advertisements in London locations where first aid had been given.

Outcomes

- One mother contacted St John Ambulance to say she had saved her daughter from choking using the iPhone app's advice.
- There was extensive media coverage (368 items) of which 98.5 per cent was positive and 55.8 per cent referenced the five first aid tips.
- Visits to the charity's website went up by 25 per cent year-on-year.
- 71,000 people received a free first aid guide in the campaign period, and a total of more than 460,000 by the end of 2010.
- 13,566 downloaded the iPhone app and there was an 18 per cent growth in Facebook fans.
- The £1 million sales target for training courses was exceeded; there were 33,853 visits to first aid advice pages.
- Doorstep donations increased by 30 per cent and the direct marketing database rose by 75 per cent.
- Spontaneous brand awareness rose by from 23 per cent pre-campaign to 32 per cent post-campaign (+ 39 per cent).

- 75 per cent of survey respondents said the campaign was effective and 72 per cent felt more positive towards St John Ambulance.

The Life Lost campaign won the CIPR's Excellence Awards for Best Low Budget campaign and Best Use of Measurement and Evaluation in 2011.

Medicare Open Enrolment: changing behaviour through PR

'One of the most vexing challenges facing executives today is planning for, managing against and quantifying the contribution of marketing and communication on behavioral impact.' That is the opening sentence of this case study about the measurement of a major national health-related campaign in the United States. Unlike the previous case studies, which included the whole campaign process, this discussion will review the measurement and evaluation methods.

The situation being measured was the annual Open Enrolment (OE) campaign when those US citizens who receive Medicare are asked to review their health insurance and prescription drug plans for the coming year. Each year they are bombarded with information about health care and its reform at a time when they are choosing the level of insurance cover during the OE period.

The task for Centers for Medicare and Medicaid (CMS), PR adviser Porter Novelli and research provider PRIME Research was to determine the effectiveness of its communication (outreach) and to identify the activities that most efficiently communicate the call-to-action for Medicare beneficiaries to review their plans during OE.

To do this, they developed a research programme that could measure standard metrics, including:

- beneficiaries' exposure to OE communications, compared with previous years;
- target audience awareness of paid television compared with previous years;
- beneficiaries' knowledge of OE;
- earned media coverage, also compared with previous years.

The research strategy the team developed was based on communication and collaboration. Rather than separately measure campaign outreach, media monitoring and marketing evaluation, they chose to develop a holistic set of metrics. To do this, the research was executed at two levels and then brought together.

- The tracking survey measured awareness and recall of earned and paid media efforts, from unprompted and prompted perspectives.

- Media monitoring and tracking studies gauged pick-up and recall of the campaign's core and supporting messages.
- All data would be matched at the regional levels on CMS's operations, thus providing data for future national and regional campaigns.

Before and after the campaign, which ran from October 2010 to January 2011, CMS conducted telephone tracking studies, while PRIME contributed media analysis data for much the same period. When the campaign was completed, the three partners combined their data into a single dataset.

Data analyses included standard frequencies and cross-tabulations to reveal recognition of campaign messages, type of content, and channels of exposure to awareness of OE, knowledge of options and key behavioural actions (for example, reviewing and comparing coverage). Through statistical analyses, the team 'captured the impact of specific campaign components on overall campaign effectives. It also enabled them to compare the performance of public relations elements of the strategy with those from marketing and other forms of communication.

This holistic approach gave a wide range of data-informed insights but a key finding was that, after controlling for exposure to paid media, demographic and decision-style variables, those 'beneficiaries who reported exposure to PR coverage and earned media about OE were 2.3 times more likely to adopt the campaign's primary call-to-action than those who were not exposed to PR'.

The CMS programme demonstrated that public relations 'profoundly and positively impacts message dissemination, comprehension and behavior at levels that are more effective and efficient than other forms of more highly-controlled marketing and communication commanding higher levels of expenditure', commented Mark Weiner, CEO, who with Chelsea Mirkin led PRIME's work on the OE campaign.

In 2012, The Changing Behavior Through PR case study won the Institute for Public Relations Jack Felton Golden Ruler Award as well as the Sabre Award from the Holmes Report and the Platinum PR Award from PR News, The programme was also award-recognized by the Advertising Research Foundation and Ragan Reports.

Westminster City Council: using evaluation to improve services

Westminster City Council is the local authority in the centre of London. It has more than 240,000 residents and welcomes more than a million visitors a day. It stretches from Buckingham Palace to London's West End. It is home to the UK government, big business, and historical sites, as well as offering leisure and cultural facilities to residents and visitors alike.

The UK government's austerity agenda has resulted in radical changes to the way that public services are delivered. Westminster sees the use of research and evaluation as an opportunity to change the way they deliver services in a way that will best meet the interests of its residents. In parallel, there is a radical shift in the way that people consume communications. Situated at the heart of London, the City of Westminster boasts a local population that leads Europe in the adoption of communication technology. Nearly nine out of 10 (86 per cent) residents have the internet at home (compared to 76 per cent nationally) and a third (36 per cent) of those aged 16 or over have an iPhone – compared to 21 per cent nationally (National figures from Ipsos MORI technology tracker early 2013; compared to council's own polling).

Strategy

Westminster City Council uses measurement and evaluation to help the council navigate the challenges associated with the provision of public services in the current climate. The aim is to keep residents engaged while also informing the council's strategic direction. The council combines communications measurement with other research techniques to develop measurable objectives and develop carefully targeted plans. For example, Westminster developed a mathematical tool (the ALBERT model) that enables the council to pre-determine the number of people to target and where to find them. Experience of using the model has demonstrated that there are three main ways to improve campaign results:

- target groups with higher levels of non-satisfaction;
- target more people;
- target people for whom messages are most relevant, or using the medium most relevant to them.

Westminster's whole approach to communications is evidence-based. On a daily basis, a summary of media coverage (including top tweets) is e-mailed to the communications team and the Council's Executive Board. Every month, a dashboard of the key metrics is reported back to the Executive Board; these metrics include public opinion and media monitoring statistics, as well as data on key issues that are likely to impact on the council – the aim is to provide insight into possible future trends, not just to review activity retrospectively.

All campaigns are reviewed quarterly and the council estimates that the achievement of annual outcomes is in the area of 80 to 90 per cent. This validates both the ALBERT model in particular and the overall communications approach in general.

Execution/implementation

The key aspects that Westminster's communications team delivers in terms of measurement and evaluation are:

- **Monthly dashboards** to inform the Council's Executive Board of key evaluation measures and the key challenges the council faces. These inform the strategic direction of the council.

- **The Westminster Reputation Tracker** which is a market research public opinion survey of 500 residents to track perception measures. Similar surveys are run for other local authorities which validates the usefulness of this approach across the sector.

- **Market research** is used to survey businesses, stakeholders, staff and other key groups.

- **Media evaluation** includes real time monitoring of social media sentiment which enables the media team to follow up comments and react immediately.

- **Regular e-mails** to the 47,000+ people who have signed up to Westminster's online services are carefully evaluated. This enables understanding how people really respond to e-mail. The 20% of local residents who report receiving e-mails are among the council's most satisfied residents.

- **Tailored navigation** on the website has been developed by the team. Unusually, less than one-fifth of visitors to the council's website arrive through the home page. This approach to navigation adapts to user behaviour by identifying what they might be interested in no matter how they come on to the site.

Conclusions

The senior leadership of the council understands that the strategy in reaction to the changing world of communications will help guide the council through broader social changes. Without research and evaluation there would be no clear path developing. Throughout this period of service change satisfaction with the council has stayed above 76 per cent which compares favourably with local government in general across the United Kingdom.

Westminster communications team's culture of research has helped:

- reinforce the legitimacy of council policies such as the sharing of services between three adjoining local authorities, by developing the first joint staff and resident survey programme across three local authorities;

- add the concept of 'fairness' to the council's radical policy review called the Civic Contract;

- defend publications such as the parents' magazine *Children First* from cuts by demonstrating their effectiveness;
- prioritize the importance of keeping the streets clean in the council's Financial Review;
- motivate senior managers through showing how the staff survey results could help council corporate initiatives;
- show the importance of research and evaluation through supporting a programme of monthly national polling on the reputation of local government and providing the data freely for all councils to use to contextualize their own findings.

This case study has been adapted from the Gold Award made to Westminster City Council in the 'Best Use of Communication Management: Not-for Profit' category of the International Association for the Measurement and Evaluation of Communication 2012 Awards.

Questions to discuss

- The Philips case study reports three common evaluation themes: speaking the 'language' of the rest of the organization, making comparisons with the competition, and a compound media score metric. Which of these approaches would be relevant to your organization, and to what extent?
- Which metric or outcome was the most impressive for you in the evaluation of the Pepsi Refresh Project? Was it 'awareness', 'social media buzz', 'website visitors' or another?
- The 'Made from Crime?' campaign in Scotland resulted in prosecutions as well as seizure of cash, drugs and vehicles. Which measurement or judgements most effectively demonstrated the PR/communication campaign's effectiveness?
- The case study for the St John Ambulance 'Life Lost' campaign had a wide range of measurements: Were there others which could have been applied to it? How valid were the objectives set for the campaign?
- Instead of separating the measurement and evaluation of PR activity from marketing and advertising (known as 'disaggregation'), the Medicare OE campaign brought all the data together. Could that approach be applied in your workplace or for clients?
- The Westminster case uses direct measurement/research (eg reputation tracker) extensively. How does this benefit the organization in general and the communications function in particular?

08
Objectives and objective setting

One of the main weaknesses in communications planning is objective setting. There are three common problems: one is objectives that describe processes (eg 'organize a press event') rather than an end point. Another is objectives that are so vague they are useless as success (or otherwise) cannot be established. Finally, there needs to be a clear linkage between the success criteria established in the objectives and the data gathered to evaluate the success of the programme. The Barcelona Principles (International Association for the Measurement and Evaluation of Communication, 2010) state that 'goal-setting and measurement are fundamental aspects of any public relations program'. Smith (2005: 72) is more specific, adding that objectives 'give the planner a reference point for evaluation'.

Probably the most common term associated with objective setting in general is 'SMART': specific, measurable, achievable, realistic, and timed. But it can be challenging to establish communications objectives whose achievement can be controlled. For example, an objective could be the result of a range of communications inputs (eg public relations, advertising and sales promotion) or an initially achievable objective could become very challenging because of external developments (eg an unanticipated economic downturn). So SMART objectives should frequently be regarded as an ideal to aspire to rather than a practical proposition in all circumstances.

Another key concept associated with public relations objective setting is the concept of a hierarchy of objectives. Stacks and Bowen (2011: 3) explain that there are three public relations objectives found in any campaign: informational, motivational and behavioural. They occur in a logical order. First, communication must occur; that is, the information must be sent, received and understood. Second, the public, stakeholders or audience must be motivated by that communication towards the intended action. And, third, the target should adopt the desired behaviour.

The final point about objective setting is the crucial connection between outcome/impact evaluation and objectives set. Evaluation falls at the first fence if it is not taken into account at the beginning of the programme when objectives are set. Quite simply, evaluation links directly back to the objectives set at the beginning of the programme.

Objectives in context

There is some confusion over the use of the terms objectives and goals. This text uses the same approach as Stacks and Bowen (2011: 2): a goal is 'a broad idea of what you would like to happen' while an objective is 'a clearly defined statement that includes an action statement (a verb), a timeline and a measurable outcome (usually expressed as a percentage) – see the discussion of SMART objectives below. Note that the Barcelona Principles use the term 'goal' in the way Stacks and Bowen (2011) define objectives above. They suggest these guidelines for writing clear, measurable campaign objectives (2011: 4) while establishing the linkages between objective setting and research (see Chapter 4):

1 Differentiate between goals and objectives.

2 Conduct research into the baseline data from which success or failure at specified campaign phases and the campaign end can be judged and evaluated.

3 Refine the research objectives associated with each objective. How will the data be gathered and evaluated – physical examination of content, in-depth interviews with opinion leaders, surveys of targeted audiences, tracking products or commentary.

The bedrock of the effective evaluation of public relations programmes and activities is setting appropriate and effective objectives. Formative evaluation is about measuring progress towards objectives and summative evaluation is about establishing whether stated objectives have been met. Indeed, evaluation becomes relatively trivial if clear measurable objectives are established at the outset. Vague, unspecific objectives lead to unsatisfactory evaluation. So objectives are pivotal to the evaluation of public relations programmes. And it is because objective setting is not simple in public relations that public relations evaluation is also not simple.

There is a widespread and almost universally uncritical assertion that effective evaluation starts with the setting of appropriate objectives. Appropriate in this context means that the objectives are clearly defined, measurable and quantifiable. Countless authorities assert that achieving objectives is the simplest (only) way to evaluate any communications programme or campaign. For example, when talking about the credibility of measurement and evaluation in communications, Lindenmann (2006: 13) stresses that the starting point is indeed to set specific, measurable communications objectives: 'This has to come first. No one can really measure the effectiveness of anything, unless they first figure out exactly what it is they are measuring that something against.' Broom and Dozier (1990: 76) develop this point further: 'To learn if your program worked, you must use the criteria established in the objectives and goals'. They then go on to point out that if at the evaluation stage the criteria for evaluation have to be refined – or even defined from scratch – then the only reason is that the criteria spelled out in the objectives were not specific enough. Indeed, a common fault of ineffective evaluation is a mismatch between (so-called) evaluation undertaken at the end of (and during) the programme, and the objectives spelled out at the start of the programme.

However, objectives are a key issue in a much broader context than public relations and communications. For example, when discussing the role of objectives in corporate strategy, Fill (2009: 324) outlines a number of reasons why objectives play an important role in the activities of individuals, social groups and organizations:

1 they provide direction and an action focus for all those participating in the activity;

2 they provide a means by which the variety of decisions relating to an activity can be made in a consistent way;

3 they determine the time period in which the activity is to be completed;

4 they communicate the values and scope of the activity to all participants;

5 they provide a means by which the success of the activity can be evaluated.

All of these general attributes of objectives have key benefits when specifically applied to public relations programming. In particular, the last two points cover the potential value that objectives can play in proving the worth and assessing the value of business activities.

Figure 8.1 shows how objectives (and goals) are the link between the organization's mission and values, and the strategies and tactics required to fulfil that mission. In this way, public relations practitioners do not derive objectives in isolation. They are identified and selected specifically so that their achievement makes some contribution to solving the problems and seizing the opportunities that face the organization. If a number of communications objectives can be established (and then met) that ultimately contribute to an organization achieving its mission, then public relations can truly be described as playing a strategic role within that organization.

FIGURE 8.1   Strategic planning pyramid (based on Austin and Pinkleton, 2001)

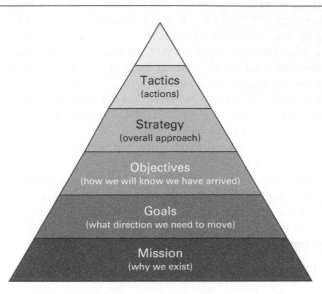

While any discussion of objectives tends to be uncritically approving, it is worth adding one note of caution. The desire to be specific and crystal clear when outlining objectives should not go to the extent of creating a straitjacket. As Mullins (2010: 549) states:

> Objectives may be just implicit but the formal, explicit statement of objectives will assist communications and reduce misunderstandings, and provide more meaningful criteria for evaluating organizational performance. However, objectives should not be stated in such a way that they detract from the recognition of possible new opportunities, potential danger areas, the initiative of staff, or the need for innovation or change.

In other words, objectives have significant benefits in providing focus and direction for a public relations campaign or programme. But this should not be at the expense of stifling creativity or eliminating the flexibility to respond to opportunities that were not anticipated when the plan was formulated. For example, the outbreak of a computer virus is a good opportunity for an anti-virus software vendor to raise its profile, irrespective of whether this type of activity was anticipated at that time.

Aims, goals and objectives

The terms 'aims', 'goals' and 'objectives' tend to be thrown around as if they are interchangeable. Attempts of varying specificity are made to distinguish between the three. For example, James Grunig and Todd Hunt, while accepting that the dictionary definition of goals and objectives is the same, move on to 'define goals as broader and more general than objectives' (1984: 116) as discussed above:

Goals are generalized ends – ends that provide a framework for decision making and behaviour but that are too broad to help much in making day-to-day decisions.

Objectives, on the other hand, are ends in view – expected solutions to day-to-day problems that we can use to deal with that problem and to evaluate whether we have solved it.

An example given to illustrate the difference is that the goal of a PR department might be to ensure public acceptance of the organization. But the practitioners working in the department will need more specific objectives in order to enable them to plan and evaluate day-to-day activities. These might be along the lines of getting a certain percentage of an important public to understand the organization's stance on a particular issue.

Here, we will be no more precise than accepting that goals and aims are frequently slightly broader and less closely defined than objectives and concentrate on understanding and applying the latter. It may be helpful to set overall campaign goals but, by and large, these will not be measurable. Indeed, many statements that are described as objectives in public relations proposals and programmes are no more than vague goals. Typical examples are 'to raise awareness of...' or 'to position as...'. Such a goal may possibly be achievable in some loose way, but is certainly not measurable unless quantifiable elements are added. Purists might even argue that if an objective is not measurable then it is not achievable, as the fact of its achievement cannot be identified. Frequently, public relations – quite appropriately – sets broad outcomes such as raising awareness but it is unhelpful (indeed incorrect) to describe these as objectives, although they are almost universally so described.

This is a key point. Virtually every public relations plan or proposal has stated objectives that are expressed in these vague terms. This reflects not so much lazy thinking on behalf of the practitioners involved, but rather (as we will see) the peculiar challenges of objective setting in large swathes of public relations activity. Simply stated, but more difficult to implement, public relations planning frequently requires the statement of broad aims and goals underpinned with more specific – and necessarily, therefore, limited – objectives.

Note that this interpretation of the relationship between goals/aims and objectives is not universally accepted. Smith (2005: 69) points out that in public relations and marketing contexts, goals are indeed couched in general terms and objectives are specific. However, some other business disciplines 'either reverse the meanings of the terms or use them interchangeably'. This is not the first time – nor will it be the last – that codifying and developing the practice of public relations is bedevilled by terminology rather than true content.

So, unhelpfully, in actual practice these terms (goals and objectives) are used differently by different people. Public relations practitioners need to decide on their preferred definition and then stick to it. We commend the use of the terms as outlined by Smith (2005: 69–72) as follows and this is the approach used here:

> A goal is a statement rooted in the organization's mission or vision. Using everyday language, a goal acknowledges the issue and sketches out how the organization hopes to see it settled. A goal is stated in general terms and lacks measure; these will come later in the objectives.

An objective is a statement emerging from the organization's goals. It is a clear and measurable statement, written to point the way forward towards particular levels of awareness, acceptance or action. Objectives often are established by communication managers responding to broader organizational goals. Like goals, objectives deal with intended outcomes rather than procedures for reaching them. A single goal may be the basis for several objectives.

This is nothing new. Indeed, Grunig and Hunt (1984) outlined this distinction between goals and objectives while also highlighting the relationship between them. This is demonstrated in Figure 8.2. Finally on this point, Broom and Sha (2013: 295) efficiently sum up the linkage between objectives and goals: 'objectives are smaller-scale outcomes that, collectively and over time, achieve the broader goal of the public relations program'.

In much the same way that the term objective is frequently used without too much care, so there tends to be confusion with the associated (but not overlapping) concepts of strategy and tactics. While the objective is the end-point that the programme, campaign or activity is attempting to reach, the strategy is the overall approach to be used in pursuance of reaching that end-point: not to be confused with tactics, the particular set of actions required in order to implement the strategy.

FIGURE 8.2   Goals and objectives

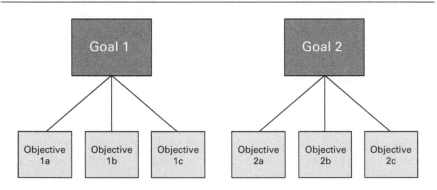

Goals are broad and abstract and cannot be tested directly.

Objectives are derived from goals. They are specific and measurable.
Meeting an objective contributes to attaining a goal.

Management by objectives

In a general business context, the term objective is most commonly associated with the concept of management by objectives (MBO). Indeed, this is nothing more than common sense in public relations where we have already established that objectives play a key role before, during and after the implementation of a communications programme, and we have established that public relations is a management process.

This reinforces the central role that objectives can, and frequently do, play in modern management thinking. As Kotler *et al* (2009: 105) explain, while most business units pursue a range of objectives, for an MBO system to work, the business unit's various objectives must meet four criteria:

- they must be arranged hierarchically, from the least to the most important;
- objectives should be quantitative whenever possible;
- goals should be realistic: goals should arise from an analysis of the business unit's opportunities and strengths, not from wishful thinking;
- objectives must be consistent: it is not possible to maximize both sales and profits simultaneously.

These exhortations will be echoed in much of the discussion of public relations objectives outlined below. For instance, a hierarchy of objectives implies the linking of public relations objectives, directly or indirectly, with organizational objectives. Taking another example, the encouragement for objectives to be quantified is a mantra oft repeated in a public relations context. In terms of being realistic, public relations objectives need to be communications objectives. Finally, realism also points towards being realistic about the effects sought. Public relations practitioners too often fall into the trap of promising/assuming over-optimistic results from their efforts. This may breed euphoria in the short term, but certainly disappointment and disillusionment follow in the medium to long term.

A more careful review of classic MBO thinking also throws up clear parallels with public relations evaluation when undertaken in a formative rather than summative guise. This parallel also illustrates the contention that public relations thinking is continually hampered by the need to reinvent the wheel: quicker and more effective progress could easily be made if practitioners had the confidence and good sense to borrow and adapt ideas that have been tried and tested in related fields of endeavour (note that the phrase 'management by objectives' has been in use for nearly half a century).

The underlying basis of a system of MBO is described by Mullins (2010: 467) as:

- the setting of objectives and targets;
- participation by individual managers in agreeing unit objectives and criteria of performance;
- the continual review and appraisal of results.

This introduces a number of ideas that are directly applicable to objective setting in a public relations context and will be echoed in the discussion of objective setting below. The use of the term 'targets' alongside 'objectives' is an indication of how objectives can made measurable without a 'near miss' condemning the programme to failure. Performance criteria firmly imply that thinking about how the success of the programme is to be measured needs to take place as soon as planning starts (not when implementation has been completed). Finally, 'continual approval and appraisal' points to a dual formative and summative approach to the evaluation of public relations activities.

Translating this thinking to PR programme management, we have another plea to concentrate on the impact of what is being undertaken rather than being sidetracked into concentrating solely on the process of the programme. As discussed below, process objectives can be useful but need to be treated with caution. They can easily result in the misplaced approach to evaluation represented by the substitution game.

Hierarchy of objectives

Broom and Sha (2013: 296–97) outline three levels of outcomes for programme objectives: knowledge outcome, predisposition (opinion) outcome and behavioural outcome. This starts to indicate what Smith (2005: 74) describes as 'an ordered hierarchy' of communications objectives. They grow out of 'a logical progression through three stages of persuasion: awareness, acceptance and action'. The word 'hierarchy' is used to indicate that higher-level objectives can only be achieved once objectives below them in the hierarchy have been achieved. For example, people will not buy your new product before they have first been made aware of it and secondly are positively disposed towards it.

Stacks (2002: 29) is another authority who confirms that there is a 'sequencing' of public relations objectives – from informational (or awareness/knowledge), through motivational to behavioural objectives:

> Informational objectives establish what knowledge should be known or is needed by the publics the campaign or program is intended for. ... Motivational objectives test whether or not the information is having an effect and whether tactical strategies are having an impact on future behaviour. Furthermore the relationship between informational and motivational objectives is interactive; that is, if motivational objectives are not being met, informational objectives can be changed to overcome identified blockages. The behavioural objectives are often what 'count', and they in the end define the success or failure of a campaign.

While instinctively we might appreciate that awareness/knowledge objectives are the most common and easiest public relations objectives to achieve, they can be relatively difficult to measure. Survey research is often required but frequently practitioners seek to infer (rather than prove) effectiveness by concentrating on measuring media coverage. However, efficient delivery of the message does not prove anything about changes in awareness and exposure to messages does not necessarily mean increased awareness.

Awareness objectives, and even motivational objectives, can be regarded as – and may on occasion overtly be – process objectives in pursuance of behavioural objectives. If so, the standard health warning associated with the substitution game applies. As Stacks points out above, behaviour is frequently the ultimate aim. However, it is not necessarily the province of public relations/communications. Product sales might reasonably be regarded as a marketing/sales objective but supported by public relations/communications objectives which concern themselves with raising awareness of the product and even motivating prospects to buy.

Behavioural objectives tend to be more difficult to achieve but ironically they are frequently easier than awareness and motivational objectives to measure. The former are based on clearly measurable results that can be quantified and observed directly, rather than implied (eg product sales or attendance at an event).

In short, behaviour is easier to observe than cognitive effects. However, it is more difficult to prompt. Below are examples of public relations objectives for three levels of outcomes:

- knowledge/awareness outcome: within six months, to increase by 20 percentage points the number of UK homeowners who are aware that smoke detectors halve the chance of death or serious injury in a house fire;
- motivational/predisposition outcome: to ensure that over the next 12 months at least 75 per cent of local residents, for example, have a positive attitude towards the regional airport;
- behavioural outcome: to increase the percentage of employees who donate to the company's chosen roster of charities through 'pay as you earn' from 13 per cent to 25 per cent by the end of the financial year.

Specifying objectives

Perhaps the most common acronym to be applied to objectives is SMART. Even here, authorities differ in their interpretation (with some extending it to SMARRTT):

- specific because objectives should be clear, precise and give direction about what is to be achieved;
- measurable because a quantified measurement statement (eg a percentage or absolute amount to be achieved) enables precise evaluation of the campaign;

- achievable because the resources must be available to achieve
  the objectives set;
- realistic because – even with adequate resources – the objectives
  should be capable of being met;
- relevant because objectives should be appropriate for the task at hand;
- targeted because all objectives should be related to the target
  audiences that are being addressed (and with more than one target
  audience there needs to be separate objectives for each);
- timed because a clear time-frame indicating when objectives are
  expected to be achieved enables the campaign to be monitored and
  evaluation to be undertaken.

Macnamara (2011: 8) makes the point that public relations and corporate communications objectives are not SMART but tend towards being 'broad, vague and imprecise'. He goes on to argue that they are also frequently so high level that it might be difficult to disentangle the contribution PR has made to their achievement.

For example, Smith (1998: 43) provides examples of communications objectives which are commendable for encompassing some of the SMART principles, even if they might not all be wholly achievable through the use of public relations alone:

- to increase awareness from 35 per cent to 50 per cent within eight
  weeks of the campaign launch among 25–45-year-old ABC1 women;
- to position the service as the friendliest on the market within
  a 12-month period among 70 per cent of heavy chocolate users;
- to reposition Guinness from an old, unfashionable, older man's drink
  to a fashionable younger person's drink over two years among all
  25–45-year-old male drinkers;
- to maintain brand x as the preferred brand (or number one brand) of
  photocopiers among at least 50 per cent of current UK buyers in
  companies with 1,000+ employees;
- to include Bulgarian wines in the repertoire of possible wine
  purchases among 20 per cent of ABC1 wine buyers within
  12 months;
- to support the launch of a new shop by generating 50 per cent
  awareness in the immediate community one week before the launch;
- to announce a sale and create 70 per cent awareness one day before
  the sale starts.

Macnamara (2011: 9) also addresses another 'failing' of objectives 'is the lack of any baseline or benchmark' because without this starting point it will not be possible to measure any progress/success achieved.

Broom and Dozier (1990: 44) go into further detail when describing the anatomy of an objective. They discuss the nature of the intended change, the target public, the outcome to be achieved, amount of change desired and a target date for achieving the outcome:

1 Begin with 'to' followed by a verb describing the direction to the intended outcome. There are three possibilities: 'to increase', 'to decrease,' and 'to maintain'.

2 Specify the outcome to be achieved. Again three possible outcomes: knowledge, predisposition or behaviour. Each objective should spell out a single, specific outcome.

3 State the magnitude of change or level to be maintained in measurable terms. The watchwords are quantifiable and realistic. A combination of judgement based on experience, and benchmark data is used to set outcome levels.

4 Set the target date for when the outcome is to be achieved. Typically, outcomes must be achieved in order with one necessarily before another.

As with SMART objectives, this guidance is frequently an ideal to be aspired to rather than anything that can be followed to the letter. Frequently, there may be major environmental influences (recession) and/or other communications efforts (failed sales promotion) that will result in a professional public relations campaign failing to (help) achieve the effects sought.

The nature of objectives

Nonetheless, on some occasions, the achievement of public relations objectives is simple to assess. Frequently, this is when public relations is not operating in a marketing context. A campaign to amend a piece of legislation will either succeed or fail and establishing this success or failure will be a trivial matter. Similarly, a company's share price will either reach a target level or it will not and the evidence will be in the public domain.

Frequently, meeting public relations objectives is not a simple pass/fail issue. The nature of the objectives themselves has a major effect on the type of the public relations campaign required, what needs to be achieved and therefore how the campaign is to be evaluated:

- the nature of public relations objectives varies according to virtually every conceivable criterion;
- the nature of the objective will determine the techniques required to evaluate the programme concerned;
- behavioural objectives are more difficult to achieve than objectives which seek to achieve simpler effects.

Chris Fill (2009: 326) confirms that there are differing opinions as to what communications seeks to achieve and the resulting complexity means that many managers fail to set promotional objectives at all. When they do, 'they are inappropriate, inadequate or merely restate the marketing objectives'. Setting sales-related promotional objectives, for example, fails to accept the contribution of other elements of the marketing mix: 'Two distinct schools of thought emerge, those that advocate sales-related measures as the main factors and those that advocate communication-related measures as the main orientation'.

There are a number of problems with what Fill describes as the 'sales school', the view that: 'the only meaningful measure of the effectiveness of the promotional spend is in the sales results'. These include:

1 sales result from a variety of influences which can be marketing related or even the wider social, political or technological environment;

2 promotional effort may influence the eventual purchasing decision but this can take some time to become apparent;

3 sales objectives do little to assist in the development of the communications programme, that is, they do not have a formative role.

However, there is an argument that, at least on occasions, sales-oriented objectives are appropriate. This is when direct response is sought from a targeted message through clearly identified channels. Frequently retail organizations operating in mature markets can use sales response to evaluate public relations effort. Such organizations often use loyalty cards and the customer database that they represent can be powerful in trying to model and evaluate customer response to communications efforts.

Sales, of course, are not the only goal and the aim of the communications campaign is to enhance the image or reputation of an organization or product. A number of models have been developed to aid our understanding of the processes involved. The challenge now is to link communications objectives to sales objectives in such a way that they are mutually consistent yet are able to be measured while recognizing that communications by itself frequently only contributes to the sales effect.

Often, the ultimate impact of a communications programme is behavioural, but cognitive effects are sought as part of the process of achieving the organization's ultimate objectives. For instance, UK marketing professor Peter Doyle (2002: 274) argues that public relations can be highly effective and that PR campaigns frequently address changes in awareness and attitudes but 'it is very difficult to disentangle the effects of PR from the variety of other factors affecting business performance'.

For example, adopters on new products are described by Kotler *et al* (2009: 567) as moving through five stages:

1 awareness: the consumer becomes aware of the innovation but lacks information about it;

2 interest: the consumer is stimulated to seek information about the innovation;

3 evaluation: the consumer considers whether to try the innovation;

4 trial: the consumer tries the innovation to improve his or her estimate of its value;

5 adoption: the consumer decides to make full and regular use of the innovation.

Imagine that a distinctive new toothpaste is launched (perhaps it incorporates baking soda to deliver a fresh taste and feel). A consumer is made aware of the innovation through a television advertising campaign, is stimulated to seek more information and does so through editorial coverage in a consumer magazine (achieved as part of the PR effort). Suitably impressed, the consumer makes a regular visit to the local supermarket and notices a sales promotion for the toothpaste (half-price trial offer) which prompts purchase.

The toothpaste would probably not have been purchased if the PR campaign had not got the right coverage in the right media. But sales objectives could not have been set for the PR effort as it was the sales promotion that 'closed the sale' (and the sales promotion agency would quickly claim the credit). So frequently, public relations is essential to the process but not the only factor in achieving the marketing/corporate objective. So objective setting in public relations is frequently problematical, and consequently so is evaluation of public relations activity. At its simplest, evaluation is no more than establishing whether the objectives set have been achieved.

It is tempting to throw up our hands in horror and take the despairing perspective that could be described as the 'curse of public relations': that any objective which is achievable through public relations alone is not worth measuring, and that any objective worth measuring is not achievable through PR (alone). This is, indeed, most applicable when public relations operates in a marketing support role.

The purpose of a marketing communications campaign may be to move a significant number of prospects from one set to the next. However, public relations tends to be effective at the early stages of the process (raising awareness, for example) while other elements of the communications mix will be more effective at the end of the process. Thus, it is the latter that 'close the sale' and maybe receive the plaudits, but all their efforts would have been in vain if the PR campaign hadn't successfully raised awareness of our new product so that it made it on to the shortlist. So, public relations does not work in isolation and its effects tend to be cognitive: towards the beginning of the adoption process rather than behavioural towards the end.

If public relations evaluation is intimately connected with objective setting, then the evaluative process must take into account the varying nature of those objectives. Frequently, those objectives whose achievement is completely within the control of public relations – and therefore relatively simple to evaluate – are at best process objectives only (eg obtaining media coverage).

The contribution of public relations to the attainment of true impact objectives may well be crucial, but nonetheless often partial and early in the process. Frequently, public relations makes the ground more fertile for complementary communications activities. Under these circumstances, disentangling the public relations contribution is complex and a pure 'evaluation by objectives' approach becomes inappropriate.

Process objectives

As well as a more realistic approach to objective setting, there is a useful concept to which we have alluded but not yet explained that can help guide us through the objective-setting maze. This is the concept of process objectives: on the surface an oxymoron, as an objective is an end-point and process revolves around reaching that end-point.

Crable and Vibbert (1986: 391–92) articulate a general theme when listing evaluation by objectives as the last of six evaluation 'standards'; they describe it as a system based on MBO. This links the discussion back to both the pivotal role that objectives play in public relations evaluation, and the concept of MBO.

When public relations is managed by a system of objectives, the measurement of those efforts is incorporated into the system. There are two key aspects to MBO in public relations: objectives are derived mutually, between public relations manager and supervisor; and these objectives set a series of intermediate goals that define what should be done and when. When public relations projects, programmes, or problems are managed 'by objectives', those objectives are the result of consultation between public relations manager and supervisor.

This introduces the concept of process objectives (or targets): a very useful concept for public relations where the process is frequently complex and the ultimate impact is a result of range of influences of which public relations is one, but only one. 'Process objectives' is an oxymoron as an objective is an end-point, not part of the process. However, the closer we are to a point of achievement, the more control we have and the easier it is to monitor and measure. So, it is possible that a combination of broad goals supported by a number of process objectives can approximate to ideal objectives. This is when the complexity of the communications process means that truly SMART public relations objectives cannot be set. Frequently, in public relations, SMART objectives are an ideal to be aimed for rather than anything that can be fully achieved.

However, there is a concomitant danger: too much emphasis on the process can prompt a mindset where communications activity is undertaken for its own sake rather than to achieve identifiable effects. So, process objectives run the risk of the substitution game. But if this risk is appreciated, they can become useful elements (but no more) of the evaluator's toolbox as they relate to milestones in the communication effort (but not the destination), to the reaching of which public relations has made a major contribution, even if other elements of the programme help us continue on to our final destination.

The role of objective setting is put into context with an evaluation questionnaire for a 'sales' seminar/workshop. The objectives associated with the questionnaire (see Table 8.1) are eminently SMART and range from pure process (event administration) through to genuine impact (sales lead generation).

TABLE 8.1   Objectives of XYZ sales seminar

At least 100 attendees, of whom 80 per cent are decision makers/key influencers.
80 per cent of delegates felt their objectives in attending were met.
80 per cent of delegates would attend another XYZ event.
The average overall rating of the event is over 3.5.
The average rating for how well the event is organized is over 3.5.
The average rating for the usefulness of information from interactive voting is over 3.5.
The average rating for speakers will be over 3.5.
80 per cent of delegates who don't already receive them will request Loaded and Currant Bun.
80 per cent of delegates wish to be invited to future XYZ events.
At least five qualified sales meetings arise directly from the event.
80 per cent of journalists who attend use material in some form within six months of the event.

Questions to discuss

- Are SMART objectives an ideal only or are they a practical proposition, at least in some instances?
- Can you derive some examples of process objectives and the broader goals that they might support/lead to?
- If we adopt MBO as a 'philosophy', might this contribute to broader recognition of the contribution of public relations among management?
- Have you come across SMART objectives in other contexts (eg appraisals) and can we learn anything from their use in these other contexts?
- What ideas do you have for disentangling the contribution of public relations to the achievement of communications and corporate goals?

09
Relationship management and crisis communication measurement

Although the term 'public relations' has been in place for many decades and definitions of PR such as 'the management of relationships between an organization and its publics (stakeholders)' have been widely used, it has *only* been in the past 15 years that the theorization of public relations as relationship management has made progress. Coombs and Holladay (2010: 5) say 'modern public relations has attempted to re-energize the term relationship' with emphasis on building better relationships with publics and ways to measure them. This reflects a corporate-centric view as organizations can derive benefits from close relationships with these groups, although it may not be clear that stakeholders (in many forms) share that perspective.

The relationship management paradigm of public relations helps move it out of the media relations and publicity model and shows that:

> public relations is captured as the value of relationship quality between organizations and their publics and the supportive behaviours from stakeholders that are more likely to result when organizations and publics have a positive relationship. (Jo, Hon and Brunner, 2004)

Bruning and Ledingham (1999: 158), who have been proponents of relationship management as the public relations model, also commented that there has been a shift 'away from the manipulation of public opinion and towards a focus on building, nurturing and maintaining organization-public relationships'. This revised conceptualization of public relations has appeal to practitioners and scholars because it changes the purpose of public relations from a persuasional practice to one that creates mutual benefit.

Ledingham (2009: 469) argues that the 'shift in central focus of public relations from a communications-centred function to one in which the management of organization–public relationships is central requires a reconceptualization of public relations theory'. It also gives the public relations industry a new focus, 'which knowing that it deals with wide-ranging objectives and methods has struggled with ways to define itself and its value' (Hibbert and Simmons, 2006: 3). Lindenmann links this emerging consensus with the standard view of PR activities producing outputs, out-takes and outcomes. But he drops out-takes and adds 'measuring the success or failure of long-term relationships' (Lindenmann, in Hon and Grunig, 1999: 5):

> As important as it can be for an organization to measure PR outputs and outcomes, it is even more important for an organization to measure relationships. This is because for most organizations measuring outputs and outcomes can only give information about the effectiveness of a particular or specific PR program or event that has been undertaken. In order to answer the much broader question – 'How can PR practitioners begin to pinpoint and document for senior management the overall value of public relations to the organization as a whole?' – different tools and techniques are required.

Hon and Grunig (1999) reviewed research that shows PR contributes value to an organization when its communications programmes result in quality long-term relationships with strategic publics (stakeholders). They identified two types of relationships, with four characteristics.

The relationships are, first, *exchange*, where one party gives benefit to the other only because the other has provided benefits in the past or is expected to do so in the future. A party that receives benefit incurs an obligation or debt to return the favour. Exchange is the essence of marketing relationships between organizations and customers. But, Hon and Grunig argue, it's not enough for a public, which expects organizations to do things for the community without expecting immediate benefit.

The second type of relationships are *communal*, where parties are willing to provide benefits to the other because they are concerned for the welfare of the other – even when they believe they might not get anything in return. 'The role of public relations is to convince management that it also needs communal relationships with publics such as employees, the community, government, media and stockholders – as well as exchange relationships with customers.' Communal relationships are important if organizations are to be socially responsible and to add value to society as well as client organizations.

The quality of relationships

> Ledingham has proposed relationship management as a general theory of
> public relations (Ledingham, 2003). There are three planks to the theory
> (Bruning, Castle and Schrepfer, 2004: 442–44):
>
> 1 there is a linkage between organizational–public relationships and
>   results such as enhanced satisfaction and improved loyalty;
>
> 2 organizations and publics should set common interests and goals;
>
> 3 public relations practitioners take the lead in preparing strategies and
>   actions that help organizations and publics to 'enhance mutual
>   understanding and benefit'.

The critique of relationship management approaches are that they may not
indicate equal balance of power between the organization and its publics/
stakeholders, the relationship may be based on factors that existed before
dialogue began or may be constructed by factors that are unrelated to the
dialogue. There is also a presumption that the publics are seeking a relationship or are aware of the relationship. For them, it may be passive, inactive
or unrecognized. As Coombs and Holladay (2010) have noted, not all ties
are equally strong: a weak tie may have more benefits than a constructed
strong one. However, as Johnston and Zawawi comment, this approach 'is
useful in helping to create a better picture of what actually goes on in public
relations processes' (2004: 60).

Measuring relationships

Hon and Grunig (1999) also nominate four outcomes that are indicators of
successful interpersonal relationships but can be applied with equal success
to relationships between organizations and their publics. Importance declines
as we go down the list:

1 *Control mutuality*: the degree to which the parties in a relationship
   are satisfied with the amount of control they have over a relationship.
   Some degree of power imbalance is natural, but the most stable,
   positive relationships exist where the parties have some degree of
   control. It doesn't have to be exactly 50:50. The ceding of some
   control is based on trust.

2 *Trust*: the level of confidence that both parties have in each other and their willingness to open themselves to the other party. Three factors are important:
   - integrity: an organization is seen as just and fair;
   - dependability: it will do what it says it will do;
   - competence: it has the ability to do what it says it will do.
3 *Commitment*: the extent to which both parties believe and feel the relationship is worth spending energy to maintain and promote.
4 *Satisfaction*: the extent to which both parties feel favourably about each other because positive expectations about the relationship are reinforced. Each party believes the other is engaged in positive steps to maintain the relationship.

The suggestion is that relationships are evaluated through a questionnaire that asks a series of agree/disagree statements (using a 1–9 scale). A complete list of the relevant statements is given at **www.instituteforpr.org**.

Grunig later wrote a paper on qualitative methods for assessing relationships between organizations and publics (Grunig, 2002) that use non-statistical methods such as interviews and focus groups to evaluate the relationship. It includes a guide to questions about the six dimensions of the relationships and the analysis of the information gathered. At least two published studies have used Hon and Grunig's (1999) or Grunig's (2002) qualitative model.

The first measured the relationship between a university and its students (Jo, Hon and Brunner, 2004: 24). Some 687 students took part in two surveys, which used a seven-point measurement scale to investigate the factors in the relationship. The researchers found that the two groups of students 'perceived the six factor measures as a valid and reliable instrument for measuring their relationship with the university'.

Hibbert and Simmons (2006: 7–8) used Grunig's qualitative approach in a quite different situation to measure the relationship between Australian political and defence media and the public affairs staff from the Australian Defence Force in the context of the 2003 Iraq War. They found it 'provided a useful guide to the research and analysis at the points of planning, exploring, labelling and reporting the relationship' but that there were limits to its facility in reporting the width of relationships because of its bilateral focus on what occurs between an organization and a public, when the real influences on the situation are more complex. They also found that some of the language had to be modified for an Australian situation and that, in its standard form, it is awkward in use.

In conclusion, the measurement of relationships is a relatively new area of public relations evaluation, although it has been widely used in other disciplines, especially psychology and counselling for interpersonal relationships. More papers are coming forwards all the time and should give a wider range of methods and case studies.

Evaluating communication in a crisis

The September 11 attacks on New York and Washington in 2001 brought the effectiveness of crisis communication into sharp focus. Many organizations whose headquarters were obliterated or severely affected by the attacks in lower Manhattan completely lost their ability to communicate externally. They lost key staff, crisis plan files, internet sites and all telecommunication capacity, as well as the buildings from which they operated.

This terrible example of a terrorist attack has had two outcomes. Corporations now organize crisis plans on a dispersed model that is not knocked out by a single act, and they are placing more emphasis on monitoring and measuring their performance in crisis situations.

The likelihood of another September 11 may be considered to be on the outer limits of probability, but there are many other crisis situations that can be considered. First, it is sensible to define a crisis and to consider the range of forms. Kathleen Fearn-Banks comments that the size of the organization is immaterial as it can range from a transnational corporation to a small business or in the case of a celebrity, an individual. She says that a crisis is:

> a major occurrence with a potentially negative outcome affecting the organization, company, or industry as well as its public, products, services, or good name ... (it) interrupts normal business transactions and can sometimes threaten the existence of the organisation ... (and) can be a strike, terrorism, a fire, a boycott, product tampering, product failure, or numerous other events. (Fearn-Banks, 2011: 2)

Essentially, a crisis is more than a problem as it 'interrupts the normal flow of business' (Fearn-Banks, 2011: 2). Another leading crisis management scholar, Otto Lerbinger, says there are eight types of crisis: natural, technological, confrontation, malevolence, skewed management values, deception, management misconduct and the more general business and economic. And crises typically have five stages, according to Fearn-Banks:

1 *Detection*: watching for warning signs; monitoring traditional and online media and feedback from stakeholders.

2 *Prevention/preparation*: monitoring for warning signs, preparing plans proactively to avoid a crisis and reactively for when they come.

3 *Containment*: taking steps to limit the crisis and effects.

4 *Recovery*: getting back to 'normal' or 'surviving' if it is a severe crisis.

5 *Learning*: evaluating what was lost or gained and how the organization performed in a crisis. Reflecting on the handling of the crisis to prevent future crises.

So the public relations practitioner has a very wide range of threats and issues to plan against and to prepare methods of evaluating their effectiveness. Within the five stages of crises, basic methods of monitoring and measuring the issues and communication efficacy can be seen. They include continuous monitoring of the environment surrounding the organization using media coverage, online discussion and feedback from stakeholders. The latter can be gathered formally through surveys, focus groups and media monitoring and informally through contact with regulators, intermediaries, journals and community contacts.

Grunig comments that: 'communication with publics before decisions are made is most effective in resolving issues and crises because it helps managers to make decisions that are less likely to produce consequences that publics make into issues and crises' (Grunig, 2001, cited in Paine, 2002a). This could be described colloquially as planning and consultation help avoid the 'law of unintended consequences'.

Grunig proposes four principles of crisis communication:

1 *The Relationship Principle*: An organization can withstand crises if it has well-established relationships with key stakeholders.

2 *The Accountability Principle*: An organization should accept responsibility for a crisis even if it was not its fault. (For example, recall a product that has been threatened or tainted by an extortionist.)

3 *The Disclosure Principle*: In a crisis, an organization should disclose all it knows about a crisis or problem. If it does not have immediate answers, it must promise full disclosure once it has additional information.

4 *The Symmetrical Communication Principle*: In a crisis, the public interest should be considered as equal in importance to the organization's interest.

To measure its performance in a potential crisis and against these principles, the organization needs to prepare itself by monitoring current issues in the media being discussed by employees, customers and stakeholders. The media scanning should also include internet chat rooms and news rooms as well as conventional print and broadcast media. Using a variation of the Lindenmann's Three-Step Yardstick (see Chapter 5), Paine (2002a) proposes three elements to measuring effectiveness:

1 *Measuring outputs and process effectiveness*: Constant monitoring of media to determine if key messages are being communicated and to whom.

2 *Measuring impact*: Determining if messages are having the desired effect, if they are being believed and whether they are swaying public opinion.

3 *Measuring outcomes*: Has the crisis impacted on reputation, sales, employee turnover, shareholder confidence and other factors?

'Which type of measurement you select should be driven by your internal needs for better decision making tools' is the pragmatic advice given by Paine (2002a: 2). In an analysis of situations that includes organizations such as IBM, Nabisco, HCA Healthcare, Levi Strauss and Kodak, Paine comments that 'a well-managed crisis gets all the bad news over with up front by aggressively dealing with a problem. A poorly handled one can drag on for months'. By 'aggressively dealing', Paine means that the response is prompt, accurate and clearly communicated.

Using case studies cited by Paine, it is possible to apply three of Grunig's four principles of crisis communication with relative ease; see the box below. It is more difficult, and probably inherently impossible, to apply the symmetrical communication principle to a crisis.

---

1 *Relationship* – Levi Strauss, famed for its branded jeans, hit a downturn and chose to close 11 plants and lay off nearly 6,400 workers. Paine says that the jeans-maker took a 'novel approach, simultaneously announcing grants to all the communities affected by the layoffs. As a result, media coverage spiked in the first week and steadily decreased after that'. Putting aside the description of best practice in stakeholder relations – simultaneous communication – as 'a novel approach', Levi Strauss's strategy minimized media comment in less than a month and allowed it to continue its negotiations and repair community relationships with less pressure than if it had taken a 'drip, drip' communication approach.

2 *Accountability* – The Odwalla natural juice organization was found to have sold batches of apple juice that caused illness and, in one tragic outcome, led to the death of a child. Paine argues that by 'owning' the problem and not blaming others, Odwalla was able to contain the crisis to a three-week period and avoid lawsuits. Media analysis showed an early peak in coverage that tapered away to almost nothing over 21 days.

3 *Disclosure* – The reverse case to Levi Strauss came when Kodak was stricken by leaks over future strategy and suffered a prolonged crisis played out in the media, as well as among other stakeholders. Paine (2002a: 5) says Kodak 'suffered a series of leaks about potential layoffs, eventually announced layoffs, and then had to announce even more layoffs because the cuts hadn't been deep enough'. Again, she says, 'the result was many more weeks of bad news. It could be argued that if Kodak had followed Levi Strauss's open and fulsome announcement, it could have built relationships that helped it manage the change'. However, the outcomes of its strategy were tracked by media analysis as three spikes of negative coverage over a three-month period.

4 *Symmetrical Communication* – This is a new usage by Grunig of his most debated descriptor of public relations practice. In essence, it is the sum total of relationships, accountability and disclosure set into a public safety scenario. The most famous of all product recalls, Johnson & Johnson's prompt and complete removal of the Tylenol branded analgesic from sale after an extortioner tainted the product, is the closest example. But this is not the same as Grunig's normal description of symmetrical communication. In the Tylenol case, J&J's action was prompted by an ethical and commercial decision to protect consumers and save the reputation of the company and the product. The fact that Tylenol remains a respected and popular product in North America is a tribute to that decision. It is not, however, an equally balanced, continuous dialogue between an organization and its publics as enunciated by Grunig for two decades or more.

After the crisis is over, evaluation can assist measurement of position and deliver lessons for future strategy and crisis communication. Paine suggests that questions to consider could include: 'Did consumers change their behaviour, did employees leave at a higher than normal rate? Did the stock drop?' To which could be added qualitative and quantitative judgements on the attitudes of regulators, the media, commercial partners, and employees and their families.

For major organizations which are listed on stock exchanges, a frequently used metric is the profile of the organization's share price recovery. Watson (2007) studied this phenomena and found that those companies which regained their share price rapidly were 'recoverers' – they continued operating with the same freedom as before; those which still had a loss of 15 per cent in share value after a year were 'survivors' and 'were vulnerable to take-over and had limited operational scope' (p 380). Those which suffered big share value losses were not likely to continue as a separate entity and could collapse. Share price value is thus an indicator of the ability to recover from a crisis which may then become a cause for further crises, as market confidence erodes.

Crisis communication is a major subject by itself but media analysis and other measurements of attitude and perception play an important role in monitoring the evolution and maturity of a crisis. They advise strategies to manage and respond. However, the principles espoused by Grunig of relationship, accountability and disclosure are the bedrock on which those strategies should be based.

Questions to discuss

- Relationships are more difficult to measure than, say, media outputs. How would you advise your workplace or clients to evaluate them?
- How would you explain 'control mutuality' to others? It's an important factor in relationships.
- Managing recovery from a crisis can be challenging. What information would be needed to monitor the progress of the crisis?
- James Grunig has proposed four principles of crisis communication: Can they co-exist or may some be more important than others?
- Some research says the share price of public companies may indicate their state of recovery from crises. Identify a company which has suffered a major recent crisis and review its share price during and after the crisis. Is this a valid measure of recovery and reputational renewal?

10
Evaluating social media

The first challenge with evaluating online public relations was monitoring: monitoring the online conversation, identifying trends, gathering information on issues and nascent crises, establishing who your promoters or detractors are, and establishing baselines to enable any progress to be measured at a later date. Now attention has moved on to 'real' evaluation in the form of analysing and using the data that this monitoring has unearthed. One immediate characteristic of evaluating social media is that there are many similar principles associated with traditional PR but the terminology is often different; frequently as part of an effort to generate spurious credibility – popularity cloaked as authority, for example.

The Chartered Institute of Public Relations (CIPR) (2011) confirms that social media 'is having a profound impact on PR practice'. There is a challenge for practitioners to monitor and analyse the volume of content available that can impinge on their professional lives. It has become much more than monitoring and tracking, it has become a question of identifying relevant conversations and then deciding if, and how, to intervene on the basis of how these conversations impact – or might – the ability of clients/employers to meet their organizational goals.

The CIPR (2011) suggests that there are tools available to:

- track blogs, forums, comments, tweets, online news, social networks and video for mentions of organizations, clients and competitors;
- analyse and reports on this content in both quantitative (eg Twitter followers) and qualitative (eg sentiment) terms;
- segment this data by geography through media type to keywords;
- present and summarize key data, normally on some form of dashboard.

This compounds the confusion that surrounds the plethora of tools (both free and paid for) that have been launched, with some of them already beginning to fade away. As Smith (2012a: 159) explains: 'The rise in interest in social media monitoring has seen a commensurate rise in technology solutions to meet this demand – solutions ranging from the free to the very costly'. Naslund (2013) makes the same point a little more vividly: 'With so many pieces of information floating around we are more pressed than ever to find something, anything that can help us make sense of the mess. Tools and apps and platforms abound, smashing together with alacrity, and pouring out more data as a response.'

Facebook and Twitter probably led the way in generating data to satisfy the demand for numbers to show that someone was doing something somewhere. Facebook likes and Twitter followers became the metrics of choice to impress managers and clients. But eventually, people began to realize that 'Influence is not reach' Paine (2011: 15). The saving grace of social media is that the traditional media lesson illustrated by the substitution game (placements do not demonstrate outcomes) is being learned relatively quickly – at least by some. There remain plenty who like to dress quantification in qualitative clothes.

Chau *et al* (2012) suggest that we should start at a higher level with the measurement of social media being regarded as a discipline rather than a tool. There is no single metric available to measure performance, impact or value. They also establish some principles of social media measurement that places it in the wider context of communications evaluation.

Social media measurement should adhere to the Barcelona Principles of Measurement. This includes setting objectives at the start, rigour in research, appreciating the hierarchy of outputs, outcomes and business results, and measurement requiring the combination of quantitative and qualitative.

Their view is that there are four key metrics for social media measurement: influence (related to specific demographics and topics); opportunity to reach (consistency and lack of multipliers are important); engagement (at different levels and related to specific goals); and sentiment (human, computer or hybrid approaches).

At its simplest, online PR is about the inevitability of there being an online conversation about the client or organization being represented and therefore a need to monitor and analyse that conversation so a decision can be made about when and how to intervene. There are similarities with the traditional, offline world – as stated above – but a clear point of difference is the loss of control online from the lack of mediation so consumers and the like communicate directly.

Message delivery is one of the prime indicators of much of the process of traditional PR. But online, the one-directional flow from organization to intended audience, mediated and authorized by journalists no longer occurs. Instead, the net's one-to-one communication, compounded by the death of deference ameliorating the authority of conventional media, leads to people turning to their own kind as a source of unbiased, authoritative information. So more pressure is placed on formative, process evaluation to generate feedback to help manage the public relations process.

Formative monitoring of who is saying what and about whom is essential to enable the rapid intervention and rebuttal necessary to influence the online conversation before it is set in stone. The digital environment has a ghostly permanence: entering 'Kryptonite bike lock' into UK Google (at the time of writing) generates a YouTube link *How To Unlock a Kryptonite Lock With a Bic Pen*. So, control online is seriously compromised without rapid and early intervention.

The credibility of offline media is well documented; many would argue that (in its media relations guise) the supposed 'killer benefit' of PR is the credibility afforded by the media's third-party endorsement; online the story, its origins and promoters are much more muddled. As a more recent phenomenon, the credibility of online media is less well established, although common sense indicates that it is likely to be high, as an extension of powerful face-to-face, word-of-mouth communications.

What should we be measuring?

The measurement and evaluation of social media allows, indeed is based on, the concept of a process or funnel that is exemplified by the horizontal axis of the valid matrix framework (see Chapter 11) which in a brand/product marketing context comprises: awareness, knowledge, consideration, preference, action. This bears similarities with long established marketing concepts such as the consumer adoption process: awareness, interest, evaluation, trial and adoption. And to provide a public relations context, PR objective setting (see Chapter 8) discusses the hierarchy of awareness/knowledge, motivation/ predisposition and behaviour.

With social media, the funnel normally has four stages with a variety of terminology that can be summarized as:

- exposure/reach/impressions;
- engagement/sentiment/tone;
- influence/respect/relevance;
- action/impact/value.

FIGURE 10.1   Social media funnel

EXPOSURE	ENGAGEMENT	INFLUENCE	ACTION
To what degree have we created exposure to content and message?	Who is interacting and engaging with our content? How and where?	How we influenced perceptions and attitudes of the target	What actions if any has the target taken?

SOURCE: Bagnall, 2012: 171

As an example, Bagnall (2012: 170–71) cites Bartholomew (2012) adapting the marketing funnel (see Figure 10.1) as exposure, engagement, influence and action. Bartholomew (2012) also accepts the framework approach championed by the International Association for the Measurement and Evaluation of Communication (AMEC) but, on the vertical axis, prefers to replace the three-stage PR process (public relations activity, intermediary effect, and target audiences effect) with what Bagnall (2012: 171) describes as 'each of the [four] integrated types of media' (see Figure 10.2, where the elements of the matrix are also populated), PESO: Paid, Earned, Shared and Owned.

Odden (2013) describes paid media as 'traditional online advertising through display ads, pay per click search ads and sponsorships'. The advantages are summarized as available on demand, offering an element of control, and scalability. Earned media is 'the result of public and media relations efforts to gain coverage in publications – on and offline. This covers content generated by enthusiastic customers themselves'. Odden (2013) describes owned media as 'media, content and assets that the brand controls' so examples would be websites, blogs, newsletters and social media accounts in the brand's name. Finally, shared media is a relatively new category that describes content which results from interaction between brands and consumers online; so it is shared in the sense that the content is created by both parties. A tweet that is retweeted with a comment is an example.

Exposure/reach/impressions

In discussing reach, Chau *et al* (2012) argue that accurate (or at least consistent) metrics for reach are very difficult to source as no two auditing bodies agree on the numbers. Information on readership is not available for some sites and most sites are not able to distinguish genuine unique visitors. The difficulty in establishing absolute numbers is further compounded by the ever-changing readership of social media content; and finally they claim that to prevent the double counting of 'readers' across multiple channels is impossible.

FIGURE 10.2   Integrated measurement – PESO

	EXPOSURE	ENGAGEMENT	INFLUENCE	ACTION
Paid	• OTS • Click-throughs • Cost per thousand	• Duration • Branded search • Cost per click	• Purchase consideration • Change in opinion or attitude	• Visit website • Attend event • Download coupon
Earned	• Message inclusion • Impressions • Net positive impressions	• Readership • Awareness • URL visits	• Purchase consideration • Change in opinion or attitude	• Visit the store • Vote for/against • Make a donation
Shared	• OTS • Comment sentiment • No of followers	• Number of links • Number of retweets • Subscribers	• Tell a friend • Ratings • Reviews	• Redeem coupon • Buy the product • Visit the website
Owned	• Unique visitors • Page views • Search rank	• Return visits • Durations • Subscriptions	• Tell a friend • Change in opinion or attitude	• Download white paper • Request more info

SOURCE: Bagnall, 2012: 171

This viewpoint is supported by Marklein and Paine (2012) who add that confusion about the definition of metrics adds to the problems, as does the use of multipliers – even suggesting that dividers are more appropriate (without explicitly recommending them). This is because not all followers read all tweets, with similar considerations for other social media.

There is plenty of confusion around basic concepts such as impressions, Opportunities to See (OTS), reach and frequency. Impressions and OTS are synonymous with the former prevalent in North America; some authorities have a preference for OTS as a more accurate description of the concept. OTS is the total number of times, potentially, that a public could be exposed to a message, usually the circulation of a publication or audience reach of a broadcaster. Confusingly, with print, OTS is sometimes calculated using readership rather than circulation; the former is usually a multiple of circulation. Readership is arguably more accurate as all readers have an opportunity see any content, but it compounds one of the drawbacks of OTS. That is, when multiple media are aggregated, numbers become so high as to threaten credibility. This brings in the concepts of reach and frequency. The reason why the Canadian case in Chapter 6 has a number of impressions (OTS) in excess of the population of Canada is because of frequency. OTS is calculated by multiplying reach (the number of people who have the opportunity to see) by frequency (the number of times they have had the opportunity to see).

Engagement/sentiment/tone

Marklein and Paine (2012) state that engagement is 'an action that happens after reach, beyond consumption' and add that it can be an outcome but is not necessarily so. They agree with Chau *et al* (2012) when the latter suggest that the way engagement manifests itself varies across different channels, and that this is normally classified as low, medium and high. This classification is 'based on the effort required, how much it reflects the user's Point of View, and how it is shared with others'.

So examples of low level engagement include Facebook likes, Twitter followers, and clicks on 'read more' links. Equivalent medium-level engagement examples are Facebook comments, Twitter retweets, and time spent viewing content. Finally, high level engagement is exemplified by Facebook shares (including e-mail), Twitter @mentions or #hashtags, and downloads.

Paine (2011: 80) expands this tripartite classification into five levels: lurking, casual, active, committed and loyalist. Lurking is exemplified by a Facebook like and indicates some sort of relationship has been formed but no more. So, at this stage the metrics to be used are click-throughs, unique visitors and likes. The casual phase is characterized by some sort of desire for further contact such as following someone on Twitter or subscribing to a blog; most relationships 'stagnate' at this point. Now, repeat visitors, Twitter followers, and comments are the orders of the day.

The minority that go further become active: characterized, for example, by retweeting and distributing links to YouTube videos. The relationship has become a communal one (rather than a simple exchange relationship) meaning that a party to that relationship will do a service for the other party even if they get nothing back in return. The key now is to try and establish an increase in engagement over time; so the metrics remain similar (eg comments, retweets and repeat visitors) but trends become important.

The committed demonstrate trust to the organization by registering or signing up or membership. So these actions need to be tracked and again it's the comparative that is important – changes over time rather than absolute numbers. The loyalist begins to contribute more actively and recruit others. Now, we have moved well away from monitoring metrics to direct measurement in the form of traditional primary research (probably some sort of tracking survey) to establish how loyalists feel about the organization. Paine (2011) suggests something along the lines of the work undertaken by Hon and Grunig (1999) on measuring relationships (see Chapter 9).

Paine (2011: 79) says that engagement covers a multitude of sins: 'engagement now means everything from the number of times that a visitor returns to a site, to the number of comments on a corporate blog, to the number of retweets of a Twitter stream'.

Paine continues by arguing that engagement is critical for three reasons:

1 *Engagement is the first step in building a relationship between your customers and your brand.* The relationships an organization has differentiate it from the rest and demonstrate it is having a true dialogue.

2 *Customer engagement helps promote and protect your brand.* Engagement prompts brand advocates or ambassadors to both promote and defend your brand.

3 *Customer engagement can make your products better.* Engagement can generate an ad hoc customer panel.

Sentiment and engagement are two of the most commonly discussed concepts in social measurement in general, and the measurement of social media in particular. But the confusion around social media is confirmed by Bagnall (2012: 169) when he mentions both of these terms when discussing where further clarity is required, saying of the latter: 'What constitutes engagement? Just because someone has clicked on a Facebook "Like" button, does this mean that they engaged with your organization or brand?'

Smith (2012a: 159) defines sentiment analysis as: 'the attempt to deduce how somebody feels about a particular person, topic, issue, or organization based on what they say'. Similarly, Sheldrake (2011: 38) suggests that sentiment analysis: 'aims to determine the author's emotional regard for, or attitude towards, something from the text alone'.

The confusion rife in social media's insistence on using new words for old concepts is exemplified here. Tone is an important, well established and well understood concept in traditional media evaluation defined by Paine (2011: 51) in these words: 'The tone of an article or mention is the attitude or opinion it expresses toward something or someone'. It's a struggle to separate the concepts of sentiment and tone based on these definitions (indeed, Paine 2011: 93 regards the terms as interchangeable) yet traditional media frequently uses the latter and rarely the former, while the situation is reversed for new media.

So it seems to parallel good, old-fashioned content analysis that is the acceptable face of media evaluation. While traditional print media is at least constrained by the number of trees left on the planet, one distinguishing feature of social media is the pure volume of words it has spawned. So technology has ridden to the rescue, in the area of sentiment analysis at least, with efforts to automate it.

Bagnall (2012) says of sentiment analysis that its most important characteristic is indeed whether it has been undertaken by man or machine. Chau *et al* (2012) support the need for clarity on how sentiment has been assessed (as well as introducing a third option): 'Was it undertaken by a machine, by crowd sourced labour, or by trained analysts?'

Similarly, Smith (2012a: 159) confirms that automated sentiment analysis is indeed 'perhaps the most interesting area' when discussing the use of technology in social media monitoring. He moves on to outline two broad approaches: the first uses lists of positive and negative words. If there are more negative than positive words in an item, it is classified as negative on the topic. Alternatively, more sophisticated systems are based on computer algorithms and semantic analysis. The former approach is low cost, but also low accuracy. Smith (2012a: 160) characterizes the more sophisticated approaches as providing: 'far more accurate analysis of far higher volumes of content as well as being able to isolate sentiment from different viewpoints'. Unsurprisingly, the downside is relatively high cost.

Sheldrake (2011: 38) confirms none of the approaches to sentiment analysis are perfect and that their capabilities vary. Humans can take into account the context in which words appear, 'infer meaning', and both appreciate and account for sarcasm and irony. However, he suggests that human intervention cannot cope with an organization generating more than a few hundred mentions a month. He also suggests that automated systems struggle to achieve more than 65 per cent accuracy.

Paine (2011) agrees that the involvement of human coders is required to get accurate results, if only because with automated systems, it is difficult to prevent irony and sarcasm being misinterpreted. She also adds a welcome reality check when she states: 'no amount of automated sentiment analysis can tell you what people are actually thinking. To know this you need to ask them' (Paine, 2011: 28).

In spite of, or maybe because of, the extensive discussion about sentiment in the context of social media, Marklein and Paine (2012) state that 'Sentiment is over-rated and over-used', which is a fairly direct comment. They argue that it is not an all-encompassing qualitative measure and there are other factors to consider. They are also concerned that the measurement of sentiment varies according to vendor and approach so that it lacks transparency. They suggest that there are other qualitative measures that are more useful and 'increasingly measurable'. Before confirming the importance of coding, consistency, and transparency, they list their preferred qualitative measures as:

- opinions ('it's a good product');
- recommendations ('try it' or 'avoid it');

- feeling/emotions ('That product makes me feel happy');
- intended action ('I'm going to buy that product tomorrow').

Influence/respect/relevance

Savell and Iannelli (2012) suggest that to stop being overwhelmed by the challenge of measuring social media, a solution is to 'measure the social influencers'. Defining influencers as 'influential people with a relevant footprint, who talk about what matters to your brand', they argue that measuring social influencers has the following benefits:

- reduces the volume of social media conversations to measure;
- reduces the time needed to measure social media conversations;
- reduces the cost to measure social media conversations;
- eliminates the complexity of measuring the 'universe' of social media;
- separates the signal from the noise;
- increases the relevance of social media conversations to measure.

Sheldrake (2011: 25) looks at influence from the perspective of those being influenced: '... you have been influenced when you think in a way you wouldn't otherwise have thought, or do something you wouldn't otherwise have done'. He stresses that influence is not popularity, nor a score, nor is it something that only exists online. Chau *et al* (2012) add that influence is domain and subject specific as well as being directly related to relevance. Influence is not a generic trait, but influencers are influential on particular topics and for particular demographic groups – this has to be established through research. Consequently, when using an influence metric, it is important to both indicate how that matrix has been calculated, and to specify how influence has been defined.

To put the discussion of influence into context, Sheldrake (2011: 18–19) maps six influence flows (see Chapter 11) as:

1 our organization's influence with stakeholders;
2 our stakeholders' influence with each other with respect to us;
3 our stakeholders' influence with our organization;
4 our competitors' influence with stakeholders;
5 stakeholders' influence with each other with respect to our competitors;
6 stakeholders' influence with our competitors.

Sheldrake (2011) argues that the first and third flows are well established in 'traditional' PR, even if the third flow rarely achieves the balance that would result from true symmetry. He then goes on to assert that in 'new PR', these two flows become subservient to the second flow – interpreted as the conversation on social media that we need to monitor and consider intervening in. And, indeed, organizations could benefit from keeping an eye on all six influence flows as they might learn something, identify risk, or leverage positive comment.

Action/impact/value

Bartholomew (2012) argues that social media impact and value follow engagement. He defines impact metrics as outcomes that result from engagement with social media content and message. Value is the next, and final, stage: value metrics show the financial implications to the business resulting from the impact created. He explains that impact is process-oriented, while value is transactional. Impact has both tangible and intangible components, while value is financial. According to Bartholomew (2012), the majority of social media programs are not designed to generate value/Return on Investment (ROI) (in the short term).

Marklein and Paine (2012) state:

- impact and value will always be dependent on client objectives;
- need to define outcomes in advance – will likely span multiple business goals, especially for social (crosses disciplines);
- 'ROI' should be strictly limited to measurable financial impact; 'total value' can be used for financial and non-financial impact combination;
- value can be calculated in positive returns (sales, reputation, etc.) or avoided negative returns (risk mitigated, costs avoided);
- key performance indicators (KPIs) and balanced scorecards are helpful to connect social media impact to business results/language.

Social media planning

This book is predicated on measurement and evaluation being an integral part of the public relations planning process, indeed threaded through the whole process. For social media, Jeffrey (2013: 4) has developed an eight-step social media measurement process that – appropriately – mirrors many a public relations planning model; demonstrating that many of the principles remain constant but the context and language evolves. Importantly, Jeffrey links the process back to the AMEC valid metrics framework – bringing social media measurement firmly into the best practice fold.

This process comprises:

1 define organizational goals;

2 research stakeholders and prioritize;

3 set specific objectives for each prioritized stakeholder group;

4 set social media KPIs against each stakeholder objective;

5 choose tools and benchmark (using the AMEC matrix);

6 public relations activity;

7 intermediary effects;

8 target audience effects;

9 analyse the results and compare to costs;

10 present to management;

11 measure continuously and improve performance.

This bears similarities to Paine's (2011: 33–44) 'Seven Steps to the Perfect Measurement Program':

1 define your goals and objectives;
2 define your environment, your audiences, and your role in influencing them;
3 define your investment;
4 determine your benchmarks;
5 define your KPIs;
6 select the right measurement tool and vendors and collect data;
7 turn data into action.

Unlike much of the discussion surrounding the Barcelona Principles, Jeffrey (2013) distinguishes between goals and objectives with the former as a broad indication of what the organization is trying to achieve, and the latter much more specific. She argues that social media goals should be kept simple, and it is important to recognize that there will be multiple channels employed to achieve them. Next is the need to prioritize stakeholders, and this is based on internal and external research: 'At the end of Step Two, one should have a good sense of the most important stakeholders, where they are active in social media, what they think of the organization/department and their competitors, and how they can be helped' (Jeffrey, 2013: 7).

She moves on to setting specific objectives for each stakeholder: 'Remember that an objective must include **an action statement, a timeline** and **a measurement outcome** (usually expressed as a per cent increase)'. Then, Jeffrey (2013) moves on to developing the communications programme in general, and the tactics in particular – appreciating that social media specifically is likely to play only part of the role.

KPI/metrics

There is a vast array of tools available to provide output and outcome measurements for social media tactics and campaigns. Texts from Katie Paine (2011) and Jim Sterne (2010) will tell you more than you are ever likely to want to know on the topic. The latter reports blogger David Berkowitz's '100 Ways to Measure Social Media' (cited in Sterne, 2010: xx–xxv) for those who want a long list to choose from.

Here we have selected eight tools to look at. We have not selected them because they are particularly good (or bad) nor are they recommended in any sense. And also, a tool that might be effective in one context might be totally unsuitable in another context. The only criteria we have used are these: two at each level of the social media process and – at each level – one free and one paid for.

There does seem to be some consensus that in the measurement of social media you do get what you pay for – to an extent, at least. Most of the paid-for tools will provide a limited (usually time limited) opportunity to trial the service, while many of the 'free' tools will invite you to upgrade to a premium (ie paid for) offering. Some of the tools are channel specific (eg Tweetreach) while others are cross-channel (eg Social Mention). There is no guarantee that the tools listed below will continue to be available in perpetuity.

One way in which the suite of social media tools also vary from traditional tools is that they 'equip you not just to listen but also participate' (Sanders, 2012: 18). So, for example, Hootsuite is an example of a free tool that enables you both to monitor and post your own content.

So, for measuring exposure/reach/impressions, we look at Google Alerts and Tweetreach.

Google Alerts (**www.google.com/alerts**) is a simple, free tool that is simply a search tool (covering web pages, press articles and blogs, for example) with some bells and whistles – its typical use is to provide e-mail alerts of defined keywords. So you can monitor, for example, what is being said about your company, or mention products mentions following a launch. You can manage your alerts by specifying frequency of delivery and categories of sources used.

Tweetreach (**www.tweetreach.com**) allows you to search for a keyword, username, phrase or URL. It claims to measure reach (what is the size of the potential audience), engagement (how are people talking about the campaign), content (what are people talking about), and contributors (who is talking about the campaign).

For measuring engagement/sentiment/tone, we look at Social Mention and uberVU.

SocialMention (**www.socialmention.com**) is a search and analysis tool that aggregates user generated content across most social media. It claims to 'to easily track and measure what people are saying about you, your company, a new product, or any topic across the web's social media landscape in real-time'. It reports on sentiment, reach, passion, and strength. The rigour and usefulness of these measure varies. Sentiment is a ratio of mentions that are generally positive to those that are generally negative. This seems to have some value (particularly as a comparative) although as a free tool, the analysis is likely to be automated. In contrast, the reach metric is more difficult to appreciate. Social Mention defines its reach metric as 'a measure of the range of influence' and calculated as 'the number of unique authors referencing your brand divided by the total number of mentions'. This seems to be more a measure of frequency than reach.

uberVU (**www.ubervu.com**) claims to identify the content that engages target audiences and who influences them. It identifies influencer mentions as well as spikes in sentiment, location and demographics.

These two tools illustrate the previously reported debate on human versus automated analysis of sentiment. Smith (2012a: 160) says:

> there is no question that free tools such as Social Mention allow any
> organisation to at least test the concept of sentiment analysis in the context of
> social media for no monetary outlay ... Low-cost tools such as UberVu will also
> give the end use the ability to easily amend the sentiment rating if inaccurate
> assessments are spotted.

For measuring respect/influence, we look at Klout and Peerindex.

Klout (**www.klout.com**) is much discussed in social media measurement circles although not always positively. There is a view that the methodology that lies behind a Klout score could be more transparent, and that influence is too complex a concept to be usefully distilled down to a number. It generates an influence score which is calculated using a proprietary algorithm although the broad concepts on which it is based are declared. A Klout score is in the range 1–100 and is normally applied to individuals (although organizations can, and do, have Klout scores). This is claimed by Klout to be a measure of how much influence (defined by Klout as 'the ability to drive actions') the individual has – the higher the better. It is calculated by looking at the interactions people have on eight different social media, including Twitter and Facebook. So for example, on Facebook, likes, comments and friends are important; on Twitter, followers and retweets matter.

PeerIndex (**www.peerindex.com**) is also based on a proprietary algorithm so suffers from the assumption that online equals transparent. Smith (2012a: 161) explains that tools such as PeerIndex offer the promise of identifying those people who are more important than others – or should be responded to more urgently. So for example, he states: 'PeerIndex ... will attempt to analyse an individual's online influence and then provide an overall score relative to a particular subject or topic' [emphasis added].

And, measuring response/action, we feature Twitter Favourites (free) and Google Analytics/Social (also free, but formerly the paid for PageRank).

Twitter Favourites (**http://support.twitter.com/articles/20169874-favoriting-a-tweet**) is a tool that is an oasis of simplicity in a sea of obfuscation, although the concept is not going to solve all of your problems overnight. It enables Twitter users to 'favourite' a tweet, normally as a means of bookmarking indicating your approval to the poster of the tweet. The poster can see which of their tweets have been favourited and is also able to identify other tweets that their endorser has also favourited. It's a pretty basic tool (so free and easy to use) but it does identify people who have acted in response to your content, and gives you information on what else prompts them to respond.

Google Analytics/Social (**www.google.com/analytics/index.html**) provides a range of free reports that comprise web analytics to enable tracking of traffic to your website. It claims to enable users to 'see which social networks and sites refer the highest quality traffic so you can refine social campaigns'.

Bhurji (2012: 183) describes Google Analytics as being 'intuitive enough for the ordinary user, has given brands and their agencies easy access to a wider range of insights on online consumer behaviour'.

Smith (2012b: 26–28) outlines the following 'quick wins for PRs' using Google Analytics data:

- bounce rate – there are issues with websites that have bounce rates of 75 per cent or more;
- segmenting website visitors – where they come from and why they are visiting;
- setting very specific goals – concrete actions by visitors;
- indications of activities that contribute both directly and indirectly to the final result – multi-channel analysis as opposed to 'last click attribution'.

Westminster Council (2011: 25) lists the advantages of Google Analytics:

- it is free;
- the user friendly dashboard makes understanding data easy;

- you can quickly see key metrics, including which are the most viewed pages on your site, where people enter and leave to site, how long people spend on your site, and how many pages they view on average;

- you can see how your site is being used by mobile devices, and what for;

- you can see what search terms people use in Google to find your site;

- you can set goals you want the site to achieve, for example to monitor how many customers complete a specific transaction or download a document from your site.

However, Westminster (2011) also outlines some concerns. For example, there is plenty of information on numbers of visitors but little on the profile and interests of those visitors (note that another free resource, **www.alexa.com**, claims to provide demographic data on website visitors). There are concerns about the sheer volume of data produced, and users are encouraged to look at trends over time and to collect historical data for future comparison.

Jeffrey (2013: 9–10) relates her discussion of the measurement of social media to the AMEC valid metrics framework. She argues that the measurement programme can be coordinated by populating the elements of the appropriate framework.

To make the Matrices easy to use, the practice of public relations has been broken down into three phases:

- the message or story is created and told;
- the story is disseminated via a third party/intermediary (such as a journalist, influencer or blogger);
- the story is consumed by the target audience, which (hopefully) leads to changes in behaviour and business results.

These three phases are thus reflected in the *Vertical Axis* of each matrix as follows:

- *Public Relations Activity* – metrics reflecting efforts in producing and disseminating messages;
- *Intermediary Effect* – metrics reflecting third-party dissemination of messages to target audiences;
- *Target Audience Effect* – metrics showing the target audience has received the messages and any resulting action-driven outcomes.

Social media examples provided by Jeffrey (2013) include:

- social media engagement (numbers of blog posts, blogger events, blogger briefings, Twitter posts, community site posts and events) as an example of PR activity;

- share of conversation, key message alignment, accuracy of facts, expressed opinions, endorsements by journalists or influencers, rankings on industry lists as examples of intermediary effect;
- surveys, statistics (eg market mix modelling) and web analytics to provide evidence of a target audience effect.

The move towards standards

Marklein and Paine (2012) outline the need for standards in social media measurement in these, perhaps a little optimistic, terms:

- social media has moved well beyond experimentation phase, moving towards justifying investment rather than chasing numbers;
- marketplace is demanding standards, in terms of terminology and common metrics across communications disciplines;
- accelerate shift from low-level counting to higher-level value, enabling comparisons, reliability, and true insight.

They add that media content analysis (media evaluation) should be buttressed by a range of complementary research ranging from web analytics to survey data. The focus in social media needs to be on conversations and communities, not just rest on a coverage culture. Finally, they assert that reliability is unreliable so experimentation and testing are the required – at least for the present.

To summarize, here are ten media measurement tips (Paine, 2013):

1 Take time to *define your social media success*. Get your managers and coworkers to agree on audiences, goals, and measures of success.

2 Develop specific *measurable goals* and objectives. Remember: SMART objectives are specific, measurable, attainable, realistic, and timely.

3 Measure *engagement* (for instance, comments, shares, or any measure related to your organization's goals) rather than old-school media metrics, like eyeballs and advertising value equivalence.

4 If you are just starting to measure your social media, then *start small*, with an easy-to-handle project.

5 Learn to *measure results*, rather than activity.

6 Learn to *measure influence*, rather than popularity.

7 Use measurement to connect your social media program with your *organizational goals*.

8 If you can't use the term ROI in a strictly financial sense, then don't use it at all. Instead, express your results in terms of your organization's goals.

9 Use your metrics to *learn and improve*. Don't just wave them around to show you've been busy, use them to develop a plan to get better results.

10 Use your measurement to *save you time*; learn how to not to waste it on efforts that don't get results.

Questions to discuss

- What are your views on the challenges for evaluation that social media pose?
- How do we handle the sheer volume of content and the plethora of tools (free and paid for) available to monitor and analyse it?
- What opportunities does the online world open up for public relations evaluation?
- What are the pros and cons of automated and human sentiment analysis?
- Are there any particular challenges associated with the planning and evaluation of integrated campaigns – using both social and traditional media?
- What lessons have we learned from the evaluation of traditional media that are applicable to the online environment?

11
Linking PR activity to business

The issue of accurately quantifying public relations and corporate communication activity in relation to business objectives and outcomes has long been a top practice issue. In times of tighter economic pressure, there is increasing need to demonstrate value. Although for some decades the use of advertising value equivalence (AVE) to show value by reference to equivalent advertising space was used, managements are now shrewder and want real results, not false ones. In this chapter the notion of Return on Investment (ROI) is critiqued, two metrics are proposed as being both more accurate and relevant than ROI and a total approach to the creation of value through communication – communication controlling – is outlined in detail.

Return on Investment

'ROI' is frequently defined in management and marketing literature as a measure of financial effectiveness concerned with returns on capital employed in (profit-making) business activities (Best, 2009; Drury, 2007; Moutinho and Southern, 2010). It is expressed as a ratio of income or earnings divided by the costs that had been applied to generate the income or earnings. In formal public relations nomenclature, the *Dictionary of Public Relations Measurement and Research* defines ROI as 'an outcome variable that equates profit from investment' but does not attempt to classify a 'public relations ROI', other than as a 'dependent variable' (Stacks, 2006: 24). In public relations practitioner language, ROI is applied in a much looser form to indicate the results of activity.

The term has been in public relations discourse for more than 40 years. The British public relations writer and educator Sam Black commented that it was 'fashionable to measure ROI in business, 'but in the field of public relations it has little significance' (1971: 100). Merims (1972), a practitioner with Motorola, proposed an ROI model in the *Harvard Business Review* that gave the concept a fillip in North America. There has been regular interest in the concept over the years by many practitioners (for example: Marken, 1988; Williams, 1992; Lee, 2002; Sierra, 2003; Sinickas, 2003; Wood, 2004). The concept of ROI has also been given expression as market mix modelling, a financial indicator promoted by some consultancies in the past decade (Likely, Rockland and Weiner, 2006).

In 2004, a report by the (then) Institute of Public Relations (IPR) in the United Kingdom defined ROI as 'a ratio of how much profit or cost saving is realized from an activity, as against its actual cost, which is often expressed as a percentage' (IPR & Communication Directors Forum (CDF), 2004: 15). The report, however, added that 'in reality few PR programmes can be measured in such a way because of the problems involved in putting a realistic and credible financial value to the results achieved. As a result, the term PR ROI is often used very loosely'.

Watson's (2005) study of more than 200 articles on measurement and evaluation found that the term was not widely used or recognized in academic literature. Gaunt and Wright (2004), however, found that 88 per cent of a sample of international public relations practitioners was interested in an ROI tool and 65 per cent considered that ROI could be applied to judgements on public relations effectiveness. Gregory and Watson (2008) also noted that use of the term ROI was widely used in practice and called for greater academic engagement with practice issues such as the use of business language, including ROI, and communication scorecards.

In the Asia-Pacific region, Macnamara (1999) advocated the use of the language of accountability embodied in concepts such as management by objectives, total quality management and quality assurance to position public relations as a contributor to strategic decision-making. Macnamara later identified that 'public relations and corporate communication practitioners are under pressure to evaluate their work, particularly in terms of outcomes and Return on Investment' (2007: 1), which indicated the increasing application of business nomenclature, as he had earlier forecast.

Professional literature and discussions and presentations at the European Summits on Measurement and the IPR Measurement Summits in the United States, however, clearly show that ROI is a term widely used, if not tightly defined. The 2004 study by the IPR in the United Kingdom found that 34 per cent of respondents considered public relations budgets in term of ROI and 60 per cent used a notion of ROI to measure public relations activity in some way. It summarized the responses as, 'some inclination towards seeking a form of ROI that could be applied universally' (IPR/CDF 2004: 6).

Recently, Watson and Zerfass (2011) researched understanding of ROI in both the United Kingdom (Watson, 2011; a pilot study) and across Europe in the annual European Communication Monitor survey (Zerfass *et al*, 2011).

The headline results for the usage of the term 'ROI' or 'Return on Investment' when planning and evaluating communication activities was a 1.1 per cent separation between those who responded Yes (47.6 per cent) and No (46.5 per cent) with 5.9 per cent giving a 'Don't know the term' response. ROI usage analysed by workplace found those in consultancies and agencies were most supportive (59.3 per cent) and practitioners in governmental organizations least supportive (28.2 per cent) and only marginally less than non-profit organizations (32.5 per cent). As regards hierarchy, Chief Communication Officers (or equivalent title) and agency CEOs showed 53.7 per cent support for usage whereas middle and junior-level staff (team members) were more reluctant at 34.5 per cent.

The second question explored practitioner perceptions of ROI, especially the linkage between the profit to costs ratio, which is expressed in business literature, and communication outcomes or the achievement of communication objectives. Seven propositions were presented and distributed. There was a continued expression by this large group of communicators that ROI and communication could be linked, but in two separated styles.

The most positive response was that 'ROI can be expressed in achievement of communication objectives' (83.1 per cent), followed by the financially-linked indicator, 'ROI requires financial assessments of the resources needed for communication' (72.5 per cent) and then 'ROI can demonstrate the non-financial value of communication' (70.5 per cent). The next three propositions dealt with communication's contribution to organizational strategy, a standardized financial valuation of communications results, and the ratio of financial profit arising from communication set against its costs. They all gained more than 50 per cent support from this large, multinational sample of communicators. Only one, 'ROI has to be defined in monetary terms' gained less than 50 per cent support.

The propositions can thus be placed into two separate and apparently conflicting categories – the financial and non-financial. The 'financial' category proposes that ROI is shaped by financial assessment of resources and a standardized financial evaluation of results which results in a ratio of profit and costs arising from communication activity. Added together, these have a mean of 61.1 per cent. The 'non-financial' are composed of ROI as an expression of achievement of objectives, the creation of non-financial value and contribution to formation of organizational strategy. These average 72.1 per cent.

Overall, responses to the transnational survey indicated that European public relations practitioners conceive ROI in a more non-financial frame, thus opposing the established understanding of the concept in business administration and management science. Watson and Zerfass (2011) considered that a 'quasi-ROI', focused on non-financial objectives and outcomes, appears to be well-supported already by European practitioners and can be fostered by methods that help practitioners to manage and advance future activities such as models of communication management, including communication scorecards and value link models. These integrate public relations and corporate communications within the whole business planning and monitoring process (the German 'communication controlling' model which is discussed later in this chapter) rather than being treated as a promotional add-on or a functional activity. However, the complexity of communication processes and their role in business interactions means it is not possible to calculate ROI in financial terms. Consequently, they concluded that public relations practitioners should refrain from using the term in order to keep their vocabulary compatible with the overall management world.

James Grunig on ROI

Following publication of Watson and Zerfass's ROI research, they engaged in an e-mail dialogue with James Grunig that was published online by the Institute for Public Relations (IPR Research Conversations, October 2011). The main elements were:

James E Grunig: I'm very interested in looking at the value of public relations in terms of nonfinancial indicators or as intangible assets. Essentially, I argue that the value of public relations can be found in the relationships it cultivates with publics/stakeholders. Relationships are intangible assets, but they can be measured. In addition, it is possible to conceptualize the financial returns to relationships; they reduce costs, reduce risk, and increase revenue. However, it is difficult, if not impossible, to measure, or attribute these financial costs to specific relationships. They are long-term, lumpy, and often keep things from happening. Thus, we should measure relationships but explain their value conceptually to understand (but not measure) the ROI of public relations.

Tom Watson and Ansgar Zerfass: We agree with all of your statement, with one exception. We are rigorous about the problems of applying ROI out of its business context, as PR's use (or abuse) of ROI does it no good with decision-making managers who have an accounting or financial management background. Research has found these views in central Europe amongst business managers in charge of 'controlling' (similar to audit) and it is beginning to be identified in the UK. These high-level managers simply don't recognize ROI in the form that it is presented to them by PR staff or consultants with 'PR metrics' or in the concept of ROI outside strictly financial parameters. Hence, we are encouraging PR folks to find their own language which is more accurate such a value creation or value links, etc. The 'Outflow' concept which came from Sweden in 1996 is more pertinent than ROI.

James E Grunig: No disagreement here. I talk more about the value of public relations than about ROI. As I said, you can explain the value of relationships; but you really can't measure a financial return to compare with the money invested in it. I tend to use the term ROI because PR people want to hear it used. I will now cease and desist from using it.

Tom Watson and Ansgar Zerfass: Glad to hear we are on the same track ... this is really a big discussion over here and we feel that a sound position will be supported by those communication officers (often with a managerial background) who are now in charge, while some suppliers still have to do their homework. Understanding that cultivating relationships, listening and issues management is more important than talking and image building is of course difficult and it will take continuous efforts to explain, (IPR, October 2011)

The importance of this particular debate is that it: a) offers a clear rejection of the ROI terminology by James Grunig – 'I will now cease and desist from using it'; b) brings the 'communication controlling' model from central Europe into the international arena; and c) is counter to the prevailing industry desire to repurpose ROI in a public relations context.

Practitioner interest in financial metrics

In 2010, the Barcelona Declaration of Measurement Principles (International Association for the Measurement and Evaluation of Communication (AMEC), 2010), discussed earlier, included a 'principle' – the effect on business results can and should be measured where possible – which was aligned to many practitioners' desire to express financial outcomes of their activity. The Barcelona Principles had barred further use of AVE which had long been the preferred method to express this form of value. The 'Barcelona Principles' were quickly adopted by public relations professionals and industry bodies in the United Kingdom, North America and globally, and have led to a revival of industry attempts to define a public relations ROI (PR ROI). At AMEC's 2011 Summit in Lisbon, over 80 per cent of delegates identified the need to define PR ROI as the main industry research need. This led to the formation of a task force in North America, led by the Council for Public Relations Firms, and involving members of AMEC and the Public Relations Society of America. However, despite a draft report being produced, no further progress has been made.

It is notable that more caution has been applied in recent industry publications to the use of 'ROI' and 'PR ROI'. Measurement firm CEO Giselle

Bodie commented in the *PR Professional's Definitive Guide to Measurement* (AMEC/Public Relations Consultants Association/International Communications Consultancy Organization 2013):

> 'Return on Investment' is a very ill understood term, and some claim that it cannot be accurately calculated for non-financial programs. However, cost-efficiency metrics such as 'cost-per-targeted impression,' 'cost-per-lead' or 'cost-per-unique visitor' can be useful. If you DO want to calculate ROI, you should use a true financial formula expressed as a percentage or ratio.

Fraser Likely – let's take the CEO's perspective

In all my years of assessing communication functions – and in the course of that work interviewing CEOs – seldom has a CEO said that he/she values the media analysis results or the town hall results or the reach of Facebook or Twitter or the communication results of a particular marketing comms campaign in determining how well the function is performing.

Yet, these are the results that the CCO wants to present – or more specifically the results that PR agencies and research firms want the CCO to present.

So, I believe it's time to look at value from the CEO perspective.

New financial metrics – BCR and CEA

In 2012, Canadian consultant Fraser Likely, whose practice specializes in improving the management, organization and performance of the PR/Communication department, suggested a set of principles for their, as well as that of ROI, appropriate and accurate application (Likely, 2012: 2). Organizations have three drivers for financial performance: increased revenue, decreased costs or expenditure, and cost avoidance through reduced operational and regulatory risks. Likely acknowledged that public relations practitioners 'have long sought to demonstrate how [their] work contributes to these three drivers'.

He said that if public relations practitioners were to employ the ROI financial indicator, they should do so in the same way that financial managers and accountants do. They should not try to redefine the term or to use it other than how it was intended. ROI is a financial metric that includes net returns and gross investments applied at the level, and only at the level, of the organization itself. Thus, the term ROI can't be used as a financial measure for a communication channel (eg Twitter or YouTube), a communication campaign (eg marketing communication or employee engagement) or a communication function (eg investor relations or public relations department).

Likely (2012: 2) has identified two other financial metrics that may be more appropriate: benefit–cost ratio (BCR) and cost-effectiveness analysis (CEA). He argues that BCR and CEA are 'more applicable and perhaps more useful than the utilization of a ROI measure'. The BCR metric and the ROI metric are similar in methodology, but the former is used to *predict* benefits or returns while the latter applies actual benefits or returns. BCR is best used to assess a proposal or to choose between several alternative ones, ie to build a business case (Schmidt, 2009).

Though it was not labelled as BCR, the most extensive discussion of the use of BCR in PR/communication has been by William Ehling (in J Grunig, 1992). The term he used was *compensating variation*, the same term employed throughout the Excellence Study. Compensating variation is a form of BCR, not ROI. Since then, both academics and practitioners have employed modifications of compensating variation and thus BCR (Shaffer, 2004; Sinickas, 2003, 2004, 2009; Smith, 2008; Weiner *et al*, 2010).

The CEA metric is different from the ROI metric (Levin and McEwan, 2001). CEA compares the relative costs and the outcomes (effects) of two or more courses of action or activities, but it does not assign a monetary value (financial return) to the measure of effect. Like the ROI metric and unlike the BCR metric, CEA applies actual, realized investments or costs. Unlike the ROI metric but like the BCR metric, it applies intangible benefits as effectiveness measures.

In public relations, effectiveness may be measures such as channel reach, accuracy of media reporting, length of time on a site, or number of retweets (Paine, 2011). Likely states that in a public relations department, BCR and CEA financial metrics have the possibility of greater utility in providing valuable financial measures for the many categories of investments – than does the utilization of a ROI measure. These two are underused currently (Likely, 2012: 19). He also argued that most of what public relations consultants and practitioners now call ROI measurement, including that of marketing mix modelling or similar approaches using multivariable statistical methods, are not true ROI metrics since they do not include time-delayed net returns as well as all-in gross investments – at the level of the organization (Likely, 2012: 14).

Valid metrics framework

The Barcelona Principles (AMEC, 2010) are clear in their rejection of AVEs and serious reservations about them are widely rehearsed elsewhere. For example, prefacing seven reasons why this approach is inappropriate, Broom and Sha (2013: 347) state: 'There is no theoretical or empirical basis for making the leap from editorial to paid advertising. In fact, the calculation of alleged advertising equivalents is seriously flawed and misleading on several grounds.'

To their credit, AMEC backed up the rejection of AVEs in the Barcelona Principles with an initiative to provide a replacement in the form of a 'valid metrics framework' (AMEC, 2011). The framework is actually much more than a replacement for AVEs; it integrates measurement and evaluation into a planning framework as well as focusing on the contribution of communications to the achievement of business/organizational results. Along the way, the framework recognizes that public relations frequently employ intermediaries as well as moving target audiences/publics through a communications funnel (see Figure 11.1).

The vertical axis of the matrix outlines a simplified three-phase public relations process (AMEC, 2011):

- PR activity: the message or story is created or told, measured by metrics reflecting production or dissemination of messages;
- intermediary effect: the story is disseminated via a third party, measured by metrics reflecting dissemination to the target audience;
- target audience effect: the story is consumed and a change in behaviour results; measured by action-driven outcomes.

The grid's horizontal axis is based on a communications/marketing funnel: awareness, understanding, interest/consideration, support/preference and action. Appropriate metrics are grouped under each stage of the funnel.

Much of this discussion has a marketing feel to it, and Figure 11.2 gives the example of a brand/product marketing grid with appropriate elements of the grid populated with generic metrics. However, a series of grids have been devised for different public relations functions. In addition to brand and product marketing, they are: reputation building, issues advocacy and support, employee engagement, investor relations, crisis and issues management, public education/not-for-profit and social/community engagement. This does not prevent adapting an existing grid or developing one's own customized grid. There are plenty of examples and further guidance available at: **http://amecorg.com**.

Communication controlling

Management and evaluation in the corporate environment are key challenges for the communication sector. There has been an international discussion about value-oriented business communication for years, driven by professional associations and academic researchers.

FIGURE 11.1 Valid metrics framework template

COMMUNICATIONS/MARKETING STAGES					
Key Area of Communication *(Brand/Product Marketing, Reputation Building, Issues Advocacy/Support, Employee Engagement, Investor Relations, Crisis/Issues Management, Not-for-Profit, Social/ Community Engagement)*	Awareness	Knowledge/ Understanding	Interest/ Consideration	Support/ Preference	Action
Public Relations Activity					
Intermediary Effect					
Target Audience Effect					ORGANIZATION/ BUSINESS RESULTS

COMMUNICATIONS PHASES

FIGURE 11.2 Completed brand/product marketing framework

Brand/ Product Marketing	Awareness	Knowledge	Consideration	Preference	Action
Public Relations Activity	• Content creation • Traditional media engagement • Social media engagement • Influencer engagement • Stakeholder engagement • Events/speeches				
Intermediary Effect	• Audience reach [traditional and social media] • Impressions/Target audience impressions • Number of articles • Video views • Frequency • Prominence • Share of voice	• Key message alignment • Accuracy of facts	• Key message alignment • Frequency of (positive) mentions • Expressed opinions of consideration • Social network Followers • Retweets/Shares/Linkbacks	• Endorsement by journalists or influencers • Rankings on industry lists • Expressed opinions of preference • Social network fans • Likes	
Target Audience Effect	• Unaided awareness • Aided awareness	• Knowledge of company/ product attributes and features • Brand association and differentiation	• Relevance of brand (to consumer/ customer) • Visitors to website • Click-through to site • Time spent on site • Downloads from site • Calls • Event/meeting attendance	• Attitude uplift • Stated intention to buy • Brand preference/ Loyalty/Trust • Endorsement • Requests for quote • Links to site • Trial	• Sales • Market share • Cost savings • Leads generated • Customer loyalty

Their approaches focused on the evaluation of PR impact but were insufficient for strategically managing the performance of corporate communication, as they did not fully comprehend the complex process of value creation through communications. Therefore, the discussion has increasingly shifted to service provision processes and intangible assets; ie success factors which can be significantly influenced by communications.

Common guidelines have become apparent only recently. In summer 2010, the Barcelona Principles were agreed; the first time joint international standards had been drawn up for PR measurement. Since then AMEC presented its valid metrics model (see above) which highlights the communication value proposition and shows performance indicators at different impact levels. These initiatives were all introduced by service providers and agencies within the communications sector.

In order to implement approved standards, however, it was considered necessary to involve the corporate practitioners in charge of communication, who develop strategies, agree on objectives, establish processes and measure performance indicators. The focus on corporate practice and cooperation between communication managers and management accountants has characterized development of the new discipline of communication controlling or communication performance management in German-speaking countries (Deutsche Public Relations Gesellschaft (DPRG), 2011). It has been introduced in varying forms by major German corporations such as Commerzbank, Deutsche Telekom, Henkel and Siemens. It is notable that communication controlling has been developed by a partnership of the German public relations association, DPRG, and the international management accountancy and performance management body, Internationaler Controller Verein (ICV).

Top managers of companies and organizations are increasingly recognizing communication as a key factor in the creation of corporate value. New requirements in the corporate world are the main reason for this shift. Since a company's success is now so dependent on intangibles, the role of corporate communication has become more important.

Factors such as reputation and trust are key differentiators potentially providing companies with significant competitive advantage. Effective corporate communication is the main driver of these factors, once they are included in the strategic management process. In addition, many typical development, process and market objectives can only be achieved if the relevant stakeholders support these goals through their opinions and behaviour.

With the rise of social media, enterprises are facing further communication challenges: if communication with stakeholders was often limited to one-way information transfers in the past, stakeholders can now make use of a multitude of interactive media to take an active part in the communication process and network with each another. This development has also contributed to the growing expectation of senior management that corporate communication executives should make their contribution to achieving the corporate goals more transparent and manage it in a more persistent way.

Communication controlling helps corporate communications departments to deal with these new requirements: it enhances the integration of corporate communication in organizational processes and provides instruments for planning communications activities, tracking their impact and evaluating the resulting contribution to achieving corporate goals. This way, it helps to increase the effectiveness, the efficiency and the transparency of corporate communication.

An essential prerequisite for communication controlling is to establish a link between communication and corporate strategy. The European Communication Monitor 2011 confirmed that this is of central importance for PR executives. More than 2,200 communication managers from 43 countries took part in the study. Nearly half said that integrating communications into the corporate strategy would be one of their most pressing tasks over the next three years (Zerfass *et al*, 2011). There are personal benefits for practitioners using this approach, which validates the work of Broom and Dozier over more than two decades on managers using research and taking a strategic approach prosper in their careers.

In practice, communication controlling is often mistakenly equated with 'monitoring' or 'evaluation'. But this is only one part of the functional tasks it needs to fulfil. From a management accountancy perspective, the term 'controlling' stands for the full management cycle comprising the planning, implementation, monitoring and evaluation of an organization's communication activities. It makes transparent how decisions are taken, how results relate to expenditure, whether resources are used efficiently and which results are achieved. As a support function, communication controlling provides methods and instruments for planning, steering and controlling corporate communication.

The purpose of enhancing and demonstrating what communication contributes to corporate value creation makes the alignment of communication activities with the corporate strategy a key deliverable. Accordingly, there is no 'one best way' for communication controlling. To be successful, it needs to take the specific conditions within a company into account and to develop a framework for steering and evaluation that matches them.

Corporate communication is responsible for supporting the goals of a company through the strategic management of stakeholder relationships. The value proposition consists of the steering of communication processes that influence the knowledge, attitudes, and ultimately the behaviour of stakeholder groups in line with corporate objectives. Then outcomes sought from communication depend on the company's goals and the actions of stakeholder groups to make this happen. Accordingly, to gain stakeholder support, corporate communicators must understand their expectations of the organization. In this way value can be created. The stakeholder model that follows illustrates the concept of corporate strategy-aligned communication.

The model shows the four classic stakeholder markets of corporate communication, which can be assigned to different communication functions. The resource market is addressed through internal communication.

FIGURE 11.3 Stakeholder model based on Rolke (2011)

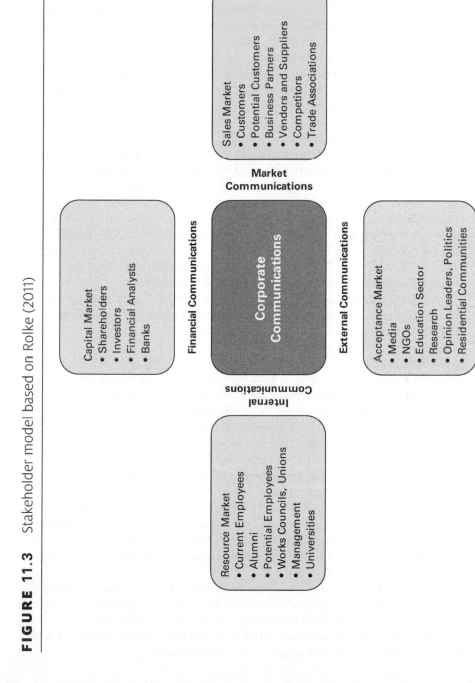

Financial Communications

Market Communications

External Communications

Internal Communications

Capital Market
- Shareholders
- Investors
- Financial Analysts
- Banks

Sales Market
- Customers
- Potential Customers
- Business Partners
- Vendors and Suppliers
- Competitors
- Trade Associations

Corporate Communications

Acceptance Market
- Media
- NGOs
- Education Sector
- Research
- Opinion Leaders, Politics
- Residential Communities

Resource Market
- Current Employees
- Alumni
- Potential Employees
- Works Councils, Unions
- Management
- Universities

It manages the relationships with former, current and potential employees, employee representatives and managers. Financial communication focuses on the dialogue with the target groups representing the capital market, such as shareholders, investors, analysts, banks and the financial media. External communication takes care of the acceptance market. It manages the relationship with and the reputation among politicians, non-governmental organizations (NGOs), residents, opinion leaders, representatives from the education sector and the media in order to legitimize the social license to operate and to secure the organizational leeway. Market communication primarily supports the sale and purchase of products and resources by building and sustaining the relationship with customers, prospective customers, business partners, suppliers, competitors, associations, trade and consumer media. They aim at creating a corporate image that supports the company's sales and procurement activities.

The model is a guide for identifying the key stakeholder groups of a company, highlighting their demands. A strategic approach to stakeholder management requires precise definitions of objectives and performance targets. Therefore, implementing such an approach paves the way towards professional communication controlling. As corporate goals can only be achieved in cooperation with other corporate functions, corporate communication should take the opportunity to become the driver of cross-functional collaboration. With this in mind, stakeholder management and communication controlling would be well-advised to follow an integrated approach.

By strategically influencing stakeholder relationships, corporate communication contributes to business success in a variety of ways. Four dimensions of communicative added value can be identified.

First, a distinction is to be made between economic and socio-political perspectives. In both areas, communication can contribute to value creation either by building intangible capital or by supporting service provision processes.

As an enabling function, corporate communication supports operational management in the ongoing creation of goods and services (products and/or services) by contributing to economic success (economic dimension) and implementing socio-political activities (socio-political dimension). Outcomes of this kind of activities are the strategic alignment of employees, the creation of room for manoeuvre and the influence of market preferences.

At a strategic management level, corporate communication influences the development of intangible assets such as reputation, corporate brand or a culture that fosters innovation. As a means of investment, it helps to build potential for future success of the company, either in terms of business (economic dimension) or regarding the license to operate (socio-political dimension).

Communication managers are asked to assess the relevance each dimension has for their company and to determine communicative goals accordingly. In this way, communication executives are able to translate the corporate strategy into communication activities with targets that are important and meaningful for the senior management of the company.

FIGURE 11.4 Value-based management in the force field of economics and legitimacy, strategic and operational management (Zerfass 2007:26; Zerfass 2008:68)

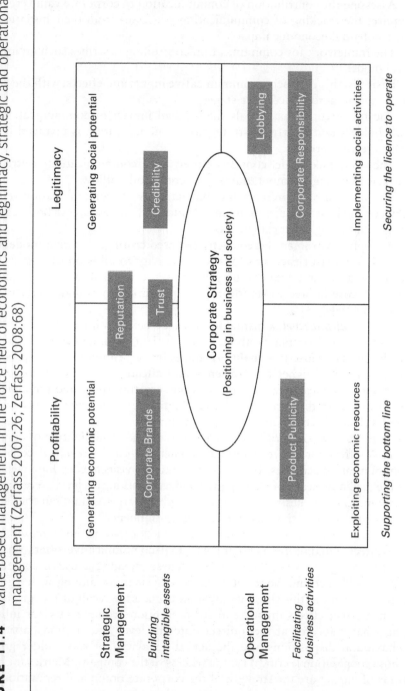

Assessing the contribution of communication to corporate value creation requires the tracking of communication processes from their initiation to their potential economic impact.

The framework for communication controlling describes such an impact level model.

Basically, this represents communicative inputs and effects, with the latter being spread across successive stages.

The framework thus reveals the gradual impact of communication on stakeholders and clearly illustrates how communication is involved in the value creation process.

The value link model connects closely with communication controlling and has four stages – input, output, outcome and outflow.

The *input level* represents the expenditures on communication-related services, such as the use of financial and human resources. Both can be measured through cost categories.

A helpful instrument here is activity based costing, a costing model that assigns the cost of each organizational activity to all products or services according to their actual consumption of resources. This allows the assignment of more indirect costs (overhead) into direct costs than conventional costing models.

On the *output level*, a distinction is made between internal and external output. Internal output is about how efficient communicative offers are produced and about the quality of the delivered communication products or services. The higher the efficiency and effectiveness of communication processes, the greater the impact on value creation (provided the activities are in tune with the corporate strategy). Suitable monitoring instruments at this level are process, concept or content analysis.

At the *external output level*, the focus is on the dissemination of communicative offers for the relevant stakeholders, ie on the reach of corporate communication activities. Typical metrics include visits to corporate websites, or the media presence of a company. Achievements at this level do not necessarily indicate the desired influence on a given target group, but they mark an essential step on the way to exerting this influence.

The actual impact on the stakeholders is located at the *outcome level*. The direct outcome refers to the effect of communicative offers on how stakeholders perceive an organization. These include the use of content by a target audience and the resulting knowledge increase among such a group. Typical metrics at this stage are awareness, message recall or recognition.

Such direct effects on stakeholder perception are necessary for influencing what is located at the indirect outcome level: the opinions, attitudes, behavioural dispositions and the actual behaviour of stakeholder groups whose cooperation is critical for the success of the company. Metrics for these kinds of impact are the strength of the corporate brand and reputation, the strategic awareness of employees and employer attractiveness among needed talent groups.

FIGURE 11.5 Levels of impact and evaluation of communications (DPRG/ICV 2009)

Levels of Impact	Input	Output		Outcome		Outflow
		Internal Output	External Output	Direct Outcome	Indirect Outcome	Value Creation
Measurement Range	Resources Employee Assignment Financial Expenses	Process Efficiency Quality of Works Product	Media Coverage Content	Perception Utilization Knowledge	Opinion Attitudes Emotion Disposition Behaviour	Impact on Strategic and/or Financial Targets (Value Chain) Impact on Tangible and/or Intangible Assets (Capital Accumulation)
Indicators (eg)	*Personnel Costs Outsourcing Costs ...*	*Budget Compliance Throughput Times No. of Shortcomings Readability/ Fogg-Index Satisfaction of Internal Clients ...*	*Clippings Visits Downloads Impact Ratio Share of Voice ...*	*Awareness Unique Visitors Session Length Reader per Issue Recall Recognition ...*	*Reputation Index Brand Image Strategic Awareness of Employees Purchase Intention Leads Innovative Ideas Project Participation ...*	*Sales No. of Project Agreements Cost Reduction Reputation Capital Brand Value Employee Performance ...*
MEASURED OBJECT	ORGANIZATION	ORGANIZATION	MEDIA/CHANNELS	STAKEHOLDERS		ORGANIZATION

Initiation of Communication Processes → | Communication Processes | → Results of Communication Processes

Low Impact on Value Creation
Strong Influence of Communications Management

High Impact on Value Creation
Weak Influence of Communications Management

The economic impact that results from the influence on stakeholder relationships exerted through corporate communication is assigned to the *outflow* level. At this stage it becomes visible what communication has actually contributed to achieving the financial and strategic goals of the organization. As described earlier, corporate communication can add value either by supporting service provision processes of other corporate functions or by creating intangible assets. As both kinds of contributions depend on the specific goals and strategy of the company, performance indicators at the outflow level are subject to a target dialogue and agreement with senior management. The range of indicators includes business-related metrics such as sales, innovations, productivity etc, or intangible capital such as monetary brand value.

The framework lays the structural foundation for communication controlling. It enables the systematic development of value chains running from corporate strategy to communication measures and their impacts onwards to corporate goal achievement. In this way, the entire process of value creation through monitoring progress, reporting results and adapting plans to changing imperatives is demonstrated.

So, communication controlling needs to provide tools for linking communications with the corporate strategy and identifying its contribution to value creation.

Operational communication controlling aims to optimize the potential for success of strategic projects. At this level, the focus is on the efficiency of corporate communication ('Are we doing things right?'). Firstly, operational communication controlling is about steering, monitoring and analysing communication activities. This comprises the evaluation of the operational quality in terms of both the production process and the availability of communicative offers (*output*). It furthermore evaluates the impact resulting from these measures (*outcome*) using empirical research methods. Success of the measures is looked at, along with their (expected) effects upon the corresponding stakeholder groups.

Secondly, operational communication controlling deals with the quality of management of communication measures, programmes and campaigns (eg cogency, resource allocation, proximity to target). Communication is made transparent. Programmes are broken down to subsequent communication objectives at each impact level, supplemented with appropriate metrics and targets. The resulting value links establish a path of plausible cause–effect relations across all levels of communicative impact.

The development and implementation of a communication controlling system follows a process flow consisting of four phases: analysis, conception, operationalization and steering/reporting.

The analysis phase comprises the collection, systematization and evaluation of survey methods, studies and data sources. To avoid redundancies, it is helpful to start with an audit of the existing monitoring, evaluation and steering instruments. Most companies already measure a variety of communication impacts. To find these data, evaluate the applied methods and

FIGURE 11.6 Implementation steps of communication controlling

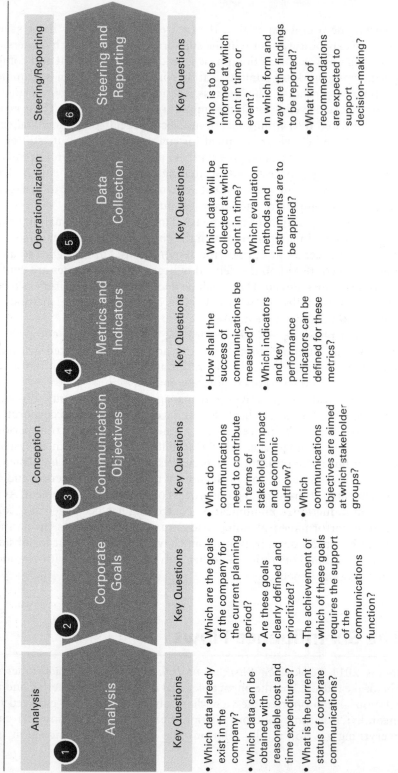

Analysis	Corporate Goals	Conception	Operationalization	Steering/Reporting

Analysis (1)

Key Questions

- Which data already exist in the company?
- Which data can be obtained with reasonable cost and time expenditures?
- What is the current status of corporate communications?

Corporate Goals (2)

Key Questions

- Which are the goals of the company for the current planning period?
- Are these goals clearly defined and prioritized?
- The achievement of which of these goals requires the support of the communications function?

Communication Objectives (3)

Key Questions

- What do communications need to contribute in terms of stakeholcer impact and economic outflow?
- Which communications objectives are aimed at which stakeholder groups?

Metrics and Indicators (4)

Key Questions

- How shall the success of communications be measured?
- Which indicators and key performance indicators can be defined for these metrics?

Data Collection (5)

Key Questions

- Which data will be collected at which point in time?
- Which evaluation methods and instruments are to be applied?

Steering and Reporting (6)

Key Questions

- Who is to be informed at which point in time or event?
- In which form and way are the findings to be reported?
- What kind of recommendations are expected to support decision-making?

integrate the useful material in the future system not only helps save cost and time expenditures but win the support from the research owners.

The aim of the conception phase is to develop a practical and company-specific framework for communication controlling. This can be summed up in a three-step process. The first task is to identify those corporate goals that can only be achieved through the support of communication. These goals are then translated into communication objectives related to those stakeholder groups whose behaviour is critical for enabling the corporate strategy. The last step is to develop and agree on (key) performance and result indicators for monitoring progress and evaluating target achievement. A detailed documentation of the management system helps communication executives to handle its complexity and adapt it to future challenges.

During the operationalization phase, data collection and analysis processes are established. In cooperation with the communication managers who will later be held accountable, roles and responsibilities are assigned to all functions involved. Based on the defined indicators, actual values are confirmed and target values agreed. These include documented clarification as to which data are to be collected, who will be in charge, timescale, methods to be applied, and the instruments used.

The last phase deals with the steering and reporting of corporate communication. Communication scorecards are a tried-and-tested steering tool, best suited for integrating the key result and performance indicators of the various areas and levels of corporate communication.

Communication executives and management accountants also need to agree how the relevant indicators and developments within corporate communication are to be processed and regularly reported. A trial period will provide first learnings regarding the usability of the management system and ideas for further optimization. Experiences made during the implementation will enable communication professionals to adapt their steering and evaluation methods, thus initiating the process of ongoing improvement. As noted in the introduction, communication controlling has been used as a communication performance planning and measurement process in many large central European organizations. Some have been applying it to subsidiaries and transnational operations in other European countries with considerable organizational benefit.

The Six Influence Flows

In his 2011 book, *The Business of Influence*, British practitioner Philip Sheldrake reflected on the impact of social media upon marketing and public relations. He supported the view that public relations had changed fundamentally: 'it is hard to avoid making the claim that "the internet changes everything" ... for public relations the unavoidable conclusion is that nothing will ever be the same again' (Phillips and Young, 2009: 3). He has separately proposed a new definition of public relations which was counter to the long-standing management of communications model: 'the planned and sustained effort to influence opinion and behavior, and to be influenced similarly, in order to build mutual understanding and goodwill' (Sheldrake in, Waddington, 2011: 235).

His emphasis, as can be seen, is upon the creation of influence and understanding its unavoidable multi-directional effects. From this, Sheldrake has proposed a model called the Six Influence Flows (Sheldrake, 2011: 19). At one end of the model is the organization and at the other is the competition. Between them are stakeholders who are communicated with and who themselves communicate with each other and with the organization and its competition. This is a pot-pourri of influences and is 'unprecedented emergent behaviour' which cannot be linked to a specific stakeholder relationship. 'It is the combination of the whole that itself exerts influence' (Sheldrake, 2011: 22).

FIGURE 11.7   Six Influence Flows (Sheldrake)

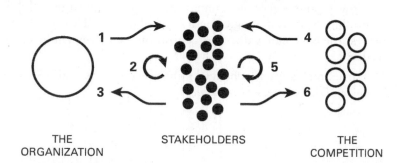

THE
ORGANIZATION   STAKEHOLDERS   THE
                                                        COMPETITION

The measurement of influence and influence flows is undertaken using a scorecard approach, similar to that proposed by Kaplan and Norton. His Influence Scorecard has measures, targets and reports in a digestible form: 'The Influence Scorecard underlines the importance of identifying measurement criteria and tracing influence, and the actual ongoing acts of measurement and single- and double-loop [iterative] learning' (Sheldrake, 2011: 98).

As the Six Influences model has been recently proposed, there are no case studies about its application. However, it is illustrative of how PR may be reconceived over time and of the increasing use of scorecard and dashboard models, which have been mentioned earlier.

Questions to discuss

- Return on Investment (ROI) is a specific financial term: is it appropriate for public relations? Or should there be a PR ROI? If so, would financially driven managements understand it?

- James Grunig says he will 'cease and desist' using ROI in a public relations context? Do you agree with him?

- One commentator says PR measurement and evaluation should 'look at value from the CEO's perspective'. How would that be expressed in your workplace or by clients?

- Fraser Likely proposes the use of benefit–cost ratio (BCR) to predict the benefits and returns from PR and communication activity. Would this be a valuable planning tool and would it be welcomed by senior management?

- Communication controlling is a holistic process that links PR strategies to organizational objectives and evaluates results (outputs, outcomes and outflows) in a range of measures. How it could be applied in your workplace or by clients.

- Outflow expresses economic impact in the communication controlling process in tangible and intangible ways. How could it express the economic value of organizational involvement in social media?

- Has social media utterly changed public relations, as Philip Sheldrake claims in *The Business of Influence*?

REFERENCES

Association for the Measurement and Evaluation of Communication (AMEC) (2010) *Barcelona Declaration of Measurement Principles*, AMEC, London, available at: http://amecorg.com/2012/06/barcelona-declaration-of-measurement-principles/

AMEC (2011) *Valid Metrics*. Available at: http://amecorg.com/important-stuff/ (accessed 30 July 2013)

AMEC (2013) *PR Professional's Definitive Guide to Measurement*, AMEC (and partners), London. Available at: http://prguidetomeasurement.org/

American Management Association (AMA) (1968) Measuring and Evaluating Public Relations Activities, *Management Bulletin No 110*, AMA, New York

Austin, E and Pinkleton, B (2001) *Strategic Public Relations Management*, Lawrence Erlbaum Associates, Mahwah, NJ

Bagnall, R (2012) Measuring social media, in *Share This: The social media handbook for PR professionals*, ed S Waddington, pp 163–74, Wiley, Chichester

Bartholomew, D (2012) Social Media Impact and Business Value, 4th European Summit on Measurement, 13–15 June 2012, Dublin. Available from: http://amecorg.com/downloads/dublin2012/Social-Media-Impact-and-Business-Value-Don-Bartholomew.pdf accessed 01/05/2013

Batchelor, B (1938) *Profitable Public Relations*, Harper and Brothers, New York

Bernays, E L (1955) *The Engineering of Consent*, University of Oklahoma Press, Norman, OK, pp 3–4

Best, R J (2009) *Market-based Management: Strategies for growing customer value and profitability*, 5th edn, Pearson Prentice Hall, Upper Saddle River, NJ

Bhurji, D (2012) Skilling up for the future, in *Share This: The social media handbook for PR professionals*, ed S Waddington, pp 177–92, Wiley, Chichester

Black, S (1971) *The Role of Public Relations in Management*, Pitman, London

Blaxter, L, Hughes, C and Tight, M (2010) *How to Research*, 4th edn, Open University Press, Buckingham

Blissland, J in Wilcox, D *et al* (2000) *Public Relations Strategies and Tactics*, 6th edn, Longman, Harlow

Botan, C and Hazleton, V (1989) *Public Relations Theory*, Lawrence Erlbaum Associates, Hillside, NJ

Broom, G M and Dozier, D M (1990) *Using Research in Public Relations*, Prentice Hall, Englewood Cliff, NJ

Broom, G M and Sha, B (2013) *Cutlip and Center's Effective Public Relations*, 11th edn, Prentice Hall, Englewood Cliff, NJ, p 6

Bruning, S D, Castle, J D and Schrepfer, E (2004) Building relationships between organizations and publics: Examining the linkage between organization-public relations, evaluations of satisfaction, and behavioral intent, *Communication Studies*, 55 (3), pp 435–46

Bruning, S D and Ledingham, J A (1999) Relationships between organizations and publics: Development of a multi-dimensional organization-public relationship scale, *Public Relations Review*, 25 (2), pp 157–70

Chartered Institute of Public Relations (CIPR) (2010) *CIPR CEO commits to leading PR measurement best practice*, Chartered Institute of Public Relations, London. Available at: www.cipr.co.uk/content/news-opinion/press-releases/6390/cipr-ceo-commits-to-leading-pr-measurement-best-practice

CIPR (2011) toolkit. Available at www.cipr.co.uk/sites/default/files/Measurement%20March%202011.pdf (accessed 29 July 2013)

CIPR (2011) Social Media Measurement Guidance. Available at: www.cipr.co.uk/content/policy-resources/for-practitioners/research-planning-and-measurement/toolkit/social-media-measurement (accessed 29 July 2013)

CIPR (2013) *About PR*. Available at: www.cipr.co.uk/content/about-us/about-pr

Chau, E, Daniels, M and Lau, E (2012) Defining Global Social Media Measurement Standards, 1st Asia Pacific PR Summit on Measurement, 29 February–1 March 2012, Hong Kong

Coombs, W and Holladay, S (2006) *It's not just PR: Public relations in society*, Wiley Blackwell, Oxford

Coombs, W and Holladay, S (2010) *PR Strategy and Application: Managing influence*, Wiley-Blackwell, Chichester

Crable, R and Vibbert, S (1986) *Public Relations as Communication Management*, Bellwether Press, Edina MN

Cutlip, S M (1965) *A Public Relations Bibliography*, 2nd edn, University of Wisconsin Press, Madison & Milwaukee

Cutlip, S M (1994) *The Unseen Power: Public relations, a history*, Erlbaum Associates, Hillsdale, NJ

Daniels, M and Jeffrey, A (2012) *International Media Analysis Made Simple*. Institute for Public Relations. Available from: www.instituteforpr.org/topics/international-media-analysis-made-simple/

Daymon, C and Holloway, I (2011) *Qualitative Research Methods in Public Relations and Marketing Communications*, 2nd edn, Routledge, Abingdon

Denscombe, M (2010) *The Good Research Guide*, 4th edn, Open University Press, Maidenhead

Deutsche Public Relations Gesellschaft (DPRG) (2011) *Position Paper – Communication Controlling: How to maximize and demonstrate the value creation through communication*, DPRG, Berlin

Doyle, P (2002) *Marketing Management and Strategy*, 3rd edn, Financial Times/Prentice Hall, Harlow Essex

Dozier, D (1984) The evolution of evaluation methods among public relations practitioners, Paper presented to the Educators Academy, International Association of Business Communicators, Montreal

Dozier, D (1985) Planning and evaluation in public relations practice, *Public Relations Review*, **11**, Summer

Dozier, D and Ehling, W (1992) Evaluation of public relations programs: What the literature tells us about their effects, in *Excellence in Public Relations and Communication Management*, ed J E Grunig, Lawrence Erlbaum Associates, NJ

Dozier, D and Repper, F (1992) Research firms and public relations practices, in *Excellence in Public Relations and Communication Management*, ed JE Grunig, Lawrence Erlbaum Associates, NJ

Drury, C (2007) *Management and Cost Accounting*, 7th edn, Cengage, London

Eden-Green, A (1963) Foreword, in *The Handbook of Public Relations*, ed N Ellis and P Bowman, p 5, George Harrap & Co, London

Fairchild, M (2002) Evaluation: An opportunity to raise the standing of PR, *Journal of Communication Management*, **6** (4)

Fearn-Banks, K (2011) *Crisis Communications: A case book approach*, 4th edn, Routledge, New York

Festinger, L (1957) *A Theory of Cognitive Dissonance*, Stanford University Press, Stanford CA

Fill, C (2009) *Marketing Communications: Contexts, strategies and applications*, 5th edn, Pearson Education, Harlow

FitzGibbon, C T and Morris, L L (1978) *How to Design a Programme Evaluation*, Sage Publications, Beverley Hills, CA

Fleisher, C S and Mahaffy, D (1997) A balanced scorecard approach to public relations management assessment, *Public Relations Review*, 23 (2), pp 117–42

Gaunt, R and Wright, D K (2004) *Examining international differences in communications measurement: Benchpoint global measurement study 2004*. Paper presented at the PR Measurement Summit, 21–24 September 2004, Durham, NJ

Global Alliance for Public Relations and Communication Management (2011) *Global measurement standard drafted*, Global Alliance for Public Relations and Communication Management, Lugarno, Switzerland. Available at: www.globalalliancepr.org/website/news/global-measurement-standard-drafted.

Gregory, A and Watson, T (2008) Defining the gap between research and practice in public relations programme evaluation – towards a new research agenda, *Journal of Marketing Communications*, 14 (5), pp 337–50

Griese, N L (2001) *Arthur W Page: Publisher, public relations pioneer, patriot*, Anvil Publishers, Atlanta

Grunig, J E (1983) Basic research provides knowledge that makes evaluation possible, *Public Relations Quarterly*, 28 (4), pp 28–32

Grunig, J E (ed) (1992) *Excellence in Public Relations and Communication Management*, Lawrence Erlbaum Associates, Hillsdale, NJ

Grunig, J E (1994) A situational theory of publics: Conceptual history, recent challenges and new research, *Paper presented to the International Public Relations Research Symposium*, Bled, Slovenia, July 1994

Grunig, J E (2002) Qualitative methods for assessing relationships between organizations and publics, available at www.instituteforpr.org

Grunig, J E and Hunt, T (1984) *Managing Public Relations*, Holt, Rinehart & Winston, New York

Grupp, R W (2010) *Research Conversations: The Barcelona Declaration of Research Principles*, Institute for Public Relations, Gainesville, FL. Available at: www.instituteforpr.org/2010/06/the-barcelona-declaration-of-research-principles/

Harlow, R (1976) Building a public relations definition, *Public Relations Review*, 2 (4), pp 34–42

Heath, R L and Coombs, W T (2006) *Today's Public Relations: An introduction*, Sage, Thousand Oaks, CA

Hering, R, Schuppener, B and Sommerhalder, M (2004) *Die communication scorecard: Eine neue methode des Kommunikations managements*, Hering Schuppener, Stuttgart

Hibbert, Z and Simmons, P (2006) War reporting and Australian defence public relations, an exchange, *PRism online public relations journal*, available at praxis.massey.ac.nz/evaluation.html

Holmes, P (2012) Why I hate the PRSA's new definition of public relations, Holmes Report, 6 March 2012. Available at: http://blog.holmesreport.com/index.php/pr/why-i-hate-the-prsas-new-definition-of-public-relations/

Hon, L C and Grunig, J E (1999) Guidelines for measuring relationships in Public Relations, available at www.instituteforpr.org

Hyman, H H and Sheatsley, P B (1947) Some reasons why information campaigns fail, *Public Opinion Quarterly*, **11**, pp 412–23

Institute of Public Relations & Communication Directors' Forum (2004) *Best practice in the measurement and reporting of public relations and ROI*, London. Available at: www.cipr.co.uk/content/policy-resources/cipr-research-and-reports

International Public Relations Association (IPRA) (1994) *Gold paper No 11: Public relations evaluation: professional accountability*, IPRA, London

Jeffrey, A (2013) *Social Media Measurement: A step-by-step approach*. Available at: www.instituteforpr.org/topics/social-media-measurement-a-step-by-step-approach/ (accessed: 31 July 2013)

Jo, S, Hon, L C and Brunner, B R (2004) Organisation-public relationships: Measurement validation in a university setting, *Journal of Communication Management*, **9** (1), pp 14–27

Johnston, J and Zawawi, C (2004) *Public Relations Theory and Practice*, 2nd edn, Allen & Unwin, Crows Nest, NSW

Kane, E and O'Reilly-de Brun, M (2001) *Doing Your Own Research*, Marion Boyars, London

Kaplan, R and Norton, D (1996) *The Balanced Scorecard: Translating strategy into action*, Harvard Business School Press, Boston

Kotler, P, Keller, K, Brady, M, Goodman, M and Hansen, T (2009) *Marketing Management*, Pearson Education, Harlow

Lamme, M O and Miller, K R (2010) Removing the spin: Towards a new theory of public relations history, *Journalism & Communication Monographs*, **11** (4), pp 281–362

Lazarsfeld, P F, Berelson, B and Gaudet, H (1948) *The People's Choice*, Columbia University Press, New York

Ledingham, J A (2003) Explicating relationship management as a general theory of public relations, *Journal of Public Relations Research*, **15**, pp 181–98

Ledingham, J A (2009) Relationship management: A general theory of public relations, in *Public Relations Theory II*, eds C Botan and V Hazleton, pp 465–83, Lawrence Erlbaum Associates, Mahwah, NJ

Lee, T J (2002) Calculating ROI for communication, *Strategic Communication Management*, **6** (6)

Levin, H M and McEwan, P J (2001) *Cost-effectiveness Analysis: Methods and applications*, Sage Publications, Thousand Oaks, CA

Likely, D F (2012) *Principles for the use of return on investment (ROI); Benefit-cost ratio (BCR); and cost-effectiveness analysis (CEA) financial metrics in a public relations/communication (PR/C) department*. 15th International Public Relations Research Conference, 8–10 March, 2012, Miami, FL

Likely, D F, Rockland, D and Weiner, M (2006) *Perspectives on ROI of Media Relations Publicity Efforts*, Institute for Public Relations, Gainesville, FL. Retrieved from www.instituteforpr.org/topics/media-relations-publicity-efforts/

Lindenmann, W (1993) An 'Effectiveness Yardstick' to measure public relations success, *Public Relations Quarterly*, **38** (1), pp 7–9

Lindenmann, W (2006) *Public Relations Research for Planning and Evaluation*, available at www.instituteforpr.org

Macnamara, J R (1999) Research in public relations: A review of the use of evaluation and formative research, *Asia Pacific Public Relations Journal*, **1** (2), pp 107–34

Macnamara, J R (2005a) Media content analysis: Its uses, benefits and Best Practice Methodology, *Asia Pacific Public Relations Journal*, **6** (1), pp 1–34

Macnamara, J R (2005b) *Jim Macnamara's Public Relations Handbook*, Archipelago Press, Sydney

Macnamara, J R (2007) *Return on investment (ROI) of PR and corporate communication*, Mass Communication Group, Sydney

Macnamara, J R (2011) *PR Metrics: How to Measure Public Relations and Corporate Communication*. Available from http://amecorg.com/wp-content/uploads/2011/10/PR-Metrics-Paper.pdf (accessed 29 July 2013)

Marken, G A (1988) Public relations and sales: There must be a measurable relation, *Business Marketing*, April

Marklein, T and Paine, K (2012) The March to Standards, 4th European Summit on Measurement, 13–15 June 2012, Dublin. Available from: http://amecorg.com/downloads/dublin2012/The-March-to-Social-Standards-Tim-Marklein-and-Katie-Paine.pdf (accessed 1 May 2013)

McCoy, M and Hargie, O (2003) Implications of mass communication theory for asymmetric public relations evaluation, *Journal of Communication Management*, 7 (4), pp 304–16

McElreath, M P (1989) *Priority research questions in the field of public relations for the 1990s: trends over the past ten years and predictions for the future.* Paper presented at the meeting of the Speech Communication Association, San Francisco

McElreath, M P (1997) *Managing Systematic and Ethical Public Relations Campaigns*, 2nd edn, Brown & Benchmark, Madison, WI

McElreath, M P and Blamphin, J M (1994) Partial answers to priority research questions – and gaps – found in the Public Relations Society of America's Body of Knowledge, *Journal of Public Relations Research*, 6 (2), pp 69–103

McGuire, W J (1984) Attitudes and attitude change, in Handbook of Social Psychology, II, 3rd edn, ed G G Lindzey and E Aronson, Random House, NYPRSA Public Relations Society of America (2012) *What is Public Relations?* Available at: www.prsa.org/AboutPRSA/PublicRelationsDefined

McKeown, D (1995) *Measuring Your Media Profile*, Gower, Aldershot

Merims, A (1972) Marketing's stepchild: product publicity, *Harvard Business Review*, November/December, pp 107–113

Moutinho, L and Southern, G (2010) *Strategic Marketing Management*, Cengage, Andover

Mullins, L (2010) *Management and Organisational Behaviour*, 9th edn, Prentice Hall, Harlow

Naslund, A (2013) www.brasstackthinking.com/2011/11/the-most-powerful-social-media-measurement-tool-money-can-buy/ (accessed 30 April 2013)

Noble, P (1994) A proper role for media evaluation, *International Public Relations Research Symposium*, Bled, Slovenia, July

Noble, P (1999) Towards an inclusive evaluation methodology, *Corporate Communications: An International Journal*, 4 (1)

Odden, L (2011) www.toprankblog.com/2011/07/online-marketing-media-mix/ (accessed 30 April 2013)

Oeckl, A (1964) *Handbuch der Public Relations*, Süddeutscher Verlag, Munich

Paine, K (2002) How to measure your results in a crisis, www.instituteforpr.org

Paine, K (2006) Designing and implementing your communications dashboard: Lessons learned, available at www.instituteforpr.org

Paine, K (2011) *Measure What Matters*, John Wiley & Sons, Hoboken, NJ

Paine, K (2013) http://kdpaine.blogs.com/themeasurementstandard/2013/04/katie-paines-top-10-social-media-measurement-tips.html (accessed 01 May 2013)

Patton, M Q (1982) *Practical Evaluation*, Sage, Thousand Oaks, CA

Pavlik, J V (1987) *Public Relations: What research tells us*, Sage, Newbury Park, CA

Phillips, D (2001) The public relations evaluationists, *Corporate Communication*, 6 (4), pp 225–37

Phillips, D and Young, P (2009) *Online public relations: A practical guide to developing an online strategy in the world of social media*, 2nd edn, Kogan Page, London

Plackard, D H and Blackmon, C (1947) *Blueprint for Public Relations*, McGraw-Hill, New York

Public Relations Consultants Association (PRCA) (2010) *PRCA announces new action on evaluation*. London: PRCA. Available at: www.prca.org.uk/PRCA-announces-new-action-on-evaluation-AMEC-PRSA

Public Relations Review (1990) *Using research to plan and evaluate public relations*. Summer 1990, xvi (2)

Public Relations Society of America (PRSA) (2010) PRSA and AMEC provide new measurement standards and metrics for business sectors, PRSA, New York. Available at: http://media.prsa.org/article_display.cfm?article_id=1843

Putt, G and Van der Waldt, D L R (2005) A quantitative matrix model for strategic management of stakeholder/issues relationships, 12th International Public Relations Research Symposium, Bled, Slovenia

Robinson, E J (1969) *Public Relations and Survey Research*, Appleton-Century-Crofts, New York

Rossi, P H and Freeman, H E (1982) *Evaluation – A Systematic Approach*, Sage, Thousand Oaks, CA

Sanders, S (2012) Kick-start your social media strategy, in *Share This*, ed S Waddington, pp 15–22, CIPR/John Wiley, Chichester

Savell, M and Iannelli, D (2012) Social Media Analytics Does Not Have to Be Overwhelming, 4th European Summit on Measurement, 13–15 June 2012, Dublin. Available at amecorg.com/downloads/dublin2012/Workshop_G.pdf (accessed 9 May 2013)

Sennott, R (1990) in *Using Research in Public Relations*, ed G D Broom and D M Dozier, Prentice Hall, Englewood Cliffs, NJ

Shaffer, J (2004) Four steps to demonstrating communication ROI, *Communication World On-Line*, November

Shoebridge, N (1989) Column, *BRW Magazine*, April, 1989

Sheldrake, P (2011) *The Business of Influence*, Wiley, Chichester

Sierra, L (2003) Sierra's theory of communicativity: Calculating the value of organizational communication through cost, effort and perception, *Communication World*, June/July

Sinickas, A (2003) Focus on behaviour change to prove ROI, *Strategic Communication Management*, 7 (6)

Sinickas, A (2004) Top tip: Calculating ROI, *Internal Communication Measurement Manual*. Available at: www.sinicom.com/Sub%20Pages/pubs/articles/article130.pdf

Sinickas, A (2009) Measure your ROI – fast, *The Ragan Report*, February

Smith, A (2012a) Social Media Monitoring, in *Share This*, ed S Waddington, pp 157–62, CIPR/John Wiley, Chichester

Smith, A (2012b) What has Google ever done for PR? in *Share This*, ed S Waddington, pp 23–29, CIPR/John Wiley, Chichester

Smith, B G (2008) *Representing PR in the marketing mix: A study on public relations variables in marketing mix modeling*, Institute for Public Relations. Retrieved 9 April 2012 from: www.instituteforpr.org/topics/pr-marketing-mix/

Smith, P (1998) *Marketing Communications: An integrated approach*, 2nd edn, Kogan Page, London

Smith, R (2005) *Strategic Planning for Public Relations*, 2nd edn, Lawrence Erlbaum Associates, Mahwah, NJ

Stacks, D (2002) *Primer of Public Relations Research*, Guildford Press, New York

Stacks, D W (ed) (2006) *Dictionary of public relations measurement and research*, Institute for Public Relations, Gainesville, FL, 26. Retrieved from www.instituteforpr.org/wp-content/uploads/PRMR_Dictionary.pdf

Stacks, D and Bowen, S (2011) The strategic approach: Writing measurable objectives. Available at: www.instituteforpr.org/iprwp/wp-content/uploads/Master-PR-Tactics-document-08-10-16.pdf

Stacks, D and Michaelson, D (2010) *A Practitioner's Guide to Public Relations Research, Measurement, and Evaluation*, Business Expert Press, New York, NY

Sterne, J (2010) *Social Media Metrics*, John Wiley & Sons, Hoboken, NJ

Swedish Public Relations Association (SPRA) (1996) *Return on Communications*, Swedish Public Relations Association (Svenska Informationsförening), Stockholm

Swinehart, J W (1979) Evaluating public relations, *Public Relations Journal*, **35** (July)

Synnott, G and McKie, D (1997) International issues in PR: researching research and prioritizing priorities, *Journal of Public Relations Research*, 9 (4), pp 259–82

Tedlow, R S (1979) *Keeping the corporate image: Public relations and business 1900–1950*, JAI Press, Greenwich, CT

Tixier, M (1995) Appraising communication: Reality or utopia?, *International Public Relations Review*, **18** (3)

VanLeuven, J *et al* (1988) Effects-based planning for public relations campaigns, presented to PR Division, Association for Education in Journalism and Mass Communications, Portland, OR, July

Vos, M and Schoemaker, H (2004) *Accountability of Communication Management: A balanced scorecard approach for communication quality*, LEMMA, Utrecht

Waddington, S (ed) (2012) *Share this: The social media handbook for PR professionals*, Wiley, Chichester

Watson, T (1995) Evaluating Public Relations: The creation and validation of models of measurement for public relations practice, Unpublished PhD thesis, Nottingham Trent University (Southampton Institute)

Watson, T (1997) Measuring the success rate: Evaluating the PR process and PR programmes, in *Principles and Practice of Public Relations*, ed P J Kitchen, Chapman and Hall, London

Watson, T (2005) ROI or evidence-based PR: The language of public relations evaluation, *Prism*, **3** (1). Available from: www.prismjournal.org/fileadmin/Praxis/Files/Journal_Files/Issue3/Watson.pdf

Watson, T (2007) Reputation and ethical behaviour in a crisis: Predicting survival, *Journal of Communication Management*, **11** (4), pp 371–84

Watson, T (2008) Public relations research priorities: A delphi study, *Journal of Communication Management*, **12** (2), pp 104–23

Watson, T (2011) An initial investigation on the use of 'Return on Investment' in public relations practice, *Public Relations Review*, 37, pp 314–17

Watson, T and Zerfass, A (2011) Return on investment in public relations: A critique of concepts used by practitioners from communication and management sciences perspectives, *Prism*, 8 (1), www.prismjournal.org/homepage.html

Weiner, M, Arnorsdottir, L, Lang, R and Smith, B G (2010) *Isolating the effects of media-based public relations on sales: Optimization through marketing mix modeling*, Institute for Public Relations, Gainesville, FL. Available at: www.instituteforpr.org/topics/media-based-pr-on-sales.

Weiss, C (1977) *Evaluation Research: Methods of assessing program effectiveness*, Prentice Hall, Englewood Cliffs, NJ

Westminster Council (2011) *Evaluating Your Communication Tools, What Works, What Doesn't? The Westminster Model*, October 2011. Available at: http://transact.westminster.gov.uk/Newdocstores/publications_store/communications/evaluating_your_comms_aw_lr-1319206316.pdf

White, J (1991) *How to Understand and Manage Public Relations*, Business Books, London

White, J and Blamphin, J (1994) Priorities for Research in Public Relations Practice in the United Kingdom, London City University/Rapier Research, London

Wilcox, D *et al* (2000) *Public Relations Strategies and Tactics*, 6th edn, Longman, Harlow

Williams, L W (1992) *Calculating your return on investment: Measuring the impact of your PR programs on the bottom-line*. Workshop at the Institute for International Research Conference, Toronto, Canada, January.

Wood, J A (2004) Communications ROI, *Communications World*, January/February

Zerfass, A (2005) *The corporate communications scorecard – a framework for managing and evaluating communication strategies*, 12th International Public Relations Research Symposium (BledCom), 1–3 July, 2005, Lake Bled, Slovenia.

Zerfass, A, Verhoeven, P, Tench, R, Moreno, A and Verčič, D (2011) *European Communication Monitor 2011. Empirical insights into strategic communication in Europe. Results of an empirical survey in 43 countries*, EACD, EUPRERA, Brussels

INDEX

NB: page numbers in *italics* indicate Figures or Tables

Accountability Principle   140, 141
action research   42, *43*
Advertising Research Foundation   114
advertising value equivalence (AVE)   27,
    30–31, 33, 34, 100, 160, 163, 167,
    169–70
aims   *see* objectives
ALBERT model   115
Alexa   159
American Management Association   28
apPRaise system   82–83, *84–87, 88–89*
AT&T   3, 26, 28
Austin, Erica and Pinkleton, Bruce   *122*
average media score (AMS)   104

Bagnall, Richard   148
Balanced Scorecard (BSC)   73–74
Barcelona Principles   30–34, 104, 119, 120,
    146, 155, 167, 169–70, 173
  advertising value equivalence (AVE)   33
  business results, effect on   32
  goals and measurement, importance of
    32
  outcomes vs outputs   32
  quantity and quality   32–33
  social media   33
  transparency and replicability   33
Barnet & Reef   4
'Barometer, The'   26
Bartholomew, Don   148, 154
Batchelor, Bronson   26–27
BBC News   77
benefit–cost ratio (BCR)   169
Bernays, Edward   3, 8, 26
Best, Roger   163
Bhurji, Daljit   158
Black, Sam   163–64
Blamphin, John
  McElreath, Mark and Blamphin, John
    16
  White, Jon and Blamphin, John
    16, 28
Blaxter, Loraine, Hughes, Christina and
    Tight, Malcolm   42
Blissland, James   18

Bluetooth   110
Botan, Carl and Hazleton, Vincent   8
Broom, Glenn
  Broom, Glenn and Dozier, David   18, 28,
    38, 39, 40, 44, 121, 128, 174
  Broom, Glenn and Sha, Bey-Ling   6, 18,
    35, 53, 55, 57, 124, 126, 169
  Cutlip, Scott, Center, Allen and Broom,
    Glenn   55
Bruning, Stephen
  Bruning, Stephen and Ledingham, John
    135–36
  Bruning, Stephen, Castle, Janessa and
    Schrepfer, Erin   137
Burson-Marsteller   4, 28
Business of Influence, The   182

Canadian Public Relations Society   83
case studies
  Lothian & Borders Police   109–11
    objectives   109
    results   110–11
    strategy   110
  Medicare   113–14
    research strategy   113–14
    results   114
  Pepsi Refresh Project   107–08
    objectives   107
    results   108
    strategy   108
  Philips   103–07
    average media score (AMS)   104
    Net Promoter Score (NPS)   103–04
    online portal   *105*
    reporting   *106*
  St John Ambulance   111–13
    objectives   111
    results   112–13
    strategy   112
  use of in research   42–44
  Westminster City Council   114–17
    ALBERT model   115
    results   116–17
    strategy   115
    Westminster Reputation Tracker   116

Center, Allen
    Cutlip, Scott and Center, Allen   6, 8
    Cutlip, Scott, Center, Allen and Broom,
        Glenn   55
Chartered Institute of Public Relations (CIPR)
        7–8, 9, 31, 36, 145
    Evaluation Toolkit   36, 62
    Excellence Awards   31, 111, 113
    Planning, Research and Evaluation (PRE)
        process   63, 63–64, 64, 68
Chau, Eddie, Daniels, Mike and Lau, Eden
        146, 148, 150, 152, 153
cognitive dissonance   14
Commerzbank   173
Commission on Measurement and
        Evaluation of Public Relations   19
communal relationships   136
communication controlling   74, 165, 170,
        173–82
    corporate strategy, translating to comms
        activities   176, 177
    Deutsche Public Relations Gesellschaft
        (DPRG)   173
    impact levels of communication
        178–80, 179
    implementing a system   180–82, 181
    Internationaler Controller Verein (ICV)
        173
    operational communication controlling
        180
    stakeholder model of corporate comms
        175
        external communication   176
        financial communication   176
        internal communication   174, 176
        market communication   176
Communication Matrix   73
Communications Scorecard   73
Cone Cause Evolution Study   107
Consultancy Management Standard   5
content analysis   52–54
Continuing model   68, 69, 70
control mutuality   137
Coombs, W Timothy
    Coombs, W Timothy and Holladay, Sherry
        7, 135, 137
    Heath, Robert and Coombs, W Timothy
        10
Corporate Communication Scorecard   73
cost-effectiveness analysis (CEA)   169
Costerton, Sally   31
Council for Public Relations Firms   167
Crable, Richard and Vibbert, Stephen   132
crisis communication, evaluating   139–43
    9/11 attacks   139
    Accountability Principle   140, 141

Disclosure Principle   140, 142
    Relationship Principle   140, 141
    share price recovery   142
    stages of a crisis   139
    Symmetrical Communication
        Principle   140, 142
    types of crisis   139
Cutlip, Scott   3, 6, 8, 26, 27, 55
    Cutlip, Scott and Center, Allen   6, 8
    Cutlip, Scott, Center, Allen and Broom,
        Glenn   55

Daniels, Mike and Jeffrey, Angela   100, 101
Daymon, Christine and Holloway,
        Immy   43, 48
Denscombe, Martyn   41, 42–43, 44, 45, 49,
        50, 51, 52–53
Deutsche Public Relations Gesellschaft
        (DPRG)   173
Deutsche Telekom   173
*Dictionary of Public Relations Measurement
        and Research*   19, 163
dimensional model   90, 91–95
    choosing analyses   95, 95
    focus   94, 94
    qualitative   92, 92
    quantitative   92, 92–93
    time   94, 94
Disclosure Principle   140, 142
domino model   14
Doyle, Peter   130
Dozier, David   19, 20, 28, 39
    Broom, Glenn and Dozier, David   18, 28,
        38, 39, 40, 44, 121, 128, 174
    Dozier, David and Ehling, William   16
    Dozier, David and Repper, Fred   18
Dudley, Pendleton   3

Edelman   107
Eden-Green, Alan   27
Editorial Services   3
'effects-based planning'   22
Ehling, William   169
    Dozier, David and Ehling, William   16
European Communication Monitor   5, 164,
        174
evaluation models   55–74
    Continuing model   68, 69, 70, 71, 72
    dashboards   72–73, 74
    Planning, Research and Evaluation (PRE)
        process   63, 63–64, 64, 68
    practitioner-derived models   67–68
    Preparation, Implementation, Impact (PII)
        model   56, 56–57, 61
    Public Relations Yardstick model   58, 60,
        60–61, 64–65, 71, 76, 141

Pyramid Model   57–58, 59, 64, 92
scoreboards   73–74
Short Term model   68–70, 69, 71, 72
Unified model   64–65, 66, 72
evaluation system, establishing a   75–101
   apPRaise system   82–83, 84–87, 88–89
   benchmark, establishing a   78
   case study   96–100
   dimensional model   90, 91–95
     choosing analyses   95, 95
     focus   94, 94
     qualitative   92, 92
     quantitative   92, 92–93
     time   94, 94
   example report   80–81
   Google News   76–77
   IMPACT criteria   77–78
   international media   100–01
     narrative analysis reports   100
     online dashboards   100–01
     translation   101
   Media Relations Rating Points
     (MR2P)   83, 89, 89–90
   Microsoft Bing   77
   'observer bias'   79
   PR objectives   76
   reader panels   79–80, 91
   sample form   79
   'substitution game'   80, 90
evaluation theory   13–24
   control over media   21
   'effects-based planning'   22
   evaluation, defining   17–19
   influence of media on behaviours   13–15
   and justifying cost   17
   McGuire's persuasion model   15
   methodological problems   21–22
   Noble's principles of evaluation   22–24
   objectives   19–20
   purpose of   21
   situational evaluation   20–21
   variables   21
evaluation-only approach (to managing PR
   programmes)   39
Excellence Theory   9–11
exchange relationships   136
experiments   44

Facebook   20, 168
   in case studies   108, 110, 111, 112
   social media, evaluating   146, 150, 151,
     157
Fairchild, Michael   62
Fearn-Banks, Kathleen   139
Festinger, Leon   14
Fill, Chris   121, 129, 130

FitzGibbon, Carol and Morris, Lynn   20–21
Fleisher, Craig and Mahaffy, Darren   73
Fleishman-Hillard   103
focus groups   47–48
formative evaluative research   38

Gaunt, Richard and Wright, Donald   164
Global Alliance for Public Relations and
   Communication Management   5, 31
goals   see objectives
Golin Harris   111
Good Purpose Study   107
Google
   Alerts   156
   Analytics   158–59
   News   76–77
Great Depression   27
Gregory, Anne and Watson, Tom   164
Griese, Noel   26
Grunig, James   6, 28, 68, 71, 138, 169
   crisis communication   140, 141–42, 143
   Grunig, James and Hunt, Todd
     12, 17, 123, 124
   Hon, Linda and Grunig, James
     136, 137, 138
   primacy   10–11
   Return on Investment (ROI)   166–67
Grupp, Robert   31

Hallmark Public Relations   82
Handbook of Public Relations   27
Harlow, Rex   6
Harvard Business Review   164
HCA Healthcare   141
Henkel   173
Hering, Ralf, Schuppener, Bernt and
   Sommerhalder, Mark   73
Hibbert, Zoe and Simmons, Peter   136, 138
Hill+Knowlton   4, 89–90
Holmes, Paul   7
   Holmes Report   114
Hon, Linda
   Hon, Linda and Grunig, James
     136, 137, 138
   Jo, Samsup, Hon, Linda and Brunner,
     Brigitta   135, 138
Hootsuite   156
Hyman, Herbert and Sheatsley, Paul   14

IBM   141
IMPACT criteria   77–78
informal approach (to managing PR
   programmes)   39
Institute for Public Relations (US)   9, 28–29
   Jack Felton Golden Ruler Award   114
   Research Conversations   166–67

Institute of Public Relations (IPR)   27, 164
International Association for the
        Measurement and Evaluation
        of Communication (AMEC)
        100, 167, 169
    2012 Awards   117
    Barcelona Principles   30–34, 104, 119,
        120, 146, 155, 167, 169–70, 173
        advertising value equivalence (AVE)   33
        business results, effect on   32
        goals and measurement, importance
            of   32
        outcomes vs outputs   32
        quantity and quality   32–33
        social media   33
        transparency and replicability   33
        valid metrics framework   30, 34, 104,
            154, 159, 169–70, *171*, *172*, 173
International Communications Consultants
        Association (ICCO)   5, 168
international media   100–01
    narrative analysis reports   100
    online dashboards   100–01
    translation   101
International Public Relations Association
        (IPRA)   4, 5, 29, 68
    Gold Paper No 11: *Public Relations
        Evaluation: Professional
        Accountability*   29, 68
International Quality in Public Relations   5
Internationaler Controller Verein (ICV)
        173
interviews   46–47
iPhone   111, 112, 115
Ipsos MORI   115
Iraq War 2003   138

Jeffrey, Anne   154–56, 159
    Daniels, Mike and Jeffrey, Angela
        100, 101
Johnson & Johnson   142
Johnston, Jane and Zawawi, Clara   137

Kane, Eileen and O'Reilly-de Brun, Mary
        47
Kaplan, Robert and Norton, David
        73, 75, 183
    Balanced Scorecard (BSC)   73–74
Ketchum (Pleon)   28, 103
Kirban, Lloyd   28
Klout   157
Kodak   141, 142
Kotler, Philip, Keller, Kevin, Brady, Mairead,
        Goodman, Malcolm and Hansen,
        Torben   125, 130

Krupp   3
Kryptonite   147

Lamme, Meg and Miller, Karen   26
Lazarsfeld, Paul, Berelson, Bernard and
        Gaudet, Hazel   14
Ledingham, John   136, 137
    Bruning, Stephen and Ledingham, John
        135–36
Lee, Ivy   3, 26
Lee, T J   164
Lerbinger, Otto   139
Levi Strauss   141, 142
Levin, Henry and McEwan, Patrick   169
Levine, Ben   104
Likely, Frazer   168–69
    Likely, Frazer, Rockland, David and
        Weiner, Mark   164
'Likert' scale   52
Lindenmann, Walter   18, 28, 29, 38, 50, 55,
        121, 136, 138
    Public Relations Yardstick model   58, *60*,
        60–61, 64–65, 71, 76, 141
Lothian & Borders Police (case study)
        109–11
    objectives   109
    results   110–11
    strategy   110

Macnamara, Jim   16, 51, 52, 53–54, 74,
        128, 164
    Pyramid Model   57–58, *59*, 64, 92
management by objectives (MBO)   125–26
Manning, Andre   103, 107
Marconi Company   3
Marken, G A   164
Marklein, Tim and Paine, Katie   149, 150,
        152, 154, 160
McCoy, Mairead and Hargie, Owen   14,
        16, 38, 39
McElreath, Mark   28, 36, 38
    McElreath, Mark and Blamphin, John
        16
McGuire, William   15, 78
    model of the persuasion process   15
McKeown, Dermot   30
measurement and evaluation, history of
        25–34
    1930s and 1940s   26–27
    1950s and 1960s   27
    1970s   27–28
    1980s and 1990s   28–29
    2000s   29–30
    advertising value equivalence (AVE)
        27, 30–31, 33, 34

Barcelona Principles   30–34
'Barometer, The'   26
Page, Arthur W   3–4, 26
*Measuring and Evaluating Public Relations
    Activities*   27–28
Media Relations Rating Points (MR2P)
    83, *89*, 89–90
media-event approach (to managing PR
    programmes)   38
Medicare (case study)   113–14
    research strategy   113–14
    results   114
Merims, Arthur   164
Microsoft
    Bing   77
    Microsoft Excel   82
'minimal effects' theories   13
Mirkin, Chelsea   114
modes of practice   9
Moloney, Kevin   46–47
Motorola   164
Moutinho, Luiz and Southern, Geoff   163
Mullins, Laurie   122, 125

Nabisco   141
Naslund, Amber   146
Net Promoter Score (NPS)   103–04
Newsom, Douglass   28
Noble, Paul   17, 22
no-research approach (to managing PR
    programmes)   38

objectives, setting   119–34
    aims vs objectives vs goals   120, 122–24,
        124
    appropriateness of   120
    hierarchy of objectives   119, 126–27
    importance of   121
    informational, motivational, and
        behavioural objectives
        119, 126–27
    management by objectives (MBO)
        125–26
    PR, understanding contribution of
        130–32
    process objectives   132–33
    sales-oriented objectives   130
    SMART objectives   119, 127–28, 129,
        132, 133
    strategic planning pyramid   121, *122*
'observer bias'   79
Odden, Lee   148
Odwalla   141
Oeckl, Albert   27
omnibus surveys   36

OneVoice   103–07
Opportunities to See (OTS)   57, 82, 149–50
Osborne-Brown, Steve   83

Page, Arthur W   3–4, 26
Paid, Earned, Shared and Owned
    (PESO)   148, *149*
Paine, Katie   72–73, 140–41, 141–42, 146,
    150, 151, 152, 155, 156, 160–61,
    169
    Marklein, Tim and Paine, Katie   149,
        150, 152, 154, 160
Parker & Lee   3
Patton, Michael   17–18
Pavlik, John   18, 28
PeerIndex   158
Pepsi Refresh Project (case study)   107–08
    objectives   107
    results   108
    strategy   108
Philips (case study)   103–07
    average media score (AMS)   104
    Net Promoter Score (NPS)   103–04
    online portal   *105*
    reporting   *106*
Phillips, David   30
    Phillips, David and Young, Philip   183
'piggyback' research   36
Plackard, Dwight and Blackmon, Clifton
    27
Planning, Research and Evaluation (PRE)
    process   *63*, 63–64, *64*, 68
Police Scotland   109
Porter Novelli   113
PR News   114
*PR Professional's Definitive Guide to
    Measurement*   168
Preparation, Implementation, Impact (PII)
    model   *56*, 56–57, 61
press agentry/publicity model   6
PRIME Research   113
process objectives   132–33
proto-PR   3
pseudo-evaluation   20
pseudo-planning   20
public information model   6
Public Relations and Survey Research   28
Public Relations Consultants Association
    (PRCA)   31, 168
*Public Relations Evaluation: Professional
    Accountability*   29
Public Relations Review   28
Public Relations Society of America (PRSA)
    7, 31, 167
    Silver Anvil   108

Public Relations Yardstick model 58, *60*,
      60–61, 64–65, 71, 76, 141
public relations, definitions of 6–8
Publicity Bureau (of Boston), The 3, 26
purposive sampling 51
Putt, G and Van der Waldt, D L R 73
Pyramid Model 57–58, *59*, 64, 92

questionnaires 49, 51–52
quota sampling 50, 51

Ragan Reports 114
random sampling 50–51
reader panels 79–80, 91
relationship management, evaluating 135–39
   commitment 138
   communal relationships 136
   control mutuality 137
   exchange relationships 136
   Iraq War 2003 138
   relationships, quality of 137
   satisfaction 138
   trust 138
Relationship Principle 140, 141
Report International 103
representative sampling 51
research 35–54
   action research 42, *43*
   case studies 42–44
   content analysis 52–54
   evaluation-only approach 39
   experiments 44
   focus groups 47–48
   formative evaluative research 38
   importance of 36–37
   informal approach 39
   interviews 46–47
   media-event approach 38
   nine steps of strategic public relations
      37
   no-research approach 38
   omnibus surveys 36
   'piggyback' research 36
   primary vs secondary research 40–41
   qualitative vs quantitative research
      41, *41*
   questionnaires 49, 51–52
   sampling 50–51
   scientific dissemination evaluation 39
   scientific management approach 39
   summative evaluative research 38
   surveys 44–45
Return on Investment (ROI) 163–69
   Barcelona Principles 167
   definitions of 164

European Communications Monitor survey
      164–65
   Grunig, views of 166–67
Robinson, Edward 28
Roosevelt, Franklin D 17, 27
Rossi, Peter and Freeman, Howard 17

sampling 50–51
Sanders, Simon 156
Savell, Margot and Iannelli, David 153
scientific dissemination evaluation 39
scientific management approach
      (to managing PR programmes) 39
Sennott, R Stephen 21
Serious Organised Crime Agency 109
Shaffer, Jim 169
Sheldrake, Philip 9, 34, 151, 152, 153,
      182–83
   Six Influence Flows 153, 182–83, *183*
Shoebridge, Neil 17
Short Term model 68–70, *69*
Siemens 173
Sierra, Lorenzo 164
Sinickas, Angela 164, 169
situational evaluation 20–21
Six Influence Flows 153, 182–83, *183*
SMART objectives 119, 127–28, 129, 132,
      133
Smith, Andrew 146, 151, 152, 157, 158
Smith, Brian 169
Smith, Paul 128
Smith, Ronald 36, 37, 53, 119, 123, 124, 126
social media, evaluating 145–61
   action/impact/value 147, 154
   Alexa 159
   control, loss of 146–47
   credibility 147
   engagement/sentiment/tone 147, 150–53
      importance of engagement 151
      lurking, casual, active, committed, and
         loyalist 150
   exposure/reach/impressions 147, 148–50
   Facebook 146, 150, 151, 157
   Google Alerts 156
   Google Analytics 158–59
   influence/respect/relevance 147, 153–54
   key metrics 146
   Klout 157
   lurking, casual, active, committed, and
      loyalist 150
   measurement processes 154–56
   Paid, Earned, Shared and Owned (PESO)
      148, *149*
   PeerIndex 158
   social media funnel *148*, 148

Social Mention 156, 157
standardization 160
tools, confusion around 145–46
Twitter 145, 146, 150, 151, 157, 159
    Tweetreach 156, 157
    Twitter Favourites 158
uberVU 157
YouTube 150
Social Mention 156, 157
St John Ambulance (case study) 111–13
    objectives 111
    results 112–13
    strategy 112
Stacks, Don
    Stacks, Don and Bowen, Shannon
        119, 120
    Stacks, Don and Michaelson, David
        19, 40, 44, 53, 126, 127, 163
Sterne, Jim 156
strategic planning pyramid 121, *122*
'substitution game' 80, 90
summative evaluative research 38
surveys 44–45
Swedish Public Relations Association
    (Svenska Informationsförening) 29
Symmetrical Communication Principle
    140, 142
Synnott, Gae and McKie, David 16, 28

Tedlow, Richard 27
theory, role of 1–2
Tixier, Maud 21
Tweetreach 156, 157
Twitter 20, 168
    in case studies 108, 112
    Return on Investment (ROI) 168
    social media, evaluating 145, 146, 150,
        151, 157, 159
    Tweetreach 156, 157
    Twitter Favourites 158
two-way asymmetrical model 6, 8, 10, 68, 71
two-way symmetrical model 6, 10, 12, 68, 71

uberVU 157
Unified model 64–65, 66, 72
Using Research in Public Relations 28

valid metrics framework 30, 34, 104, 154,
    159, 169–70, *171*, *172*, 173
    horizontal axis 170
    vertical axis 170
VanLeuven, James *et al* 22, 70, 71
Vos, Marita and Schoemaker, Henny 73

Waddington, Stephen 183
Washington, George 26
Watson, Tom 16, 18, 29, 67, 142–43, 164
    Continuing model 68, *69*, 70
    Gregory, Anne and Watson, Tom 164
    Short Term model 68–70, *69*
    Watson, Tom and Zerfass, Ansgar
        164, 165, 166–67
Weber Shandwick 107
Weiner, Mark 114
    Weiner, Mark, Arnorsdottir, Liney, Lang,
        Rainer and Smith, Brian 169
Weiss, Carol 19
Westminster City Council (case study)
    45, 114–17, 158–59
    ALBERT model 115
    results 116–17
    strategy 115
    Westminster Reputation Tracker 116
White, Jon 17, 19, 21
    White, Jon and Blamphin, John 16, 28
Wilcox, Dennis, Ault, Phillip and Agee, Warren
    18
Williams, L W 164
Wilson, Jane 31
Wood, Julie 164
Wright, Donald 28
    Gaunt, Richard and Wright, Donald
        164

YouGov 111
YouTube 150, 168

Zerfass, Ansgar 26, 29, 73–74, *177*
    Watson, Tom and Zerfass, Ansgar
        164, 165, 166–67
    Zerfass, Ansgar, Verhoeven, P,
        Tench, R, Moreno, A and Verčič, D
        164, 174